# RACE, GOVERNMENT AND POLITICS
## IN BRITAIN

*Also by Zig Layton-Henry*

THE POLITICS OF RACE IN BRITAIN

CONSERVATIVE POLITICS IN WESTERN EUROPE (*editor*)

CONSERVATIVE PARTY POLITICS (*editor*)


*Also by Paul B. Rich*

WHITE POWER AND THE LIBERAL CONSCIENCE:
Racial Segregation and South African Liberalism.

RACE AND EMPIRE IN BRITISH POLITICS

# RACE, GOVERNMENT AND POLITICS IN BRITAIN

EDITED BY

## Zig Layton-Henry

*Senior Lecturer in Politics*
*University of Warwick*

AND

## Paul B. Rich

*Research Fellow*
*Centre for Research in Ethnic Relations*
*University of Warwick*

MACMILLAN

First published 1986

Published by
THE MACMILLAN PRESS LTD
Houndmills, Basingstoke, Hampshire RG21 2XS
and London
Companies and representatives
throughout the world

British Library Cataloguing in Publication Data
Race government and politics in Britain.
1. Great Britain—Race relations  2. Great
Britain—Politics and government—1979–
I. Layton-Henry, Zig  II. Rich, Paul B.
323.1′41    DA125.A1
ISBN 0–333–39349–X
ISBN 0–333–39350–3 Pbk

# Contents

*List of Tables*                                                    vii
*Acknowledgements*                                                  viii
*Notes on the Contributors*                                         ix

Introduction    Zig Layton-Henry and Paul Rich                      1

1   Continuity, Autonomy and Peripheralisation:
    the Anatomy of the Centre's Race Statecraft
    in England                                                      17
    *Jim Bulpitt*

2   Conservative Ideology and Race in Modern British
    Politics                                                        45
    *Paul B. Rich*

3   Race and the Thatcher Government                                73
    *Zig Layton-Henry*

4   Opposition Parties and Race Policies, 1979–83                   100
    *Marian Fitzgerald and Zig Layton-Henry*

5   The House of Commons Home Affairs Sub-Committee
    and Government Policy on Race Relations                         125
    *Jaqi Nixon*

6   Non-White Policy Preferences, Political Participation and
    the Political Agenda in Britain                                 159
    *Donley T. Studlar*

7   Political Dilemmas in Multi-Racial Education                    187
    *Sally Tomlinson*

8   Training for What?: Government Policies and the
    Politicisation of Black Youth Unemployment                     204
    *John Solomos*

9   Spiral of Decline: Race and Policing                          227
    *John Benyon*

Index                                                            278

# List of Tables

3.1  Total acceptances for settlement, 1973–82                         92
3.2  Illegal entrants detected and removed, 1976–83                    93
6.1  Problems perceived as important                                  166
6.2  Main problems in local area                                      167
6.3  Reasons for immigration                                          168
6.4  Two most important issues, 1979                                  169
6.5  Two most important issues, 1983 (Gallup)                         170
6.6  Two most important issues, 1983 (Harris)                         171
6.7  Party preference and political participation                     173

# Acknowledgements

The idea for this book originated at a conference on 'Race and Politics in Britain' held at St Hugh's College, Oxford, in September 1984. This conference was sponsored by the Government and Law Committee of the Economic and Social Research Council. We are grateful to the ESRC for their support. We wish to thank the participants at the conference for their helpful and stimulating contributions both as paper-givers and discussants. All of the contributions to this book have either been substantially revised in the light of these discussions or have been commissioned and written since the conference.

We are grateful to Pion Ltd for giving us permission to reprint 'Continuity, Autonomy and Peripheralisation: the Anatomy of the Centre's Race Statecraft in England' by Jim Bulpitt. This first appeared in *Government and Policy* (vol.3, 1984, 129-147), and a revised version is published in this book. We also wish to thank Rose Goodwin and Gurbaksh Hundal for typing the various drafts of this book and the Centre for Research in Ethnic Relations for their support.

ZIG LAYTON-HENRY
PAUL RICH

# Notes on the Contributors

**John Benyon** is Lecturer in Politics and Public Administration in the Departments of Adult Education and Politics at the University of Leicester. He is editor of *Scarman and After* and co-editor of *The Police: Powers, Procedures and Proprieties*.

**Jim Bulpitt** is Senior Lecturer in Politics at the University of Warwick. He is author of *Territory and Power in the United Kingdom*.

**Marian Fitzgerald** is an independent researcher into race relations. She is the author of *Political Parties and Black People* and articles on black political participation.

**Zig Layton-Henry** is Senior Lecturer in Politics at the University of Warwick. He is author of *The Politics of Race in Britain* and editor of *Conservative Party Politics* and *Conservative Politics in Western Europe*.

**Jaqi Nixon** is Senior Lecturer in Social Administration in the Department of Community Studies at Brighton Polytechnic. She was formerly Senior Research Officer at the Civil Service College. She has published articles on the implementation of race relations policy and the work of the House of Commons Social Services Committee.

**Paul B. Rich** is Research Fellow at the Centre for Research in Ethnic Relations at the University of Warwick. He is author of *White Power and the Liberal Conscience: Racial Segregation and South African Liberalism* and *Race and Empire in British Politics*.

**John Solomos** is Research Fellow at the Centre for Research in Ethnic Relations at the University of Warwick. He is editor of *Migrant Workers in Metropolitan Cities*, a contributor to *The Empire Strikes Back* and has contributed papers to edited books and academic journals on the politics of black youth unemployment, race relations policies and theories of racism.

**Donley T. Studlar** is Associate Professor of Politics at Centre College, Kentucky. He is co-editor of *Dilemmas of Change in British Politics* and author of numerous articles on race and politics in Britain. His PhD dissertation, The Impact of the Coloured Immigration Issue on British Electoral Poltics, 1964-70, was awarded the first Samuel H. Beer prize of the British Politics Group of the American Political Science Association.

**Sally Tomlinson** is Professor and Head of the Department of Educational Research at the University of Lancaster. She is author of *Ethnic Minorities in British Schools 1960-72: A Review of the Literature* and *Home and School in Multi-Cultural Britain*, *A Sociology of Special Education*.

# Introduction

Ethnic minority politics have progressively increased in importance in Britain. The 1980s have witnessed the emergence of a vocal and articulate group of Afro-Caribbean and Asian politicians. The election of an Asian Mayor of Bradford, Mohammed Hajeeb, and an Afro-Caribbean, Bernie Grant, as leader of Haringey Council, are evidence of non-white progress in electoral politics. A number of politicians from the ethnic minorities, including Bernie Grant, have been selected for safe Labour parliamentary seats so it is likely that the first postwar Asian and Afro-Caribbean members of parliament will soon be elected to Westminster.[1] In contrast to these manifestations of non-white involvement and progress in electoral politics there have been the serious anti-police riots in Bristol in 1980 and in Brixton and Toxteth in 1981. The repetition of further rioting in Handsworth and Tottenham in 1985, which in Tottenham included the use of firearms and the horrific murder of a policeman, show the alienation of young people, especially young blacks, in declining inner city areas. The high levels of unemployment, poor housing and lack of opportunities and facilities cause a smouldering resentment which blames an uncaring government and a racist society for subordinating blacks socially and economically. The police as highly visible symbols of authority, being closer to the community than other institutions and being more immediately responsible for upholding law and public tranquillity, have become the focus of much of this general alienation. The politics of race in Britain has thus reached a major watershed and it is appropriate to assess the contribution that scholars have made to analysing and explaining the migration and settlement of Britain's ethnic minorities.

Early studies of non-white settlers in Britain were carried out by social anthropologists who described the settlements that had become established in seaport towns. They also analysed early West Indian migration after the Second World War.[2] By the 1960s a new field of race relations was becoming established and it was dominated by sociologists. There thus emerged a school of race

1

relations analysts who were concerned with particular policy issues associated with immigration and settlement. The key policy area which researchers focused on was housing. Early migrants to Britain quickly found jobs but met with massive discrimination in the housing market, which quickly led to ethnic minority concentration in inner city areas and subsequent obstacles to extensive resettlement in suburbia. Some researchers emphasised the interests of 'housing classes' actively seeking segregation to preserve the white suburbs.[3] Other major concerns were to establish the relationship of the ethnic minorities to the class and social structure of British society and to expose racial discrimination in employment, education and health provision as well as housing. The general pattern of settlement of black ethnic minorities into working class inner city areas and their integration into manual work has caused many researchers to focus on their position in the working class and their relations with trade unions, local authorities and white neighbours.[4] A heated controversy has arisen over whether there has emerged in British towns and cities a new black 'under-class' which, because of racial discrimination and disadvantage, largely fell outside of the facilities provided by the welfare state.[5]

These sociological studies were dominated by a strong concern to rectify the manifest injustices that racial discrimination imposed on non-white ethnic minorities. They thus included considerable criticisms of local government policy and often urged national government action as well.[6] Strong support was given to policies designed to encourage racial harmony and reduce racial discrimination through Community Relations Councils, the Race Relations Board, the Community Relations Commission and later the Commission for Racial Equality. But there was no theoretical model or explanatory theory developed within this sociological literature to explain the course and direction of policy at government level, despite the fact that this was in many respects one of the most important dimensions of the process of race relations that was developing in Britain.

This lacuna in academic research can also be explained by the general reluctance of political scientists to engage in extensive work on the politics of race in Britain. British political science has traditionally been dominated by the theory and practice of government and concerns of central decision-makers. Immigration and the numbers and origins of non-white settlers were defined as sociological problems of little interest to political scientists. Even the campaign for immigration control and its success in 1962, when the Commonwealth Immigrants Act was passed, generated little academic interest. In the 1960s and early 1970s the major parties were uncertain how best to manage immigration and race relations issues and attempted to play down the issue and reduce its salience by subjecting it to a bipartisan consensus. This strategy became increasingly untenable after 1968 when the speeches of Enoch Powell and the rise of the National Front put race issues forcefully on the political agenda. However, the reluctance of politicians to define race and immigration as central issues seems to have been followed by political scientists who had published very few major studies before the 1980s.[7] This reluctance to focus on race as a source of political action and conflict was reinforced by two factors: first, a belief in the primacy of class as the basic concept for analysing political behaviour and decision making; and secondly, a feeling that racism was both irrational and immoral and therefore distinctions based on race should not be given credence by using 'race' as a category of political analysis.

Early research, therefore, on the political consequences of New Commonwealth immigration has largely been conducted by scholars outside the political science establishment. Major examples would include the work of Nicholas Deakin and Paul Foot.[8] The major contributions by political scientists have often been made by American graduate students influenced by the experience of ethnic and racial conflict in the United States and particularly by the civil rights movement in the early 1960s and the urban riots of 1968.[9] Even now in the 1980s, much of the political research on race relations by British Scholars continues to be done by researchers based outside of mainstream political science departments, in independent research institutes or other social science disciplines. This is true for a number of the contributors to this book.[10] One exception to this neglect by political scientists has been the analysis of the electoral participation of Asian and Afro-Caribbean voters and the impact of the race issue on voting behaviour.[11]

This absence of a systematic political science interest has contributed to a relative paucity of theoretical models to illuminate the political response to the migration and settlement of New Commonwealth immigrants. Sociological analysis has been dominated by Marxist and Weberian theories but political science analysis has tended to be highly descriptive and lacked a strong theoretical dimension. Recently a number of neo-Marxist political scientists have begun to acknowledge the importance of analysing race, as well as other non-class categories such as gender, as a source of political action, and their writings may stimulate a theoretical debate.[12] This volume seeks to stimulate greater political science interest and analysis in race politics in Britain. A variety of models and styles of analysis are included in the book which all show the central place of politics for any analysis of issues with a race dimension including education, unemployment and policing which have hitherto been the sole reserve of sociologists.

The first chapter by Jim Bulpitt is a good example of macro-political analysis. He applies the concept of elite statecraft within a centre-periphery model to the analysis of race politics and argues that the British political centre has attempted to keep the issue of race from intruding upon matters of 'high politics' which are the concern of the central decision makers in Westminster and Whitehall. The strategy that Bulpitt describes is reminiscent of the British colonial policy of 'indirect rule' in some African colonial territories in the inter-war years. This may indicate a continuation of certain styles of political management among political elites even though the imperial experience is now largely over. However Bulpitt argues that the evolution of the British 'Dual Polity' goes back to the eighteenth century distinction between court and country and it is therefore not surprising that such a long tradition is still strongly rooted in central decision making processes.[13] Too rigid a distinction, however, between high and low politics should not be made. Richard Rose, in a recent survey of West European states, has shown how the concerns of high politics have widened dramatically in the twentieth century from a narrow focus on the maintenance of state power through expenditure on defence, the courts, administration and payment of debt interest to wider concerns centred around managing the economy, education and welfare services.[14] The widening scope of high politics in Western Europe, especially since 1945, has occurred at a time when a consensual form of liberal democracy has achieved unparalleled ascendancy. The issues that have divided parties and politicians in this period of liberal consensus have revolved around tangible and negotiable economic and related benefits, such as more or less resources for health services, education, arts, or social security. Such issues are negotiable and in a growing economy they are 'positive-sum' so that all sides can have something of the extra they wish for. Non-negotiable or zero-sum issues such as national identity, religion or racial identity have not been a major factor in Western European politics in recent times.[15] Negotiable economic issues have thus been relatively easy to accommodate to the Dual Polity model of the political process, especially as it has been the concern of politicians at the centre to divide on the broad issues of policy and leave the details of implementation to the administrative machinery of the civil service, local government or to quasi-autonomous government agencies ranging from the Arts Council to the University Grants Committee and the Whitefish Authority.

The issues surrounding the immigration and the settlement of people from the New Commonwealth posed a threat to the traditional consensual nature of post-war British politics. Neither Harold Macmillan, Harold Wilson nor Edward Heath wished race to become an issue of party politics. A high political salience for race and immigration was clearly a threat to Labour's electoral hopes in the 1960s and also to its priorities. This threat was highlighted for Labour by the Smethwick result in the 1964 general election and the subsequent defeat the following year of Patrick Gordon Walker at the Leyton by-election. The Labour Cabinet acted rapidly to neutralise the issue by tightening immigration controls and hoping that reduced immigration would allow those already settled to be integrated more easily into the community. While Labour wished for a consensus on race for electoral reasons, the Conservatives also had powerful reasons for wishing to minimise the political impact of the issue. These reasons related to abhorrence of racism, the importance of the increasingly multiracial Commonwealth and Britain's international standing.[16]

Politicians at the centre have thus sought to minimise the impact of race in national politics and exclude it as far as possible from the sphere of 'high politics'. The centre's political statecraft to achieve these ends has involved the devolution of difficult decisions to local authorities, particularly in education and housing and the establishment of intermediatory institutions like the Community Relations Councils and the Commission for Racial Equality. Problems of social control have largely been left to the police. Naturally, the centre was unable to exclude race and immigration matters completely from the national political agenda as the successive immigration and race relations Acts show. Also the riots of 1980 and 1981 forced central intervention particularly with regard to the financing of urban programmes and policing policy. It is too early to say whether the riots of 1985 in Handsworth and Tottenham will lead to more finance to combat the effects of unemployment and inner city decline or whether priority will be given to strengthening police powers and equipment. The latter response seems most likely.

The centre-periphery model employed in Bulpitt's chapter provides an alternative insight into the actions of successive governments and the 'management' of race relations in contrast to marxist theories based on economic determinism. It also provides a wider perspective than the studies of electoral behaviour and specific institutions which have so often defined political scientists' contributions in this area.[17] The model does have to be treated with caution as the distinction between the centre and the periphery is not rigid and issues may move from one area to another depending on political pressures and priorities. Moreover actions which are in fact ad hoc reactions to specific events may, with hindsight, appear to be careful statecraft when in fact they were fortuitous. The centre is not always able to prevent the periphery influencing high politics and may, on occasion, be forced to intervene in the periphery to ensure implementation of its policies.

The dearth of political research in this important area has resulted not only in a lack of general theories to explain ethnic politics in Britain but also in a failure to develop middle range theories between the general marxist and centre-periphery models and local empirical case studies. Donley Studlar's chapter on agenda-setting offers an important excursus into the area of middle range theory. He is concerned to examine how and in what circumstances race issues in Britain become salient on the political agenda. Drawing on the work of Roger Cobb and his colleagues,[18] he presents three models of agenda setting to describe the various ways in which issues became incorporated as government policy. These models are the *outside initiative* model which indicates that outside groups have been successful in pressing the government to take up issues. Secondly the *mobilisation model* in which case issues are initiated from within the government but outside support has to be mobilised before the issues are formally adopted as official policy. Thirdly the *inside initiative model* by which issues attain agenda status within the government sphere without the need to appeal for support from the mass public. While these three models afford a more detailed analysis of policy-making at the political centre, they complement rather than conflict with the centre–periphery approach presented by Bulpitt. Studlar has been concerned to demonstrate the formal nature of the agenda status of race in British politics and to refute the view that government policy-making on the issue has been simply hidden behind a series of buffer institutions centred on the race industry and the bureaucracy of community relations organisations.

Drawing on poll data indicating the views of Afro-Caribbeans and Asian voters on political issues in Britain, Studlar shows that the attitudes of most ethnic minority voters in Britain are stable and centred around the same issues for the most part as those of white voters. There was some variation between the attitudes of ethnic minority and white voters; unemployment, for example, was more important for non-whites while international issues were much less salient. Generally non-white voters indicated a general preference for central government intervention on economic and welfare issues. Similarly, relations with the police have emerged as a more important issue for non-whites since the 1980 and 1981 riots but there is no evidence, Studlar argues, to suggest the existence of a separate 'non-white political agenda' in British politics.

The ethnic minorities in Britain are relatively weak in terms of political resources. They form a very small proportion of the electorate, only 3%, and are divided on policy issues such as immigration, education, housing and law and order. There is thus only a small chance for non-white interests to make an impact on the political agenda. Which strategy is likely to be the best for them to press their interest successfully? Studlar suggests that the *mobilisation model* is likely to be the least successful in the long run. At present this strategy is being pursued by some ethnic minority politicians in the Labour party in their campaign for black sections but it is unlikely that they can mobilise enough support to achieve their aims. The other two strategies have to some extent been tried. The *outside initiative model* in an extreme form has been tested by the riots of 1980 and 1981. These riots did raise the salience of the race issue in inner city areas, despite the fact that not all the rioters were black. The government was forced to take various initiatives to improve police–community relations and ameliorate urban deprivation. The resulting government response included the inquiry into the riots by Lord Scarman and the diversion of more resources to inner city areas. Lord Scarman has taken up issues especially in the area of police–black relations which is an example of the *inside initiative model*. Studlar argues it is this latter strategy which is likely to provide the most political success for non-whites in the British context.

The general pattern of agenda management in the British political system, however, shows that issues can be effectively excluded from the political agenda by being ignored. If there is a long delay in taking up issues, their proponents may become disillusioned, the media loses interest and the issue becomes cold. The central decision-makers thus have considerable discretion in deciding whether or not to respond to issues.[19] This may lead politically weak groups to conclude that violence or the threat of violence is the only way to draw attention to their demands and force the government to pay attention to their needs.

Studlar's pessimistic conclusion is partly confirmed by the papers of Layton-Henry and Rich discussing the policy and ideology of the Conservative party, especially since the beginning of the Thatcher government in 1979. Layton-Henry shows how opposition to liberal policies on race supported by Hailsham and Whitlaw in the mid-senventies grew as the Conservative party leadership, under Mrs Thatcher, steered the party towards a more populist right-wing style. The triumph of this populist authoritarian trend on race and immigration issues was dramatically underlined by Mrs Thatcher's statements in her television interview on 30 January 1978, that British people were rather afraid that this country and the British character might be swamped by people with a different culture. She said that the Conservative party should hold out the prospect of an end to immigration except in compassionate cases and suggested that the neglect of the immigration issue was driving some people to support the National Front. She also stated that she wished to attract to the Conservative party voters who had been supporting the National Front.[20] Her intervention seems to have increased the popularity of the Conservative party, at least in the short term, and may have helped to bring about the subsequent electoral collapse of the National Front at the general election of 1979.[21] In office, however, the populist promises of the Conservatives on immigration were forced to retreat before Whitehall pragmatism and the commitments to the European Convention on Human Rights. While many on the right wing of the Conservative party pressed for full implementation of the manifesto promises, the Cabinet dropped many of the toughest proposals on immigration control. They decided that, once the status of British citizenship was clarified, the problems of immigration control would be more easily resolved.

However, the political costs of tough immigration policies were highlighted by the 'virginity test' scandal which took place before the Conservatives took office. This caused the widespread censure of Britain's immigration practices both at home and abroad. It stimulated an investigation into the immigration service by the Commission for Racial Equality which the Home Office failed to prevent by going to the courts. More seriously, the riots of 1980 and 1981 showed the tremendous resentment and alienation that had built up among sections of the inner city population and these forced changes in government policy and priorities. More resources were diverted to inner city areas to help stem urban decline, particularly in Liverpool. The government also had to respond to Lord Scarman's report and to his subsequent campaign to get more of his recommendations implemented than were initially accepted by the government. There has also been the emergence of a number of Labour local authorities, led by the Greater London Council, which have adopted dual policies of combating manifestations of racism on the one hand and positively aiding disadvantaged minority groups on the other. Government policies on race and immigration are thus increasingly being challenged.

On the right of the Conservative party, initial resentment at the failure to implement the manifesto promises led to ugly scenes at party conferences, despite the best efforts of party managers to prevent this happening. The Monday Club, also, continued to press the government to adopt tougher measures on immigration and to abolish the Commission for Racial Equality. Paul Rich, however, confirms that even the emergence of a right-wing intelligentsia in the Conservative party partly organised around the *Salisbury Review* has had little impact on policy making, despite extensive publicity for articles on race and immigration themes.[22]

The Thatcher government, however, cannot be described as merely opportunistically reacting to political circumstances, for, unlike many previous governments, it has been driven by a fairly cohesive set of economic and political ideas for restructuring the economy on free market lines, reasserting law and order and establishing a renewed sense of national identity and purpose. Despite the fact that unemployment and crime have risen relentlessly during its period in office, the government has been characterised by a marked unwillingness to modify its key political goals even though these have proved impossible to achieve through the policies it has espoused. Some writers have argued that the present economic difficulties represent an 'organic crisis of capitalism' which is causing the leaders of the British state to resort to racist and nationalist appeals to dampen rising class conflict.[23] Rich argues that in fact the reverse has occurred and that Conservative political discourse has significantly shifted away from the theme of race since the 1960s, even though it continues to be employed by a small number of MPs such as Ivor Stanbrook and Harvey Proctor. The main thrust of Conservative rhetoric has been the emphasis on national unity and the need to regenerate the economy, including the inner cities, under the guiding hand of an economically prosperous middle class. This approach accords with Mrs Thatcher's professed admiration for Victorian values and a revitalised vision of Manchester liberalism. It owes little to traditional Tory ideas of a united, organic society whose leaders intervene to help poor and disadvantaged groups.

It is thus premature to conclude that race and immigration have permanently increased in political saliency under Mrs Thatcher's administration though these issues may have become subsumed under the more general nationalist discourse employed in the government's populist style. Political scientists have been reluctant to investigate the complex and multi-faceted meanings of nationalism in the British, or rather the English context. Beyond the ethnic nationalisms of the 'Celtic fringe' there is an important historical tradition of nationalist discourse which goes back to the mid-Victorian era before the advent of imperial expansion and jingoism of the 1880s and 1890s, which led to its temporary demise from English politics in favour of wider Establishment conceptions of 'Empire' and 'Commonwealth'. With the decline of the Commonwealth in the 1970s there has been an attempt to revive past notions of English nationalism, particularly by Enoch Powell (but others as well) who wish for a resurgence of English national values against the foreigner and 'the enemy within'. Thus it may be possible to conclude that *race* has become so closely linked with this nationalist rhetoric that it does not need to be formally stated, having been transformed in Britain from being a 'sign' of physical difference to a 'symbol' with a large store of implicit connotations which can be commonly understood without being actually stated.[24] Thus, there may be a regressive effect in popular reasoning encouraged by the media whereby crime and violence is portrayed as un-British and foreign (doubly ironic given the reputation of the British in Europe for mindless hooliganism and violence both on holiday and at football matches), so the portrayal of minorities as criminal also stigmatises them as un-British.

The dilemma for the left has been how to counter racism and respond positively to the aspirations of its black supporters without jeopardising its wider electoral support, especially among working class voters. There is no doubt that whenever race becomes a salient electoral issue, the parties of the right tend to benefit. This was true in the mid-1960s when Richard Crossman described immigration as 'the hottest potato in politics' and concluded it could be 'the greatest potential vote-loser for the Labour party if we are seen to be permitting a flood of immigrants to come in and blight the central areas in all our cities'.[25] Studies of the 1970 general election confirm the view that the Conservative party benefits when race and immigration issues are salient. Studlar estimated that the immigration issue benefited the Conservative party by a massive 6.7% swing. In an independent study Miller estimated that the net benefit to the Conservative party was 2.5%. In either case this represents a substantial impact on the election results.[26] However, appeasing pressure for tough immigration controls only brought the Labour party a temporary respite in the mid-1960s and this was followed by demands, led by Enoch Powell, for even tougher policies. The Labour party stimulated by Powellism and the activities of the National Front has decided to go on to the offensive against racism, and as Fitzgerald and Layton-Henry argue, has increasingly adopted policies aimed at meeting black demands such as the commitments to repeal the 1971 Immigration Act and the 1981 Nationality Act. Both the Labour party and the Alliance hope that their policies will attract the strong support of black voters in key inner city constituencies. The results of the 1983 general election show that Labour was successful in holding the allegiance of black voters while the Alliance, whose policies are very similar to Labour's on race and immigration issues, failed to make significant gains among these voters.

Recently, new issues have emerged as being of crucial importance for Britain's indigenous black population. These are education, youth unemployment and policing. The 1970s have seen major developments in each of these policy areas and it is likely that future political conflict will revolve around these issues rather than those of immigration and nationality. Tomlinson argues that local education authorities were taken unawares by the rising demand for multi-cultural curricula as a reaction against former policies of educational and cultural assimilation. There has been strong resistance to multi-cultural education and the resulting politicisation of the debate has led to sharp conflict in a number of local education authorities between right and left over the direction of policy. Some local authorities, notably Berkshire and the Inner London Education Authority, have formally adopted 'anti-racist' education policies that stress positive action in favour of their ethnic minorities. The Swann Committee has urged a national policy to resolve these local differences around the concept of 'Education for All', though the degree of ideological division in the debate suggests that multi-cultural education may well become an issue of considerable political controversy.

The area of youth unemployment has also emerged as critically important as the economic recession has hit young people particularly hard. Solomos argues that the popular notion of black youths as a 'social problem' has been perpetuated in some government policies despite warnings from bodies like the Youth Training Board not to 'replicate inequality' in the treatment of blacks and whites. The central motivation behind much government policy in the wake of the 1980 and 1981 riots, argues Solomos, was to implement a social control strategy whereby young blacks could be removed from the dole queues and the streets. At the centre of the Youth Training Scheme there is still the lingering image of young blacks being linked to a 'problem' of race, even if it is not formally stated, and this is likely to remain so as long as schemes of special help are subordinated to a wider economic policy of economic regeneration.

Youth unemployment has become closely linked with the issue of policing and Benyon argues that black confidence in the police has declined considerably since the 1970s. The police have become more embroiled in politics as polarisation has taken place on left and right and they have also had to bear the brunt of increased social tensions generated by rising unemployment, crime and racist attacks. The Scarman Report and the 1984 Criminal Evidence Act have led to the implementation of some reforms but Benyon considers these to be highly bureaucratic and unlikely to lead to a major improvement in safeguards against abuse. The improvement of relations between the police and the ethnic minorities is clearly of vital importance but Benyon links the issue of racism in the police to the wider issue of institutional racism and sees little likelihood of the establishment of close police–community relations as epitomised by the fictional Dixon of Dock Green. The hopes placed in community policing and the Scarman reforms have been further undermined by the rioting in Handsworth and Tottenham which are likely to increase police–black hostility and fuel racial hostility in society as a whole.

The chapters by Tomlinson, Solomos and Benyon (7, 8 and 9) show the degree to which the political centre in Britain has increasingly intervened in such areas as education, employment policy and policing. This intervention has changed the former balance of responsibilities between the centre and institutions in the periphery. Such central intervention has been a marked feature of the Thatcher administration though the process began under previous governments as they struggled, for example, to control local authority spending. Increased central intervention in areas previously delegated to other institutions bring the danger of greater conflict and the need to raise further resources to intervene effectively, which may also be resisted. This suggests that controversy over the issues of race and immigration may reflect in an acute form a deeper crisis of legitimacy behind the authority of government in British politics. Early race relations legislation from the first Race Relations Act in 1965 and the Immigration White paper of the same year[27] were designed to perpetuate as far as possible a political agreement on the definition of the issues as well as in a more manipulative sense of avoiding divisions of opinion in the interests of the status quo.[28] The gradual collapse of this consensus in the late 1960s has left few areas in British political life where the issues surrounding race can be dealt with in a consensual fashion.

However, as Nixon shows, the House of Commons Home Affairs Sub-Committee on Race and Immigration can be seen as one of the last repositories of the mid-1960s consensus. The Sub-Committee normally presents unanimous reports despite the fact that it is composed of Conservative and Labour MPs with widely differing views. The Sub-Committee and its predecessor, the Select Committee on Race Relations and Immigration, have acted as valuable sources of information on a wide variety of topics with a race dimension. They have also acted as an important bridge between central decision-makers and the periphery. Organisations, experts and individuals active in race relations work have provided evidence and information which the Sub-Committee and its predecessor have used to prepare reports and make recommendations to Parliament. The government always responds to these recommendations and, while it may not accept them, it has to justify its policies. The Sub-Committee has been influential in providing a source of parliamentary expertise on race matters and in pressing the government to act, for example, on the matter of abolishing the 'sus' law.

The consensus that the Sub-Committee has maintained in such a controversial area as race and immigration is illuminating because it mirrors the political centre's remarkable cohesion in this area, whose maintenance has puzzled political analysts.[29] Perhaps more research on the politics of race needs, like Bulpitt's analysis, to explore the manner in which the political culture of the centre is maintained and reinforced through the symbolism and exercise of power and authority. To the extent that these symbols and practice are anchored in the operation of the institutions of Westminster and Whitehall, they reinforce a political culture of national homogeneity and the legitimate authority of governing power at the centre. This in turn limits the possibilities for a more pluralistic and decentralised process of delegation of authority on ethnic minority issues. It is in this area of the functioning of power and authority that political scientists can make their most valuable contribution to the study of race. For here must be the ultimate location behind the concept of 'institutional racism', a concept which has spread throughout social science literature but which is ill-defined and is not anchored in any theory of institutional power and practice. In this context political scientists can return to one of their basic concerns, the definition and analysis of institutional power and authority and how they affect members of minority groups.

## NOTES

1. There have been three Asian Members of Parliament: Dadabhi Naorji, Liberal, Central Finsbury 1892–95; Sir Mancherjee Merwanjee Bhownaggree, Conservative, Bethnal Green, 1895–1906; and Shapurji Saklatvala, Labour 1922–23, Communist 1924–29, North Battersea.
2. K. Little, *Negroes in Britain*, rev. edn (Routledge & Kegan Paul, 1972).
3. J. Rex, 'The Concept of Housing Classes and the Sociology of Race Relations', *Race*, 12, 3, 1971, 293–301.
   J. Rex and R. Moore, *Race, Community and Conflict* (Oxford University Press, 1967).
4. D. Beetham, *Transport and Turbans: a Comparative Study in Local Politics* (Oxford University Press, 1970).
   A. Phizacklea and R. Miles, *Labour and Racism* (Routledge & Kegan Paul, 1980).
5. J. Rex, 'Black Militancy and Class Conflict', in R. Miles and A. Phizacklea (eds), *Racism and Political Action* (Routledge & Kegan Paul, 1979); J. Rex &

S. Tomlinson, *Colonial Immigrants in a British City* (Routledge & Kegan Paul, 1979).

6. Rex and Moore, op.cit.; S. Abbott, *The Prevention of Racial Discrimination in Britain* (Oxford University Press, 1971); E.J.B. Rose *et al.*, *Colour and Citizenship* (Oxford University Press, 1969).

7. One of the best early political science studies is D. Schoen, *Enoch Powell and the Powellites* (Macmillan, 1977). There was also a collection of essays edited by I. Crewe in the *British Political Sociology Yearbook*, vol. II, *The Politics of Race* (Croom Helm, 1975).

8. N. Deakin, *Colour, Citizenship and British Society* (Panther Books, 1970); P. Foot, *Immigration and Race in British Politics* (Penguin Books, 1965).

9. I. Katznelson, *Black Men, White Cities* (Oxford University Press, 1973); B. Heinneman, *The Politics of the Powerless: a Study of the Campaign Against Racial Discrimination* (Oxford University Press, 1972); D. Schoen, op.cit.; G. Freeman, *Immigrant Labor and Racial Conflict: the French and British Experience 1945–75* (Princeton University Press, 1979); D.T. Studlar, *Policy Voting in Britain: the Coloured Immigration Issue in the 1964, 1966 and 1970 General Elections*, American Political Science Review, 72, 1, 1978, 46–72.

10. e.g. M. Fitzgerald, *Political Parties and Black People* (Runnymede Trust, 1984).

11. M. LeLohé, 'Participation in Elections by Asians in Bradford' in I. Crewe, op.cit.; D.T. Studlar, op.cit.; Z. Layton-Henry and D.T. Studlar, 'The Electoral Participation of Black and Asian Britons', *Parliamentary Affairs*, 38, 3, 1985; M. Anwar, *Race and Politics* (Tavistock Press, 1986).

12. Centre for Contemporary Cultural Studies, *The Empire Strikes Back: Race and Racism in '70s Britain* (Hutchinson, 1982).

13. J. Bulpitt, *Territory and Power in the United Kingdom* (Manchester University Press, 1983).

14. R. Rose, 'From Government at the Centre to Nationwide Government' in Y. Mény and V. Wright (eds), *Centre–periphery Relations in Western Europe* (Allen & Unwin 1985), pp. 13–32.

15. There have, of course, been notable exceptions such as the campaign by Basque nationalists in Spain and Republicans in Northern Ireland.

16. Z. Layton-Henry, 'Race, Electoral Strategy and the Major Parties', *Parliamentary Affairs*, vol.31, no.3, 1978, 268–81.

17. M. LeLohé, 'Participation in Elections by Asians in Bradford' in I. Crewe, *British Poltiical Sociology Yearbook*, vol.2, *The Politics of Race* (Croom Helm, 1975); S. Taylor, *The National Front in English Politics* (Macmillan 1982).

18. R.W. Cobb and C.D. Elder, *Participation in American Politics: the Dynamics of Agenda Selling* (John Hopkins University Press, 1972).

19. J.K. Stringer and J.J. Richardson, 'Managing the Political Agenda; Problem, Definition and Policy-Making in Britain', *Parliamentary Affairs*, vol.33, no.1, 1980, 23–9.

20. Granada Television, verbatim report of part of an interview with Mrs Thatcher by Gordon Burns, extract by courtesy of *World in Action*, 30 January 1978.

21. C.T. Husbands, 'Race and Immigration' in J.A.G. Griffiths (ed.), *Socialism in a Cold Climate* (Unwin Paperbacks, 1983).

22. J. Casey, 'One Nation: the Politics of Race', *The Salisbury Review*, no.1, 1982; R. Honeyford, 'Multi-Ethnic Intolerance', *The Salisbury Review*, no.4, 1983; A. Flew, 'The Race Relations Industry', *The Salisbury Review*, no.6, 1984.

23. J. Solomos, B. Findlay, S. Jones and P. Gilroy, 'The Organic Crisis of British Capitalism and Race: the Experience of the Seventies in Centre for Contemporary Cultural Studies', *The Empire Strikes Back* (Hutchinson, 1982).
24. S. Wallman, 'Refractions of Rhetoric: Evidence for the Meaning of Race in England', in R. Paine (ed.), *Politically Speaking: Cross Cultural Studies of Rhetoric* (Philadelphia Institute for the Study of Human Issues, 1981), pp. 122–3.
25. R. Crossman, *Diaries of a Cabinet Minister*, vol. I (Hamish Hamilton and Jonathan Cape, 1975), pp. 149–50.
26. D. Studlar, op.cit.; W.L. Miller, 'What Was the Profit in Following the Crowd?: the Effectivenes of Party Strategies on the Immigration and Devolution Issues', *British Journal of Political Science*, 10, 1, 1980.
27. *Immigration from the Commonwealth*, Cmnd 2739 (HMSO, 1965).
28. R. Williams, *Keywords* (Fontana, 1981), pp. 76–8.
29. A Brier and B. Axeford, 'The Theme of Race in British Social and Political Research', *British Political Sociology Yearbook*, vol.2, op.cit.fp

# 1 Continuity, Autonomy and Peripheralisation: the Anatomy of the Centre's Race Statecraft in England

JIM BULPITT

## INTRODUCTION

This chapter attempts an overview of what can be called the statecraft adopted by successive national governments to the race issue in postwar Britain. It highlights the continuity of a code of territorial management operated by and from the centre – the Cabinet and senior civil servants – towards governmental agencies, politicians, and citizens in the periphery. This code (or statecraft) reflects, in its essentials, a set of more general and traditional ideas concerning the appropriate power configuration in territorial politics or relations between centre and periphery. More particularly, it involves a view of the most advantageous stance which can be taken by the centre on those matters it regards as either unimportant or replete with potentially awkward political consequences for its own authority and prestige.

This prospectus requires some amplification. First, some of the terms employed may provoke objections or cause confusion. Race politics, for example, is equated with the politics of colour, with the relations between blacks and whites, on the one hand, and between both of these groups and governments – central or local – on the other. But, as has often been pointed out, 'race' and 'racism' are difficult concepts for academics to manage.[1] However, in Britain at least, the connection between race and colour is a sufficiently popular one to provide an easy justification for its employment in the present context. Again, the use of 'blacks' and 'whites' as generic labels undoubtedly obscures the fact that no such homogeneous categories exist in practice.[2] They are employed here for the sake of convenience, and because many of the alternatives, such as 'ethnic minorities', are even more confusing. Similar comments can be made about 'centre' and 'periphery'. These are now given a mainly territorial connotation in the literature. But they were originally conceived to describe two different cultures or value systems.[3] In practice, it is often extremely difficult to separate these two meanings and they will be employed in both senses below.

Secondly, the major aim of the exercise is to examine the centre's statecraft regarding race politics. Thus the emphasis lies not so much on the particular policies and actions of successive governments at the national level, but rather with the broad strategy behind those policies and actions. In this sense, statecraft is situated uneasily between party ideologies on the one hand and government policies and policy implementation on the other. It resembles, and perhaps can be regarded as synonymous with, related concepts such as 'the official mind' and 'the operational code'.[4] Perhaps it is time for statecraft to be rehabilitated as a conceptual device.[5] It is certainly useful in this arena because it enables us to evade the difficult problem of linking ideology to political behaviour and, at the same time, avoids the 'ad hocery' inherent in much policy analysis.

Finally, most blacks have settled in England, especially English urban areas, rather than the other two territorial sections of Britain. There are, of course, black communities in Scotland and Wales, but the political impact of their presence is inevitably complicated by the issues of nationalism and the English 'connection'.[6] Hence the race issue, as commonly defined, is primarily and most directly a phenomenon of English politics and especially of centre–periphery relations in England. In these circumstances it seems reasonable to concentrate on the English rather than the British experience of race problems. This has a certain appropriateness because the statecraft applied to race by the centre had its origin in the 'custom and practice' of territorial politics as it developed over time in England.[7]

## A RACE–CONFLICT MODEL

The development of an officially recognised multiracial society in Britain, more especially in English urban areas, constitutes one of the major social changes of the postwar era. It seems reasonable to suggest that the migration and settlement of relatively large numbers of blacks, primarily from the Asian subcontinent and the West Indies, possessed all the characteristics necessary to rank as an issue of continuous high salience and conflict in the English polity. Certainly the dominant social science paradigm, accepted both by liberals and by Marxists, appears to support this view. In pluralist or capitalist societies, so the argument runs, social changes are inevitably translated into the political arena. Moreover, it is generally admitted that racial (and ethnic) political conflicts are awkward to manage because they often assume a zero-sum character – the demands of one group can only be granted by rejecting the demands of other rival groups.[8] In addition, any comparative survey of race and ethnic relations soon reveals numerous examples of the intense and often bloody conflicts which they cause. Thus both social science theory and empirical observation suggest that the creation of a multi-racial society in large parts of England was likely to pose severe and continuous political problems.

This argument, however, can be presented in more specific terms. The available evidence with regard to English politics since 1945 makes it relatively easy to construct a race–conflict model which, potentially at least, provides additional support for these empirical and theoretical predictions. The principal items in this model are as follows.

(1) According to official estimates, the black population in Britain was less than 70 000 in 1951. By 1981 it had risen to 2.2 million.[9] This represents a thirty-fold increase over three decades. In percentage terms, the black population rose from much less than 1% of the population to some 4%. On one estimate, about 70% of all blacks are at present located in about 10% of the census enumeration districts.[10] About 50% of the black population is composed of Asians, precisely that group which differs so markedly from whites in terms of culture and language. By the early 1980s some 50% of blacks had been born in Britain, and the age profiles of black communities differed significantly from those of the whites. The official estimate for the black population at the end of the

century is about 3.3 million, some 6.7% of the total population. Data of this kind provide support for the predictions of the conflict model. Probably no other Western polity has witnessed such a rapid creation of a multiracial society, granting in formal terms at least, full political rights to the immigrants, without an initial explicit commitment by the government to such a development, and with a marked absence of any formal agreement by the bulk of its citizens to such a policy.

(2) 'We do not attempt to import blacks, coolies and Polynesians into Great Britain. The opposition of the working classes at home would be furious'.[11] This statement, made by a liberal academic at the beginning of this century, points to another item in the model. England, by tradition, was hardly the easiest polity in which to create a harmonious multiracial society. Even in the late medieval period, foreign visitors noted the extreme xenophobia of its inhabitants. Subsequent developments, especially the Reformation and imperialism, only compounded this problem. Anglo–Irish relations, even within the Union after 1800, were one example. Early 20th century attitudes to Jewish immigration were another.[12] Whatever the multiracial Empire or Commonwealth meant for the political elite, it seems clear that most ordinary English people did not want it on their doorstep, and after 1945 England was an imperial society in decline, hardly an ideal background for black immigration.[13] Moreover, as Studlar[14] has pointed out, the English culture with its emphasis on the importance of common life-styles, individual liberties not backed by constitutional enactment, and the functional necessity for inequality between groups, was not designed to cope effectively with the complex problems posed by a multiracial society.

(3) Opinion polls have indicated heavy and continuous opposition from whites to black immigration, hostility which cuts across party and class lines.[15] As one junior minister put it in 1968, all the evidence suggests that there are 'millions of Alf Garnetts in this country'.[16] Significantly, legitimate doubts exist concerning the ability of polls and surveys to reflect accurately the extent and depth of white emotions on the subject.[17] At the same time, it is well known that many blacks suffer considerably from racial discrimination and disadvantage.[18] Most blacks believe that government policies to remedy the situation have failed, whilst many whites view such policies with hostility or suspicion. Considerable pessimism about the future of race politics appears to exist. One poll in 1979,

for example, found that more people predicted serious race riots (59%) than the onset of an economic depression (43%).[19] The urban disturbances of 1980 and 1981 in several English cities appeared to confirm this pessimism. 'Smouldering apathy' is one phrase used to described contemporary black attitudes; 'antagonistic acceptance' is its equivalent for white opinions.[20]

(4) In a pluralist polity formally committed to electoral democracy and elite responsiveness to citizen (and especially majority) opinion, it seems reasonable to expect that the attitudes described above would insert themselves immediately and continuously in the political and governing process. Three specific points give added weight to this general argument. First, since the early 1960s, England has become a better informed and more querulous society, strongly addicted to single-issue group politics. Secondly, the multiracial society which developed after 1945 was not a 'guest-worker' society; most black immigrants to England received immediate political (voting) rights. And the growing number of blacks born in the country merely confirms this potential for political action. Thirdly, conflicts between blacks and whites are reflected in the party system. Labour is regarded as 'softer' than the Conservatives on immigration and race relations. Not surprisingly, perhaps, most blacks who vote support the Labour party.[21] If, as many political scientists suggest, parties are the major articulators and processors of citizens' opinions in modern politics, then these particular dimensions of the race issue would seem to raise its potential salience and conflict character even further.

(5) The development of the multiracial society in England has produced three very different intellectual responses, or languages of analysis. The disagreements between these are so many and so intense that they can be regarded as a final and significant item in the conflict model. These languages can be labelled the liberal, the radical, and the high Tory. Each requires some brief description.

*The liberal language.* This is the public language of most politicians, pressure group leaders, bureaucrats, and important sections of the quality media. In other words, it is primarily the language of a London-based, or London-oriented, political establishment. It has three major themes. First, black immigration to England was a perfectly legitimate operation, the product of domestic labour shortages and the harmonious relations between Britain and her colonies or new Dominions. Secondly, it admits that the multiracial society contains some conflict potential. But conflict, if and when it occurs, will be largely artificial, the result of mistakes by public persons and/or the actions of extremists and misguided people. Thirdly, governments in London have sought to deal with the race issue in a sensible and sane way. Black immigration has been rightly curbed and yet every attempt has been made to ensure that blacks who have settled here are treated as equal citizens. With time, education, and patience by all concerned, the problem will 'wither away'.

*The radical language.* This has obvious connections with Marxist, or neo-Marxist, analyses. But the link is not a complete one because arguments along similar lines can be presented by non-Marxists. It is this language which dominates the academic literature on the subject. Black migration to England is explained mainly in terms of colonial exploitation ('We are here, because you were there') and the economic interests of British capital. The inference here is that British governments, and whites generally, 'owe' the blacks a fair deal. Again, elite policies on the issue have been far from evenhanded. Successive governments, by emphasising the problems posed by blacks, have stimulated white racism, itself the legacy of imperialism. Since the early 1960s, governments have severely restricted black immigration and yet at the same time suggested, illogically, that blacks must be treated as equal citizens. The whole sorry story represents an almost complete victory for racism. At this point an interesting division occurs. One version of the argument emphasises that the prime source of racism has been the centre itself, which has 'institutionalised' the phenomenon from above. The other version stresses the continual and immoral responsiveness to racist attitudes in the electorate by the elite. The radical language rejects the idea that the problem will just 'wither away'. Racism will only be defeated by counter-organisation and a determination to apply sanctions against its supporters.

*The high Tory language.* Although this has only a minority displacement in the public discourse of politicians and the literature, it nevertheless reflects much popular opinion at the grass roots level on the subject. Its main themes are as follows. First, black immigration was essentially a private enterprise operation. Hence there are no debts to be paid. Secondly, the multiracial society was the result of a great betrayal, a pernicious exercise in elite autonomy, which, either from lethargy or expediency, failed to respond to majority opinion until too late. Thirdly, the black presence in English urban areas is a kind of reverse colonialism, forming a Trojan horse complex to be used by left-wing extremists. Moreover, given the attitudes of most whites, black demands can never be satisfied. Attempts to respond to those demands will produce only ludicrous policies, having little connection with English political traditions. Hardline Tories talk in terms of voluntary repatriation or guestworker status for blacks. The rest curse the great betrayal in private and emphasise the folly of most policies designed positively to favour black communities. All, however, are agreed that the future development of the issue can only be regarded as a very bleak one.

Whatever view is taken of the separate items in this model, few would reject the general message. Yet one point is clear: its dire predictions have not been fulfilled in practice. At no point between the late 1940s and the mid-1980s has the race issue occupied a continuous and important place on the national political agenda. Race conflict has had only a sporadic impact on the English polity. Two important questions arise from this. First, why, given its conflict potential, was the multiracial society allowed to develop in the first place? Second, what role has the centre played in defeating the predictions of the model?

The contention here is that plausible answers to both these questions can be provided if we assess the development of race politics in the light of the centre's statecraft, and if that statecraft is related to the nature of English territorial politics, in particular its centre–periphery, or court–country, power configuration. This approach reveals four major themes. First, the twofold continuity of race statecraft: it reflected the traditional 'custom and practice' of the centre, and its basic character remained little changed over the four decades of the era. Secondly, the major aim of the centre was to achieve as large a degree of relative autonomy as possible on the issue. 'Autonomy' here means the centre's insulation from citizen (white and black) demands, and its determination to off-load prime responsibility for the matter on to other people and other agencies. Thirdly, in practice this has involved the peripheralisation of race problems: their injection into local government and local politics as operational issues. Finally, this statecraft has been enormously successful. The management of race politics must rank as one of the great political 'jobs' of the 20th century. The interests of the centre were satisfied. The interests of blacks and whites in the periphery were left to chance.

This general argument can be amplified and supported if we examine the centre's operations in three periods important in the development of the race issue, namely 1945–61, 1962–75, and 1976–84.

## THE ORIGINS OF MULTIRACIAL SOCIETY, 1945–61

Why, given its conflict potential, was the multiracial society allowed to develop in the first place? One obvious response is that after 1945, for a variety of reasons, successive governments at the centre were not prepared to obstruct its growth, at least, that is, until 1961–62. But this raises a further question: why, given the early opposition to this development, was the centre able to delay its action on the matter for so long? The answer suggested here is that this lack of elite responsiveness was closely connected with the structure of territorial politics operating in England at the time.

This structure had emerged, in its complete form, following the period of political turbulence in the United Kingdom before and after the Great War. As an item of deliberate statecraft, however, its basic operational principles were first conceived during Lord Salisbury's regime at the end of the 19th century. As an aspiration of centre personnel its origins go back even further.[22] The principal features of this territorial 'system' can be itemised as follows.

(a) Its intended and actual power map was a single one-centre and one-periphery model. In terms more suitable to English political development, what existed was a court-country dichotomy. The centre, or court, was 'a political–administration community' of senior ministers and civil servants, operating in and around the Cabinet.[23] The periphery, or country, was all other places and agencies.

(b) To the outside world, the centre displayed considerable unity and cohesion – the result of its small size, social composition, and its jealousy of other institutions of government. Within Whitehall, however, departmentalism was rife. Hence, on those matters not regarded by the centre as important, policy was liable to be heavily influenced by 'interested' departments.

(c) Parliament's formal role in this system was to play the essential intermediary between the centre and the periphery. By the mid-1920s, however, the pressure of the party system, the party whips, and MPs' increasing fear or dislike of constituency politics, had ensured that Westminister had lost many of its former connections with the periphery. Put another way, this meant that the influence of peripheral interests in both Parliament and the centre was extremely limited, and this was furthered by the general divorce between national and local pressure-group activity at the time.

(d) The prime concern of the centre was with a relatively small number of matters which it categorised as high politics; these were foreign affairs, defence, the Commonwealth, sterling, and, after 1945, the macromanagement of economic demand via Keynesian techniques. The administration of local, or peripheral, affairs was regarded as an aspect of low politics. On these matters the centre, as far as it could, took no great interest: local decisions were left to local governors (elected and non-elected). Most aspects of the welfare state, for example, were farmed out to local politicians or officials to manage. Fortunately, in this period local politicians were prepared to collaborate with the centre in this grand design. The result was that both centre and periphery gained a degree of autonomy from one another. Territorial politics was depoliticised and bureaucratised.

(e) This insulation or autonomy of the national centre from peripheral pressures and management was replicated at the local level. The institutions and personnel of local governments in this period operated largely in a political vaccum. They had few close contacts with local party and pressure group organisations, even less with ordinary citizens. As a result, the prevailing ethic of local government was a bureaucratic and professional one. Nevertheless, in the midst of this system there existed a huge paradox. In spite of, or perhaps because of, this idiosyncratic structure of local politics, the (white) working class, especially in those areas in which it was the dominant electoral force, had been able to develop a number of institutional supports to further its interests. Council housing, neighbourhood schools (including grammar schools), the police, the health service, even jobs in local authorities, were all operated on principles which were perceived to be supportive of working-class values. Newcomers, especially to urban areas, would encounter a bureaucratised local-political world, yet one which, to a considerable extent, had been 'proletarianised'.

Combined, these items produced a structural of territorial politics (and much else besides) which can be labelled a dual polity.[24]

National and local politics were largely insulated from one another. This divorce between centre and periphery (and between local politicians and local citizens) was, in comparative perspective, one of the most important distinguishing features of the English polity in the 1950s.

What relevance has all this for the centre's statecraft regarding immigration and for the birth of the multiracial society? One immediate point is that it enables us to reject any thesis which argues that to deal with the problems of race, governments adopted some new and typically colonial administrative style – indirect rule and 'buffering' institutions – totally alien to English tradition.[25] If these were the tactics employed, it is clear that the pattern of centre statecraft and territorial politics which existed provided an adequate model to buttress any such designs. And historically, the causal link was the reverse of that suggested: it was shire government in England which supplied the model for colonial experiments with indirect rule. Of more immediate interest is that popular thesis which stresses the early and rapid elite responsiveness to white hostility regarding black immigration. Specifically, the 1962 Commonwealth Immigrants Act was the result of the centre's precipitate action to curb immigration once the race riots of 1958, and the subsequent pressures in the Conservative party, demanded such a move. Further discussion is required to assess (and reject) this argument.

Dating the beginnings of race politics in England is a difficult exercise. Public debate and pressures for action developed at different levels and in different institutions in a largely uncoordinated way, at least until the early 1960s. Although some objected to black immigration itself, others were more concerned about the absence of positive action from the centre to deal with its domestic, and largely local, implications. The important point, however, is that white 'concern' about immigration emerged well before the 1962 Act. Nevertheless, given the nature of the evidence, this is a difficult argument to advance. Some of the literature on race politics and problems in this period provides data which sustain this thesis.[26] But in the nature of things, much of the evidence is, and will remain, unrecorded, a part of the private history of the English periphery, especially its urban working class. As radical social scientists have learned, explaining 'non-decisions' and 'false consciousness' poses many problems. It is known, however, that starting in the early 1950s the Cabinet discussed on a number of occasions the possibility of limiting immigration.[27] But it always rejected taking positive action. It seems reasonable to suggest that discussions at this high level would not have taken place without some awareness of attitudes at the grass roots. After all, given English history and culture, there was every reason to believe that black immigration would pose problems. It follows that the race riots of 1958 are best viewed not as the beginnings of race antagonisms sponsored by agitators, but as one relatively late state in a protest movement against continued centre inaction on this matter. Even then the centre delayed giving any firm public commitment to immigration controls until late in 1961, three years after the riots and more than a decade after the Cabinet had first discussed the matter. In short, during the 1950s, the centre achieved a considerable degree of autonomy from citizen opinion on this issue. The principal reasons for this were undoubtedly the Westminister *laissez-faire* consensus on immigration and the weak position of the peripheral dissidents within the overall structure of territorial politics operating at the time.

What were the major factors which lay behind this exercise in relative autonomy? Clearly one, as Churchill noted, was the natural and traditional reluctance of governments to confront new problems.[28] Some arguments, such as the necessity to tackle the postwar labour shortage, were of only temporary importance. Others, such as the political necessity to import cheap labour in conditions of full employment and in the absence of an incomes policy, appear to have been stressed only by some politicians and officials.[29] Moreover, the centre seems to have been more willing to discuss these questions under Attlee and Churchill than under Eden and Macmillan. This said, three factors appear to have assumed continuous importance in determining the centre's approach to the problem. First, the free movement of people within the Commonwealth was a political and moral principle worth defending and preserving. To the extent that it held to this line the centre was more liberal than the periphery. Secondly, the sort of people demanding immigration controls represented (to recoin a phrase) the unpleasant and unacceptable face of English society. They were 'white trash', and governments would be failing in their duty if they gave in to the crude clamour emanating from such quarters. Once again the centre was more liberal than, and more remote from, popular opinion than has often been suggested. Thirdly, and most significantly, restrictions on black immigration, it was argued, would adversely affect the unity of the

Commonwealth, at a delicate stage in its development, and so essential, especially after the Suez crisis, in supporting the great power pretensions of the United Kingdom. In short, immigration controls were sacrificed on the altar of high politics, something enormously facilitated by the influence of the Foreign Office and the Colonial Office on these decisions.[30] It should be noted that this determination to avoid any foreign policy with race implications, because of the potentially disastrous impact on the Empire or Commonwealth, dated back to Lloyd George's statecraft pursued at the Imperial Conference of 1921.[31].

These characteristics of the 'official mind' on race politics, plus the existing structure of territorial politics, were instrumental in producing the three principal operational characteristics of the centre's response to the issue in this period. First, despite white protests and the centre's own sense of impending trouble, blacks were allowed to migrate to England without controls and, once settled, were granted full political rights. Again, the centre refused to accept any responsibility for protecting blacks from discrimination or to assist those local authorities into which they migrated.[32] Finally, 'any discussion of immigration and race relations, any suggestion that they were legitimate and important subjects for political debate, was frowned on. It was as though no one could talk about immigration controls without being racist'.[33] This strategy may not have amounted to a conspiracy, but it did indicate 'a common inclination, shared by most members of the upper and middle classes of British institutions, towards keeping Britain "civilised" in racial matters'.[34] Nondecisions, the mobilisation of bias, the institutionalisation of conflict, are all statecraft techniques usually attributed to capitalist governments in their continuous conflicts with the working class.[35] On this occasion they were employed by a relatively liberal centre (and were supported by radical opinion) against the demands of ordinary citizens in the periphery. The fact that in England this was an old trick does nothing to reduce the irony of their employment on this matter.

Why, then, was the 1962 Immigrants Act eventually placed on the statute book? One obvious answer is that by the early 1960s, race politics had developed to the point where even the English centre could no longer hold its autonomy against peripheral pressures. But there was another factor involved. The Commonwealth was beginning to lose its importance in the centre's foreign policy strategy. Not only had its members refused to cooperate on the matter of voluntary immigration restrictions (and the Indian Supreme Court declared illegal in 1960 the withholding of passports), but in 1961 South Africa left the organisation. Clearly in the future it was going to be a very different kind of Commonwealth, one far less amenable to direction by the United Kingdom than previously. In short, the Commonwealth showed all the signs of developing into a nuisance. More positively, 1961 was the year which signalled the centre's new external strategy, membership of the European Economic Community. Hence, in a paradoxical way the 1962 Act reveals the continued importance of high politics calculations to the centre and the impact of these on its relations with the periphery.

## THE TRIUMPH OF CENTRE STATECRAFT, RACE POLITICS, 1962–75

In the early 1960s two developments of considerable general significance occurred in British politics. On the one hand an elite culture emerged in which perceptions of Britain's relative decline as an economic and military power in the world assumed marked importance. On the other hand, the domestic political response to that culture, supported in its essentials by all major parties, was the construction of a remodernisation programme designed to arrest the international decline and, in the process, ensure the continuing effective management of the polity.

Remodernisation meant a number of things. The crux of the new strategy, however, was concerned with economic policy. Here the largely negative Keynesian demand-management posture of the postwar era was dropped in favour of more positive, neo – or pseudo – Keynesian policies, all of which involved a much greater concern for the supply side of the economy. As a result a more active, interventionist centre emerged in the early 1960s. This new statecraft was to continue largely uninterrupted, until the sterling crisis of 1976, and consequent International Monetary Fund demands, forced a reconsideration of this vital aspect of elite strategy.[36]

The consequences of this new political climate for British territorial politics were twofold.[37] First, from the early 1960s the centre began to impinge more positively than hitherto on the affairs of peripheral governments and their politicians. In doing so it dropped the relatively passive role it had played under the dual polity: the parameters of high politics were shifted to cover much more than before. Secondly, at one and the same time, the new centre policies raised general peripheral expectations concerning their benefits (which, in practice, were not fulfilled) while annoying or endangering many of the traditional political forces in the periphery. The result was a series of peripheral revolts, all of which challenged specific items of the centre's policies, and some, such as Welsh and Scottish nationalism, represented an outright attack on the traditional structure of the British Union. Hence by the mid-1970s, the old dual polity, with its fine balance of relative autonomy for both the centre and the periphery, appeared to have collapsed.

What relevance has all this for the race issue in England between 1962 and 1975? On the surface, race politics appears to have reflected many of these wider developments. The 1962 Commonwealth Immigrants Act has been described as 'the decisive turning point in contemporary British race relations', decisive in the sense that it marked an important change in centre policy and because it politicised the whole problem.[38] This Act, plus the other more restrictive immigration controls instituted in 1965, 1968, and 1971, seemed to indicate a very obvious end to the *laissez-faire* strategy of the 1950s. Moreover, the race relations legislation passed in 1965 and 1968 can also be cited as further evidence supporting this general argument. And to these new policy initiatives from the centre must be added its various urban aid programmmes dating from 1966 and 1968. In sum, it can be argued that these three policies gave the centre the resources to control black immigration, established sanctions against race discrimination, and gave the centre the ability to direct financial aid to those inner city areas in which most blacks had settled. Together, they placed the management of the race issue on a seemingly quite different plane from that operating before 1962. Moreover, change in this period was not confined solely to the centre's activities. The unfortunate halt to Patrick Gordon Walker's political career in Smethwick and Leyton, the birth of the National Front, the grass-roots activities of the Monday Club, and the increasing resentment felt in black communities (and white liberal circles) at the many iniquities of immigration controls and race discrimination, all appear to support the argument that race politics had altered radically in the periphery as well.

Above all, of course, there was the emergence of Enoch Powell, the breaker of the elite consensus on the issue, seemingly the effective champion of peripheral white opinion, and the man who brought centre and periphery together in a much more positive (if malign) relationship than existed hitherto. The combination, in 1968, of Powell's West Midlands Conservative Political Centre speech with further legislation concerning immigration and race relations plus the announcement of a new comprehensive urban programme seems to provide yet more conclusive evidence that the parameters and contents of race politics had altered radically.

Many would not accept the thesis presented above without some important qualifications. In particular, the lack of operational success both of the race relations legislation and of the urban aid initiatives would be emphasised. Nevertheless, the general argument that race politics entered a totally new phase after 1962 would command widespread support. This is surprising because, viewed in the general context of British political developments between 1962 and 1975, the significant point is how little race politics reflected these events. In other words, where the race issue is concerned, the period witnessed in its basic essentials not change but continuity, the continuity of the old centre's autonomy statecraft and the dual polity associated with it. Several points can be made in support of this alternative view.

First, for almost the whole of the period, a bipartisan line on the issue was sustained at Westminster. It is true that the Parliamentary Labour party, especially Hugh Gaitskell, initially opposed the first Immigration Bill when it was introduced. However, even by the third reading of that bill there were already signs that the gap between the parties had narrowed considerably.[39] Certainly, occasional rhetoric apart, Harold Wilson's accession to the Labour leadership ensured that every effort would be made to rehabilitate the old national party consensus. Similar comments could be made about Edward Heath after 1965. The substance of the consensus was simple: limits on immigration were necessary, but these were to be accompanied by efforts to reduce race discrimination and deprivation. Of course, the policy contents of this consensus differed from that operating before 1962, but the causes and consequences remained the same. The pressures to maintain it were the old ones; only by this means could important divisions over the race issue be avoided in Parliament, and only by this means could the centre (and Westminster) retain its autonomy from peripheral pressures on this matter. To this must be added the very real fears, after 1964, that this issue, if not properly managed, could impose electoral penalties on the major parties.[40] In this way a significant element of continuity was inserted into race politics: whichever party controlled the centre, the policies and statecraft were liable to be pretty much the same. Two further points need to be noted. Despite considerable pressures[41] the Conservative leadership under Heath never broke the broad lines of this consensus. Specifically, they did not mount any explicit electoral campaign designed to garner votes on the issue. Also, the consensus meant that Powell's influence was much less than it might have been. It is true that Powell may have contributed to the Conservatives' electoral victory in 1970[42] but he received very little reward for this in terms of any radical change in the centre's policies between 1970 and 1974. More generally, Powell's career is significant for what he has not achieved or done. He has always been a Parliamentary politician unwilling to develop any organisational base for his race campaign. He talked down to his peripheral supporters, he did not join them. As a result he may well have furthered the centre's interests on this matter. He gave the impression that 'somebody up there' understood white peripheral views. In doing so he may have further reduced the impact of the National Front.[43] From the centre's viewpoint, if Powell had not existed it may have been necessary to invent him. Like Joseph Chamberlain and Lloyd George, he found his talents were suffocated by the strength and elasticity of English Whiggism.

Secondly, it is often argued that since 1962 'the flow of Black immigrants has been virtually stopped'.[44] There is no doubt that entry controls did cause much trouble and hardship for many blacks. But they did not stop immigration. The 1962 Act, for example, was drawn up in considerable haste and confusion. As one commentator has noted, 'no one had the slightest idea what sort of effect the Immigrants Act would have on the rate of immigration into Britain'.[45] In practice, this Act, and those succeeding it in this period, merely restricted the entry of new adult black males. Dependants, and children under 16, continued to be allowed free entry. Indeed, after 1964 the bulk of black immigration was made up of dependants.[46] More generally, official figures for the period 1963 to 1975 show that net immigration from the New Commonwealth and Pakistan totalled about 710 000, with an annual average entry of some 50 000.[47] In other words, the number of blacks coming to Britain each year equalled the population size of such towns as Leamington Spa, Crewe, and Margate. Only a very skewed perspective could represent this as the end of immigration and a victory for white racism. To this must be added the considerable confusion and scepticism which surrounded the official entry and settlement statistics and the number of dependants awaiting entry on the Indian subcontinent.[48] Thus, from the point of view of many whites in the periphery, there was, after 1962, a less than full-hearted attack on the immigration problem. Once again it was the centre's interests which had triumphed over all others and once again it is difficult to argue plausibly the existence of a significant degree of elite responsiveness to majority white opinion on this matter.

Thirdly, by the mid-1970s, the official judgement was that both the antidiscrimination legislation and the various urban aid initiatives designed to remedy black disadvantage had failed.[49] Several curious and well-known aspects of these policies need to be noted.

(a) The relevant statutes were often timid and confused in content. The two Race Relations Acts, for example, were excessively narrow in their aims and lacked sufficient sanctions to make them workable.[50] The anti-deprivation programmes were concerned primarily to assist individuals in certain strictly defined districts within cities. Little attempt was made to tackle such deprivation via a comprehensive attack on the urban economies concerned. Moreover, these programmes were not explicitly designed to help blacks. It was constantly emphasised that all citizens in the relevant districts were expected to benefit.[51]

(b) Responsibility for the urban aid initiatives was scattered throughout Whitehall. Coordination between the departments involved, which changed over time, does not appear to have been very good. Moreover, the department supervising the two most important initiatives – section 11 of the 1966 Local Government Act, and the 1968 Urban Programme – was the Home Office, traditionally the centre department most insulated from the rest of Whitehall and the periphery.[52] In addition, these policies were underfunded. Hence, although they had little impact on the centre's budget, they were bound to force a series of awkward political choices on local politicians if and when they decided to implement these policies.[53]

(c) The extradepartmental agencies established to implement the race relations legislation – the Race Relations Board and its regional offices, the Community Relations Commission, and local community relations councils – suffered from a number of defects.[54] In the present context, two of these require special comment: they were understaffed, and as nominated bodies, in receipt of public money, they were expected to operate in a nonpolitical manner. Not surprisingly, they never developed any political constituency of their own; they existed in a political and institutional vacuum, relying for the most part on uncoordinated local voluntary effort. In these circumstances they could be easily ignored by governments both at the national and at the local levels. Similar comments have been made about much of the special institutional infrastructure designed to implement important parts of the urban aid programme.[55]

(d) Throughout this period, primary operational responsibility for race relations and race policies remained with elected local authorities. They were expected to initiate and supervise much of the urban programme; they administered key policy areas such as the police (outside London), education, and housing; they were important in the employment field; and it was their attitudes and responses which determined the outcome of much of the antidiscrimination legislation. The institutional framework of local government was, of course, radically altered by the London Government Act 1963 and the Local Government Act 1972. But the important point is that the structure of local politics – principally the relative autonomy of most councils from their own citizens and the centre itself – remained pretty much the same throughout this period.[56] Equally significant, despite the centre's more positive stance towards the periphery after the early 1960s, it did little to alter this vital aspect of territorial politics. No comprehensive and efficient field administrative system was established, the degree of control, especially financial control, possessed by the centre in relation to local authorities remained low, and national and local party organisations continued to operate, by and large, in separate worlds. All this meant that blacks were faced with a fundamentally unhelpful local political structure, highly resistant to their political demands.[57] In addition, those initiatives which were taken by local authorities were often unsystematic and ineffective, and the centre's financial aid did not always go to those areas most in need.

In combination these items make understandable the perceived failure by the mid-1970s of both the anti-discrimination legislation and the urban aid initiatives. They do not explain, however, why the centre allowed this particular combination to develop. Liberals have argued that these defects and mistakes were inevitable in such a new policy sector. Radicals have suggested that the centre's failure was a deliberate strategy, designed to give the blacks the appearance of positive action, whilst ensuring that few positive benefits would result in practice. Some have even suggested the whole system was an example of institutionalised racism. A more plausible view would be that the whole operation was more subtle and complex than either of these schools of thought suggest. Two points stand out. First, what the centre did was to peripheralise race politics. Major responsibility for these matters was placed on institutions outside the Cabinet and Whitehall. Hence the centre avoided most of the difficult decisions and criticisms involved. Second, the centre, as a relatively liberal actor on this stage, was not totally indifferent to the outcome of these policies. It did not deliberately will their failure, even less did it will racism. But, when it came to the crunch, it usually regarded its peripheralisation strategy as more important than the policy impact. In this sense there was more 'manipulation' than many liberals were prepared to admit,[58] yet much less, or of a different kind, than most radicals have perceived. The result was that black interests concerning these policies suffered in the same way as white interests concerning immigration, they were both largely ignored. The only winner was the centre itself.

## THE NEW RACE POLITICS? 1976–83

The previous section stressed the continuity of race statecraft between the early 1960s and the mid-1970s. The centre sought and largely obtained a considerable degree of autonomy from peripheral (black and white) forces. The Parliamentary consensus, the ambiguous immigration controls, and the peripheralisation and depoliticisation of race management were cited as factors contributing to, or resulting from, that centre autonomy strategy.

What can be called 'the mess of 1976' marked the collapse of the remodernisation statecraft pursued by each party controlling the centre after the early 1960s.[59] The period since then has witnessed the emergence of monetarism as the basis of a new centre statecraft. As an economic doctrine, monetarism is by no means coherent or comprehensive. Nevertheless, in its British context, and especially in the hands of Mrs Thatcher's governments since 1979, it has approximated to a new political economy, stressing not only the necessity to control the money supply but also wider objectives such as the reassertion of centre authority, 'privatisation', and public expenditure cuts.[60] On the territorial front, the period since 1976 has seen the somewhat fortuitous defeat of Scottish nationalism and determined attempts by the Thatcher administration to curb local government expenditure, attempts which led eventually to a policy of increasing centre control over local finances and the proposed abolition of the Greater London Council and the metropolitan county councils in the provinces. Clearly, in both system-wide and territorial terms, British politics changed considerably after the mid-1970s.

Has the management of the race issue witnessed similar changes in the centre's statecraft? More generally, has race politics altered significantly during this period? It is not difficult to provide positive answers to both these questions.

First, a number of important developments have taken place with regard to the policies pursued by the centre in this field. In 1976, for example, the Labour government passed a new Race Relations Act and in the following year it embarked on a comprehensive expansion of the urban aid programme. The Race Relations Act established a new agency, the Commission for Racial Equality, which combined the functions of the old Race Relations Board and the Community Relations Commission. On the surface this legislation gave the new Commission sweeping powers. In particular, it extended the concept of discrimination to include both direct (intentions) and indirect (effects) dimensions. Section 71 of the Act also placed a positive duty on local authorities to make 'appropriate arrangements' to ensure that their functions were carried out in such ways as to eliminate racial discrimination and promote equality of opportunity for all racial groups.[61] Labour's enhanced urban programme also indicated a significant change in centre policy. The White Paper on the matter promised to give this new initiative 'an explicit priority in social and economic policy, even at a time of particular stringency in public resources'.[62] Spending on the programme was planned to rise from £30 million to £125 million, administrative responsibility was transferred from the Home Office to the Department of the Environment, and the general focus of action was shifted to more comprehensive operations in fewer inner-city areas. Later, in 1979, Labour also attempted, via the Local Government Grants (Ethnic Groups) Bill, to direct financial aid to black groups in a more explicit and specific fashion than hitherto.[63]

The 1979 Conservative manifesto committed the party to a comprehensive change in the citizenship laws. This was duly enacted as the British Nationality Act 1981, a measure opposed both by Labour and by the Liberals on the grounds that it was essentially racist in character. Others have emphasised that the Act signalled the end of the immigration dimension to race politics.[64] In addition, the Conservatives instituted new and stricter immigration rules in 1980 and 1982.[65] And, after an initial review, the Thatcher government cut expenditure on the new urban programme while emphasising the importance of private enterprise initiatives in urban redevelopment. The CRE also suffered from Conservative policies; its financial aid was cut, five commissioners were replaced, and in 1982 its first chairman resigned after the government made it plain that his appointment would not be renewed. Finally, the 1981 Brixton and Toxteth riots led to new increases in urban aid expenditure and to the formation of the Merseyside Task Force. Michael Heseltine, as Secretary of State for the Environment, was given additional responsibilities for all inner-city areas, especially Merseyside.

Two other developments in the nature of race politics during this period also require some comment. One was that important aspects of the issue tended to go 'out of court'; race politics increasingly occurred outside the limited confines of Westminster and Whitehall. In other words, the periphery's traditionally passive role of responding to centre initiatives declined. The beginnings of this trend dated from 1977 and 1978 with the significant increase in National Front activity, activity which was opposed by the newly formed Anti-Nazi League and allied organisations. This led to often violent street-clashes between these groups. In addition, the number of racial attacks on individuals and families mounted, as did the tensions between blacks and many local police forces. One result of this increase in street activity was the emergence in the late 1970s of more positive attitudes to race problems and policies by some local authorities, unions, business groups, and police authorities. Finally, the race riots of 1980 and 1981 marked a more obvious politicisation of black peripheral demands. But a second development also needs to be noted. As the period progressed, black pressure groups began to assume a larger and more conventional role in 'normal' politics. The 'race lobby' became more vocal and respectable, a process greatly assisted by the 1981 riots and the later publication of the Scarman Report.[66] In addition, blacks began to enter local government politics and, by the 1983 general election, their presence was looked on less as a problem to be debated between white politicians, and more as an established feature of voting behaviour which might influence results in key marginal seats.

In combination, it could be argued that these developments represented the emergence of a new race politics, not by any means a coherent phenomenon, but something definitely different from the situation prior to the mid-1970s. For several reasons, however, this thesis must be viewed with considerable scepticism.

To begin with, the Labour Government's approach to race policies was a less radical break with the past than was suggested above. The 1976 Race Relations Act, the enhanced urban programme, and even the Ethnic Groups Bill of 1979 were not opposed by the Conservatives. The Parliamentary consensus was sustained. Again, what radical character these policies did possess was often the result of the actions of individual Labour politicians; section 71 of the 1976 Act was inserted at the Committee stage of the Bill by Fred Willey and much of the general ideology behind the measure belonged to Alex Lyon, a junior Minister at the Home Office until he was sacked by James Callaghan in March 1976. Moreover, it is interesting to note what Labour did not do: it made no effort to repeal the 1971 Immigration Act, it did little to improve the institutional infrastructure for the urban programme at the local level, and it produced only a very cautious, even timid, Green Paper on the question of new citizenship laws.[67]

Furthermore, the extent to which blacks experienced any real improvement in either their material or their political conditions during this period is open to question. Clearly, the riots of 1980 and 1981 suggest that there was no noticeable improvement on either count before the early 1980s. The increase in black unemployment after 1979 can be taken as further support for this point. The facts of racial disadvantage continued to be obvious for any investigation.[68] The implementation of section 71 of the 1976 Act by local authorities has also been shown, on examination, to be patchy and of limited impact.[69] Moreover, given the disarray at the CRE it is doubtful if the 'race lobby' has increased its influence as suggested. Certainly, considerable suspicions of the Commission continue to be expressed by members of the black community.[70] Of more general importance is the argument that the influence of black voters on national elections may well have been overemphasised. Put brutally, in electoral terms there are simply too few blacks and they are too dispersed and too divided to have any significant impact on election results.[71]

Thus far, the evidence seems to point to a considerable element of continuity with the past rather than to any radical change in race politics after 1975. This impression receives further support if we look carefully at the activities of the first Thatcher Government. It is true that a number of policies pursued by this administration annoyed liberal and radical opinion. It is also true that in this period certain elements in the Conservative Party became increasingly vocal on race, a development which led some people to argue that Thatcherism can be equated with a populist state-intervention stance on this issue.[72] But any considered assessment of this matter requires that attention be paid to three points: what many Conservative supporters thought this Government would do or what they wanted it to do; developments after 1979 in the Government's territorial strategy; and the Government's response to the 1981 riots and the Scarman Report.

The 1979 Conservative manifesto promised a number of initiatives on immigration and race relations. In particular, it promised a register of dependants and a general quota system for immigrants from outside the European Community. But when the party took office both these measures were quietly dropped. Moreover, after considerable trouble with some of its backbenchers, the Government decided, early in 1981, not to implement fully another manifesto promise, namely to 'end' the entry concessions to husbands and male fiances, which were introduced by Labour in 1974. Nor, despite considerable pressures from within the party, did that Government abolish the CRE, repeal all race relations legislation, and actively seek to implement the existing voluntary repatriation policy. In other words, whatever the party leaders' responsiveness to grass roots opinion before 1979 (for example, Mrs Thatcher's 'swamping' remark) they managed to achieve considerable autonomy from that opinion when in office.

Second, when the Conservatives won the 1979 election, there was a very close correspondence between its monetarist statecraft and its territorial strategy. On both counts the aim was to increase the autonomy of the centre and to reduce its interference in either the economy or the periphery. In short, early Thatcherism wished to recreate the old dual polity.[73] In office, however, this initial territorial strategy was altered: centre autonomy was to be achieved by increasing control over peripheral governments and their politicians.[74] The important point, however, is that this new strategy of greater interference and control was not extended explicitly to the race issue. After the 'urban disturbances' of 1981 the Cabinet refused, despite pressure from Michael Heseltine, to adopt more interventionist policies. Even those initiatives it did sanction, such as Heseltine's special powers on Merseyside, were later criticised as unsatisfactory in many respects and less innovative than often suggested.[75] Consequently, the scale of this government's direct response to the most serious race riots in modern English history was very limited indeed. And in so far as it did pursue radical territorial policies, these appeared likely only to increase the centre's autonomy and the already considerable obstacles in the English polity to the effective articulation of peripheral demands. Thus the management of the race issue by this supposedly radical Conservative-dominated centre was marked by very considerable efforts to preserve the statecraft of the previous four decades.

## CONCLUSIONS

The analysis above yields three principal messages, each of which needs to be expressed in the subjunctive mood.

First, the analysis of postwar race politics in England might benefit from a perspective which emphasises the centre's statecraft on the issue. This approach may serve to highlight two obvious points. One is that on this issue both blacks and whites had legitimate political claims on the centre. Whatever we think of the morality of the position taken by the majority of the whites, in a pluralist polity the centre had to consider these views seriously. It could not afford to dismiss white opinion from its calculations simply because that opinion was 'nasty'. The other point is that in these circumstances the centre may be prone to develop an interest of its own. Its operations cannot simply be viewed as a mere expression of some other interest or ideology (even 'democracy'). Second, within this framework it is possible to conclude that the centre's race statecraft over nearly forty years was characterised by continuity, involving a search for some relative autonomy on the issue and extensive peripheralisation of its management. This strategy ensured that, whatever happened, its interests would appear in the winners' enclosure.

Finally, although predicting political developments is a difficult exercise, the evidence currently available suggests that this statecraft may well persist in the future, whichever party, or combination of parties, holds power at the centre. Put bluntly, the benefits it bestows on the national political elite are too many to allow it to be easily jettisoned. Of course, some changes will occur. Future administrations, perhaps prompted by further race disturbances, may enact additional primary legislation on these matters. But the general management of the issue will probably remain the same. Radical developments are likely to stem less from newsworthy events, such as the election of black MPs (remember Bernadette Devlin?), and more from changes in the periphery involving some local parties, some trade unions, and some local governments. Education, not law and order, may well be the policy sector posing the most awkward dilemmas for this multi-racial society, not least because it is so difficult to identify what a 'liberal' posture on this issue should involve. It seems safe to suggest, however, that the centre will avoid any national initiative in this particular sector. It will prefer (as it always has done) to allow the matter to be fought over, and perhaps resolved, by local politicians, local bureaucrats, and local pressure groups.

## NOTES

1. W. Louis, *British Strategy in the Far East 1919–1939* (Clarendon Press, 1971), p.1.
2. A. Flew, *Education, Race and Revolution* (Centre for Policy Studes, 1984), pp.8–10.
3. J. Bulpitt, *Territory and Power in the United Kingdom* (Manchester University Press, 1983), p.55.
4. R. Robinson and J. Gallagher, *Africa and the Victorians: the Official Mind of Imperialism* (Macmillan, 1961); A. George, 'The Operational Code: a Neglected Approach to the Study of Political Parties and Decision-Making', *International Studies Quarterly*, June 1969, 190–222; J. Bulpitt, 'Conservatism, Unionism and the Problems of Territorial Management' in P. Madgwick and R. Rose (eds), *The Territorial Dimension in United Kingdom Politics* (Macmillan, 1982), pp.139–76.
5. P. Marsh, *The Discipline of Popular Government: Lord Salisbury's Domestic Statecraft, 1881–1902* (Harvester Press, 1978).
6. R. Miles, 'Racism and Nationalism in Britain' in Charles Husband (ed.), *Race in Britain* (Hutchinson, 1982), pp.270–300.
7. J. Bulpitt, *Territory and Power*, op.cit.
8. D. Rustow, 'Transition to Democracy: Towards a Dynamic Model', *Comparative Politics*, 2, 1970, pp.337–63.
9. T. Rees, 'Immigration Policies in the United Kingdom' in D. Kubat, *The Politics*

*of Immigration Policies* (New York, Centre for Migration Studies, 1979) pp.67–91; Runnymede Trust, *Britain's Black Population* (Heinemann, 1980); Z. Layton-Henry and D. Studlar, *The Political Participation of Black and Asian Britons*, Department of Politics, University of Warwick, Working Paper No.36, 1984.

10. D. Smith, *The Facts of Racial Disadvantage* (London, PEP) 1976; I. Martin, 'Racial Equality' in N. Bosanquet and P. Townsend (eds), *Labour and Equality* (Heinemann, 1980) pp.135–52.

11. G. Murray, 'The Exploitation of Inferior Races in Ancient and Modern Times' in W. Hirst, G. Murray and J.L. Hammond (eds), *Liberalism and the Empire* (Johnson, 1900).

12. A. Lane, *The Alien Menace* (Boswell Publishing Co, 1934); L. Gartner, *The Jewish Immigration in England 1870–1914* (Allen & Unwin, 1960).

13. J. Rex and S. Tomlinson, *Colonial Immigrants in a British City* (Routledge & Kegan Paul, 1979) pp.91–2.

14. D. Studlar, 'Political Culture and Racial Policy in Britain' in R. Rose (ed.), *Studies in British Politics* (Macmillan, 1976) pp.104–14.

15. A Marsh, 'Who Hates the Blacks?', *New Society* 23 Sept. 1976, pp.649–52; D. Butler and D. Stokes, *Political Change in Britain* (Macmillan, 1978); D. Studlar, 'Policy Voting in Britain: the Coloured Immigration in the 1965, 1966 and 1970 General Elections', *American Political Science Review*, 72, 1978, 46–64.

16. D. Hiro, *Black British, White British* (Penguin Books, 1973) p.212.

17. I. Crewe and B. Sarlvik, 'Popular Attitudes and Electoral Strategy' in Z. Layton-Henry (ed.), *Conservative Party Politics* (Macmillan, 1980) pp.244–75.

18. W. Daniel, *Racial Discrimination in Britain* (Penguin Books, 1968); Smith op. cit., Home Affairs Committee (House of Commons), *Racial Disadvantage* (HMSO, 1981).

19. D. Studlar, 'Waiting for the Catastrophe: Race and the Political Agenda', *Patterns of Prejudice*, 19, 1985.

20. Z. Layton-Henry, *The Politics of Race in Britain* (Allen & Unwin, 1984); D. Studlar, 'Waiting for the Catastrophe', op. cit.

21. Z. Layton-Henry and D. Studlar, op. cit.

22. J. Bulpitt, *Territory and Power*, op. cit., ch.3.

23. H. Heclo and A. Wildavsky, *The Private Government of Public Money* (Macmillan, 1974).

24. J. Bulpitt, *Territory and Power*, ch.5.

25. I. Katznelson, *Black Men, White Cities* (OUP, 1973) pp.123–4.

26. R. Kee, 'Is There a British Colour Bar?', *Picture Post*, 2 July 1949; P. Foot, *Immigration and Race in British Politics* (Penguin Books, 1965); N. Deakin, 'The Politics of the Commonwealth Immigration Bill', *Political Quarterly*, 38, 1968, 25–45; D. Hiro op. cit.; I. Katznelson op. cit.

27. H. Macmillan, *At The End of the Day* (Macmillan, 1973); D. Wood, 'Origins of a Multiracial Britain', *The Times*, 6 Mar. 1978; I. Bradley, 'Why Churchill's Plan to Limit Immigration was Shelved', *The Times*, 20 Mar. 1978; P. Hennessey and K. Jeffrey, 'Unnecessary immigration controls rejected', *The Times*, 23 Jan. 1982.

28. I. Bradley, op. cit.

29. D. Wood, op. cit.

30. E.J. Rose *et al.*, *Colour and Citizenship: a Report on British Race Relations*

(OUP for the IRR, 1969) pp.213, 218, and 220; Wood, op. cit.
31. W. Louis op. cit., p.58.
32. P. Foot op. cit; I. Katznelson op. cit; J. Edwards and R. Batley, *The Politics of Positive Discrimination* (Tavistock, 1978).
33. C. Patten, *The Conservative Case* (Longman, 1983) p.52.
34. D. Hiro, op. cit., pp.287–8.
35. J. Westergaard and H. Resler, *Class in a Capitalist Society* (Penguin Books, 1976).
36. S. Fay and H. Young, *The Day the £ Nearly Died* (*The Sunday Times*, 1978); J. Barnett, *Inside the Treasury* (Andre Deutsch, 1982).
37. J. Bulpitt, *Territory and Power*, ch.6.
38. G. Ben-Tovim and J. Gabriel, 'The Politics of Race in Britain, 1962–79', in Husband, op. cit., pp. 145–71.
39. I. Katznelson, op. cit., p.143.
40. R. Crossman, *Diaries* (Magnum Books, 1979) p.73.
41. D. Butler and M. Pinto-Duschinsky, *The British General Election of 1970* (Macmillan, 1971); P. Norton, 'Intra-Party Dissent in the House of Commons: a Case Study – the Immigration Rules 1972, *Parliamentary Affairs*, (Autumn 1976), 404–20.
42. R. Johnson and D. Schoen, 'The "Powell Effect" or How One Man Can Win', *New Society*, 22 July 1976, 168–172; D. Studlar, 'Policy Voting in Britain', op. cit.
43. M. Steed, 'The National Front Vote', *Parliamentary Affairs*, Summer 1978, 282–93; S. Taylor, *The National Front in English Politics* (Macmillan, 1982).
44. D. Ashford, *Policy and Politics in Britain* (Basil Blackwell, 1981) p.234.
45. P. Foot, op. cit., p.141.
46. J. Cheetham, 'Immigration' in A. Halsey (ed.), *Trends in British Society Since 1900* (Macmillan, 1972) pp.451–508; R. Rhodes James, *Ambitions and Realities* (Weidenfeld & Nicolson, 1972) p.151.
47. Z. Layton-Henry, 'Immigration' in Z. Layton-Henry (ed.) *Conservative Party Politics*, op. cit., p.74.
48. J. Brown, *The Unmelting Pot* (Macmillan, 1970); Race Relations and Immigration Committee (House of Commons), *Immigration I Report* (HMSO, 1978).
49. Home Office, *Racial Discrimination*, Cmnd 6234 (HMSO, 1975).
50. Runnymede Trust, 1980, op. cit.
51. J. Edwards and R. Batley, *The Politics of Positive Discrimination* (Tavistock, 1978); D. McKay and A. Cox, 'Confusion and Reality in Public Policy: the Case of the British Urban Programmes', *Political Studies*, 4, pp.491–506; K. Young, 'Ethnic Pluralism and the Policy Agenda in Britain', in N. Glazer and K. Young (eds), *Ethnic Pluralism and Public Policy* (Heinemann, 1983) pp.287–300.
52. J. Nixon, 'The Home Office and Race Relations Policy: Coordinator and Initiator', *Journal of Public Policy*, 2, 1982, 365–78.
53. D. McKay and A. Cox, op. cit.; D. Ashford, op. cit.
54. M. Hill and R. Issacharoff, *Community Action and Race Relations* (OUP, 1971); A. Sivanandan, 'Race, Class and the State', *Race and Class*, XVII Spring 1976; A. Dummett and M. Dummett, 'The Role of Government in Britain's Racial Crisis' in C. Husband (ed.), op. cit.
55. D. McKay and A. Cox, op. cit.; D. Ashford, op. cit.; S. Booth, D. Pitt and W. Money, 'Organisational Redundancy: a Critical Appraisal of GEAR Project',

*Public Administration*, I, 1982, 56–72.
56. J. Bulpitt, *Territory and Power*, op. cit., ch.6.
57. D. Beetham, *Transport and Turbans: a Comparative Study of Local Politics* (OUP, 1970); B. Coard, *How the West Indian Child is Made Educationally Subnormal in the British School System* (New Beacon Books, 1971).
58. D. McKay and A. Cox, op. cit.
59. J. Bulpitt, 'Thatcherism and Monetarism: the Development of Territorial Management', in I. McAllister and R. Rose (eds), *The Nationwide Competition for Votes: The 1983 British General Election* (Francis Pinter, 1984) pp.45–63.
60. D. Heald, *Public Expenditure* (Martin Robertson, 1983); W. Keegan, *Mrs Thatcher's Economic Experiment* (Allen Lane, 1984).
61. Runnymede Trust, 1980, op. cit., pp.42–5; Commission for Racial Equality, *Local Government and Racial Equality*, CRE, 1982.
62. Department of the Environment, *Policy for the Inner Cities*, Cmnd 6845 (HMSO, 1977).
63. T. Burgess, 'A Racialist Bill?', *New Society*, 22 Mar. 1979; 'Help Areas Not Ethnics', *The Economist*, 17 Mar. 1979; K. Young, 'Ethnic Pluralism and the Policy Agenda in Britain' in N. Glazer and K. Young (eds), *Ethnic Pluralism and Public Policy* (Heinemann Education Books, 1983).
64. D. Studlar, 'Waiting for the Political Catastrophe', op. cit.
65. Home Affairs Committee: *Proposed new Immigration rules and the European Convention on Human Rights, Minutes of Evidence, House of Commons* – Session 1977–80, 347-ii (HMSO, 1980); Sir John Eden, *Revised Immigration Rules*: Home Affairs Committee, House of Commons, Session 1981-82 (HMSO, 1982).
66. P. Evans, 'The Lobby that Just Grew and Grew', *The Times*, 21 Nov. 1978; Ashford, op. cit.; Young, op. cit.; Benyon, op. cit.; Lord Scarman, *The Brixton Disorders 10-12 April 1981: Report of An Inquiry by the Rt. Hon. Lord Scarman, OBE*, Cmnd 8427 (HMSO, 1981).
67. Home Office, *British Nationality Law*, Discussion of possible changes, Cmnd 6795, (HMSO, 1977).
68. Home Affairs Committee, *Racial Disadvantage*, op. cit.
69. K. Young and N. Connolly, *Policy and Practice in the Multi-Racial City* (Policy Studies Institute, 1981).
70. See the remarks of Tony Huq reported in the *Birmingham Evening Mail*, 16 June 1980.
71. D.T. Studlar, 'The Ethnic Vote 1983: Problems of Analysis and Interpretation', *New Community*, 11, 1983, 92–100.
72. R. Behrens and J. Edmonds, 'Kippers, Kittens and Kipper Boxes: Conservative Populists and Race Relations', *Political Quarterly*, 3 (1981), 342–348.
73. J. Bulpitt, *Territory and Power*, op. cit., ch.7.
74. J. Bulpitt, *Thatcherism and Monetarism: the Development of Territorial Management*, op. cit.
75. Environment Committee (House of Commons), *The Problems of Management of Urban Renewal, I Report* (HMSO, 1983).

# 2 Conservative Ideology and Race in Modern British Politics

## PAUL B. RICH

Until recently many scholars analysing race in British politics have viewed the immigration control legislation and the policies of racial integration as operating largely within a paradigm of political consensus. Donley Studlar, for example, argued in 1976, that the 'pragmatic' element in British political culture ensured that British racial policy was 'extremely non ideological'[1] and was concerned with separating race relations from politics as far as possible. This view gained credence because, in the years following the 1965 White Paper of Harold Wilson's Labour Government, *Immigration from the Commonwealth*,[2] there did appear to be a basic party political consensus on immigration. This resulted to a considerable extent from the fears of several senior Labour ministers, in the aftermath of Conservative election victories at Smethwick in the 1964 General Election and the 1965 by-election at Leyton, that immigration was an issue on which they could not hope to upstage the Conservatives in popular public opinion.[3]

However, radical analysts have not viewed British political culture as being especially pragmatic on this issue and have instead stressed the continuing racialisation of British politics and discourse within what Stuart Hall has termed 'the great moving right show'.[4] Martin Barker, for example, has argued that race relations policy in Britain has been formulated in the ideological context of a 'new racism' closely linked to the new Tory values of the 1970s and early 1980s.[5] Since at least 1968, this thesis has maintained, Tory ideology has been increasingly dictated by the 'new right' which developed a new theory of racial differentiation in terms of a 'pseudo biological

45

culturalism'.[6] This has replaced earlier 'pragmatic Conservatism' with an 'organised ideology of human nature'[7] which Barker sees as derived from the philosophy of David Hume, but reinforced by more recent ethnological and sociobiological theories of individual and group differences. Furthermore this ideology of the Tory 'new right' has linked the notion of 'nation' far more closely with 'race' than the earlier pragmatic tradition which, Barker argues, saw the nation as 'a working unit of disparate groups.'[8] With the rise of Powellism, the emphasis in recent Conservative rhetoric has been on national homogeneity, such as Margaret Thatcher's fears of Britain being 'swamped' by immigrants. This 'was an immediate application of Tory ideological principles to the issue of immigration'.[9] This racism, though, was different in kind from the earlier tradition of 'scientific' racism in European and North American thought which culminated in the experience of German National Socialism. For this tradition of 'classificatory racism' has now been superseded by a more modern 'motivational racism' which 'tells people it is only natural to meet strangers with hostility'.[10] This political theory of 'instinctivism' thus has important political consequences and Barker's analysis has resulted in a perception by some sections of the left that contemporary Conservative ideology is linked, if only tangentially, with a new biological determinism.

This reformulation of Conservative ideology has also been seen as part of an authoritarian response to mounting class conflict and economic and political crisis in British capitalism.[11] Errol Lawrence, for example, has seen the 'new racism' as a means of undermining the remaining 'wet' Conservatism left in the Tory party, and so leading it into similar political contours as the organised fascist parties of the extreme right, many of whose voters had defected to the Conservatives in the 1979 General Election.[12] A more portentous conclusion has recently been reached by Robert Miles and Annie Phizacklea who have argued that this racism leads to the emergence of a coherent nationalist ideology of Britain as a 'white man's country' with a continuous 'drift towards "repatriation"' as a result of rising unemployment and a political need to remove black 'alien' labour.[13]

The significance, therefore, of the new racism thesis is profound both for analysis and political debate. The validity of its assumptions and conclusions is thus the substance of this paper, which will begin by discussing the nature of modern Conservative ideology and its linkage, if any, with race. This will be followed by an analysis of the effect of Powellite discourse in British politics from the late 1960s, particularly in the light of the growing sophistication of Conservative electoral strategy towards the Asian vote which, it will be argued, substantially qualifies the assertion that there is an inherent trend towards the repatriation of blacks out of British society.

## THE EVOLUTION OF CONSERVATIVE THOUGHT ON RACE

The 'new racism' thesis has helped to focus attention upon political ideologies in British race relations, and it may throw light on how anti-immigrant feeling at the local level has so successfully influenced policy in a manner almost unique in postwar British politics.[14] The isolated calls for immigration restriction in the House of Commons during the 1950s from such MPs as Cyril Osborne and Norman Pannell were successfully resisted by the consensus-orientated Conservative leadership of Harold Macmillan and R. A. Butler, but the more organised campaign for immigration control at the local level was a different matter. In particular, on 13 December 1960 the Birmingham Immigration Control Association was formed which initially had a Conservative councillor, Charles Collett, on its committee. The Association began a letter-writing campaign to MPs and helped collect signatures for a national petition organised by Cyril Osbourne intended to influence policy making at the centre. The tactical style at this time was limited to conventional lobbying and avoided more direct political action at the local level. Indeed, in April of 1961 right wing Tory MPs in Birmingham such as Harold Gurden (Selly Oak) and John Hollingworth (All Saints) urged the BICA not to field independent candidates in the local elections whilst the MPs were lobbying the Conservative leadership for a bill to restrict immigration.[15] With a Gallup poll finding in May that 73% of the electorate wished for immigration control, clearly there was a tide of opinion which the government found hard to resist.

At the October conference of the Conservative Party in Brighton there were 39 resolutions in favour of immigration control, though the language of most speakers was carefully moderate. Councillor D. Clarke of Hayes and Harlington, in moving for the Government 'to take action quickly' on the issue, denied that the demand for control was influenced by colour considerations, and made a distinction between those immigrants who were 'good, honest folk' and the 'bad immigrants' whom there was no reason to tolerate. He then reinforced this paternalist distinction that was strongly reminiscent of colonial attitudes by expressing a wish that Britain should maintain Commonwealth links.[16] Though some speakers such as Nigel Fisher urged that any genuine concern for the Commonwealth implied a strictly 'colour blind' immigration policy,[17] there was no manifest enthusiasm even at this time for the Commonwealth notion in Conference circles despite the importance which had been attached to it in British colonial policy in the postwar years as a cushioning mechanism in the withdrawal from empire. Norman Pannell, for Liverpool Kirkby, argued strongly for control, expressing a more parochial concern for British national identity. Though, he argued, 'the immigrants' were 'not necessarily inferior to us' they were nevertheless 'different – different not only in colour but in background, tradition and habits'. This implied only two courses: either full integration through intermarriage and 'the mingling of their blood with ours throughout the population' or the forming of 'minority groups set apart from the general population – a sort of second class citizenship'. Either course, Pannell considered, would be 'unfortunate'.[18]

As early as 1961, therefore, in these Conservative arguments for immigration control there was an implicit notion of national homogeneity which even liberal Conservatives found hard to counteract. Nigel Fisher, for example, refused overtures from Martin Ennals of the National Council for Civil Liberties to ally himself to a broad-based campaign against the proposed immigration control bill, arguing in August of 1961 that he preferred 'to choose my own time and place for any further speeches when I know the precise proposals which may be made'.[19] By leaving the initiative to the government, the liberal Conservatives appeared somewhat half-hearted in their objections and once the bill became law their political commitment to the ideal of the Commonwealth continued to decline as the withdrawal from empire continued during the 1960s. 'What is the Commonwealth, held up in the raw light of day', wrote Elspeth Huxley in 1964, a year after the independence of her beloved Kenya. It was indeed:

> An idea in minds that, like all human minds, recoil from uncongenial reality and want to go on believing that as things were, so they remain. A sort of mummy-case in which we have embalmed an empire that's dead but that we can't bring ourselves

finally to bury, because we want to go on feeling that something's still there. The Emperor's clothes.[20]

This loss of faith in the Commonwealth extended to considerable sections of the Conservative elite whose benign paternalism on the issue of Commonwealth immigration was probably already considerably eroded by the early 1960s. While much attention has been paid to such a paternal figure as Rab Butler, it is also necessary to look at the wider climate of opinion within Conservative clubland and high Tory circles as a whole. One interesting figure who provides a sharp contrast to the liberal paternal tradition is Lord Elton, who in the 1930s had been a supporter of the MacDonald National Government and of corporatist economic management as a British compromise between capitalism and socialism.[21] In the 1940s he was an enthusiastic supporter of the Commonwealth ideal and wrote in *Imperial Commonwealth* of the British Empire as possibly forming the nucleus of some wider organisation in which the values of British liberal imperialism bequeathed by the nineteenth century could yet be maintained for 'it may well be that the island from which the world learned the art of freedom will yet teach it the art of unity'.[22]

These ideals were dashed over the following two decades as the real nature of the British position in the international system became evident. Until 1945 British economic management had been fairly successful in shoring up her position in the world economy, but over the following years there were mounting economic difficulties and large scale debts to the United States that led to harsh financial stringencies culminating in the 1949 devaluation of the pound. The Suez debate of 1956 dramatically confirmed Britain's decline as a major world power and meant, as Bernard Porter has recently argued, that Britain's 'natural pattern of development' was interrupted, and was superseded by a pattern of development determined by the interests of other powers.[23] This change in political status internal British political discourse sought as far as possible to conceal from the public arena, notably by the Churchillian rhetoric of national greatness.[24] The race theme therefore became a component part of this rhetoric as black immigration was seen as a significant threat to British national homogeneity and hence greatness. Thus, as early as 1956, Elton began echoing Cyril Osborne's pleas for immigration control in the House of Lords by laying down the ideological basis for the

patriality notion eventually incorporated in the 1971 British
Immigration Act:

> may we not come to a time when we shall have to return to some
> such conception of the indefensible right inhering only in those
> who will be returning to the home which they, or their forbears,
> once left: and for the rest of our fellow citizens of the British
> Commonwealth, rights roughly reciprocal and analogous with
> those which our own citizens enjoy with them overseas? The time
> has not yet come to answer this question – but it may come one
> day.[25]

As a former lecturer in modern history at Oxford, Elton brought
a strong sense of historical change to bear on the issue, realising as
Elspeth Huxley was to do, that the Commonwealth concept was
rooted in a set of political illusions. In 1965, he published a bitter
attack on black immigration in a book entitled *The Unarmed
Invasion*. Here he set down the notion of *returning* to the
'indefensible right' for residence in Britain only for those with
ancestral links, and fortified his argument by reference to a tradition
of Victorian liberal racialism which had opposed imperial federation
on the grounds that it would lead to its domination by India and its
large Asian population.[26] Elton now saw the Commonwealth
'almost as far as it could possibly be from multiracialism in the sense
in which Britain is becoming multiracial' since the majority of the
population in the Commonwealth consisted of 'coloured citizens'.[27]
These arguments that Britain should recognise that its interests were
in opposition to wider Commonwealth ones were also reinforced in
some sections of right wing opinion by more explicitly racist
assertions. In particular there was some publicity given to a
Eugenics Society pamphlet at the time of the 1958 disturbances,
which argued that black intermarriage or 'miscegenation' with the
white British population would lead to the eugenic deterioration of
the popular racial stock since the immigrants brought 'measurable
and largely inheritable physical attributes below the average for the
United Kingdom'.[28]
. However in the late 1950s this explicit or 'classificatory' racism
was becoming a source of political embarrassment in mainstream
Conservative circles, as the party sought to dissociate itself from
South African apartheid and promote a policy of racial 'partnership'
in the short-lived Central African Federation.[29] By the time Elton

published *The Unarmed Invasion*, combining an attack on the Commonwealth ideal of multi-racialism with a more inward nationalism, his views epitomised an atavistic racism that hearkened back to the climate of thought on race in British governing circles in the pre-war years. In the following year a more sophisticated presentation came, somewhat surprisingly, from Peter Griffiths, the notorious victor of Smethwick in the 1964 general election who had refused to condemn the slogan 'If you want a nigger neighbour, vote Labour'. Griffiths's *A Question of Colour?* was written in part to try and clear his tarnished reputation, though the book failed to re-establish him as a mainstream politician in parliamentary Conservative circles. Nevertheless, the book was an important pointer to the direction Conservative thought was taking on race and immigration while in political opposition and helped to shift discussion away from explicitly racial notions based on colour. Griffiths rejected any arguments centred around the concept of 'pure' races, for the doctrine of white racial superiority was 'the last spasm of a completely demolished proposition. Scientific facts will make it quite impossible for educated people to hold such ideas in the future. Only among the illiterate or semi literate can such doctrines find acceptance unless prejudice blinds people into rejecting what is clearly proven'.[30] Reacting essentially as a politician to the modern consensus of scientific and anthropological thought on races, Griffiths realised that the issue had to be seen in the context of man as one species, though this still left room for attention to be paid to genetic diversity for there was 'no evidence that either individuals or races are equal in their natural endowment. Moreover, it is clear that some of these inequalities are genetic or inborn'.[31] This somewhat confused position was nevertheless subordinated to Griffith's main plea which – in a tradition long upheld by anthropologists – implied 'respect for racial and cultural differences' and the recognition that these differences were 'among equals'.[32]

It was this argument for racial and cultural 'differences' which nevertheless led Griffiths into an argument supporting South African apartheid on the grounds that from 'the historical evidence', 'urban civilisation' was 'natural' for 'Caucasian and Mongoloid peoples' but was certainly not the 'natural environment for Negroes' for 'no Negro society has ever created cities or industries. Rural life on a pastoral and agrarian basis has been the creation of Negro societies throughout the centuries. . . . To impose (European life) on unwilling people seems to be wanton cruelty'.[33] Such a line of reasoning was a re-application of nineteenth and early twentieth century imperial arguments that colonies were rural and frontier areas whose colonised, and especially black inhabitants were adapted to a 'natural' terrain, and so had inherent cultural attributes antithetic to western, white and urban 'civilisation'.[34] Griffiths's argument contained no particularly strong plea for British national re-assertion and was couched more in terms of a negative warning that 'the failure of our people to meet the challenges of the age would condemn us to a place in the backwater of the nations'.[35] In one sense, his argument was still based on an imperial mode of reasoning centred on the notion that, provided the mother country was uncontaminated by foreign or alien bodies, then its natural genius would ensure it did not become a 'backwater' of nations. To this extent, Griffiths's argument reflected a more general failure at this time to understand how Britain's position had become transformed through its interests being shaped by external forces outside its control.

Enoch Powell, on the other hand, not only had a populist and dramatic style which caught the public imagination but also realised by 1968 that the race and immigration issue had to be linked to a wider theme of conscious national reassertion in an effort to reclaim control over a national destiny he realised was rapidly passing from the hands of the British political elite. Powell had moved from a position at the start of his political career in the late 1940s of extreme imperialist enthusiasm to one of resigned acceptance in the wake of the Suez crisis of 1956 that the British Empire was no longer a viable political entity. In 1947, he had seen the Empire as 'the structure on which we are dependent for our very existence',[36] though it was the power relationships underpinning this imperial structure which he thought really mattered and for which the Commonwealth could be no adequate substitute. In the early 1960s he began to reconsider his idea of British nationalism and saw that the link of the British nation with a wider Empire had been only a momentary one, stemming from the phase of late nineteenth century jingoist euphoria. It was, more particularly, a political invention which he saw as gripping the imagination of first the Conservative Party and then 'the British people', and so preventing a more realistic assessment of the British position in world politics. It was now the task, as Powell saw it, to destroy the myth of empire and return to a more introspective conception of English national identity:

Thus our generation is like one which comes home again from years of distant wandering. We discover affinities with earlier generations of English, generations before the "expansion of England", who felt no country but this to be their own. We look upon the traces which they left with a new curiosity, the curiosity of finding ourselves once more akin with the old English.[37]

This was in essence an opportunistic appeal to an ethnocentric nationalism in which Powell employed the notion of a white racial identity in a rather derivative manner. In the mid-1960s, Powell was essentially a national politician with an appeal to the political centre and his roots in his Wolverhampton South West constituency did not run especially deep: Paul Foot, for instance, has shown that in 1968 Powell did not know of the Council for Racial Harmony in Wolverhampton or how it was financed.[38] It appeared that in repeating racial folk myths such as stories of people having excreta pushed through their letter boxes, he was the adopting a more populist style after years of political frustration playing a tactical waiting game at Westminster hoping that through private persuasion the Conservative leadership could be cajoled into adopting more stringent immigration control policies. The tactic clearly paid off in a manner that Griffiths's essentially localised campaign could never have done, for in his graphic appeal to British national identity in his rivers of blood speech he undoubtedly struck a popular chord: of the 3537 letters he initially received after the speech, no less than 1128 saw immigration as linked to a threat to British culture and traditions while only 17 or 0.3% were explicitly racialist in content against the immigrants' race *per se*.[39] Some form of dialectical interaction between this grass roots mood and Powell's definition of the issue occurred for, when pressed on the issue of race in an interview with David Frost, he did not even consider the 'scientific' aspects of race 'relevant to the policies with which as a politician I am concerned'.[40]

The significance of Powell's appeal to nationalism lay in its forming the third and binding element within three main strands of his political thoughts. These were, first, a corporate philanthropy in the tradition of 'One Nation' Conservatism, secondly an economic neo-liberalism and belief in the limitation of the state's role in the regulation of the economy, and thirdly, a living conviction in the ideal of national homogeneity. A close relation can be discerned between the first two for both revolved around the *role* of the state in the body politic and a coherent logic can be discerned between policies which release market processes, on the one hand, and social welfare policies which act as a mode of political stabilisation by offering support for those unable to compete in the free market competition for material goods on the other. In contrast, the third element of nationalism related more to the *nature* of the state and was a product more of contingent historical circumstances than of any inherent ideological relationship between the state's governing ideology and social welfare capitalism.[41]

The appeal of nationalism however to the British electorate in the late 1960s had a considerable political rationale. Douglas Schoen in his analysis of the Powellite phenomenon has distinguished between the period 1968–70 and the years following. In the first period, Powell's appeal was to the more disillusioned sections of the electorate at a time when electoral turnout dropped from 79% in the 1959 election to 72% in 1970. Not surprisingly Powellites felt most strongly on immigration but were also very biased towards the Conservatives. The Butler–Stokes data for 1969–70, for example, showed that in 1968, 68%, and in 1970, 63% of people who gave Powell a 78–100 rating were Conservatives while only 28% in 1969, and 16% in 1970 of those who gave him a low 0–34 rating were also Conservatives.[42] Powellites tended to be weak class identifiers and to some extent were less strongly rooted in British status structures without being the atomised individuals of mass society theory.[43] It was to these people that Powell in the initial period of 1968–70 made a strong appeal through his rhetoric of national will and strong statecraft; asserting for example that 'The supreme function of statemanship is to provide against preventable evils.' This support, however, became more diffuse after 1970 and Schoen believes the dissatisfied elements in Powellism evolved into a wider coalition of those dissatisfied with the workings of the political system. Powellism thus played 'a preparatory role in making the electorate more receptive to those who took up positions outside the mainstream of British politics'.[44] This clearly helped to act as a catalyst for the growth in support for the extreme right wing in the 1970s during a time of political malaise when the Heath, Wilson and Callaghan governments were plagued by industrial strife and mounting economic difficulties. Powell himself though moved from the political centre after 1974 into the peripheral sphere of Ulster politics.

## THE IMPACT OF POWELLISM

The Powellite message was not lost on Conservative Party circles. In some respects it acted as a model for the emerging 'new right' of aspiring professionals, small businessmen and some working class supporters who were increasingly taking over from the older aristocratic and paternalist right, now associated with an aristocratic grouse moor image and obsolete imperial connections. In the early 1960s Powell had still seemed a relatively lone voice calling for a remoralisation of Conservative policy from a lofty, Delphic platform. By the late 1960s, however, this process began to change as some more professional and educated people began to emerge in the party, some of whom were attracted to free market and libertarian ideas, and also to nationalist and anti immigrant principles.[45] In the debate on race in the Party at this time a certain failure of political nerve by those more liberally inclined became increasingly apparent. This was in part because of the decline in political influence by the liberals in what was coming to be termed the 'race industry' following the demise of the Campaign Against Racial Discrimination in 1967. Furthermore those involved in prosecuting racial discrimination through the Race Relations Board appeared to a number of Conservative politicians as aloof and elitist after it had been established under the 1965 Race Relations Act.[46] The Act, though, gained the support of liberal Conservatives organised through the pressure group PEST (Pressure for Economic and Social Toryism).[47] Despite its limited power, many Tories saw the Race Relations Board as trying to engineer legislation without parliamentary debate. In August 1968, in the wake of Powell's Birmingham speech and before the passage of the Race Relations Bill enhancing the Board's powers in respect of discrimination in jobs and housing, William Deedes wrote of 'government without consent' illustrating 'a failing which has bedevilled race relations for nearly a generation – a lack of political candour in presenting controversial issues to the public.'[48]

The explicit language employed by Powell certainly did not produce a lack of candour on the Tory right for his message served as a catalyst for a more wide-ranging attack on the political consensus in race relations from politicians centred around the Monday Club. In 1969 George Young capitalised on the failure of the white liberal group in CARD by initiating a more direct attack on the notion of 'integration' in race relations which he saw as a complete fallacy in the light of growing racial tensions world wide.[49] He claimed that there was a 'neurotic process' involved in what he termed the 'liberal humanitarian' outlook which had dominated the British political vocabulary for a century and a half, for the liberal humanist concept of man failed to 'stand up to the new demands of self-interested diversity'.[50] Young employed the term 'communalism' to describe the political behaviour of ethnic minorities and so echoed similar rhetoric of Enoch Powell the previous year. The term had an ancestry, as Sir Keith Hancock has shown, in British colonial discourse stretching back to the 1930s.[51] However, logically this line of argument leads to an aggressive ethnocentric politics of a kind already familiar in what the Monday Club regarded as an ideal social model, South Africa.

By the early 1970s, divisions began to emerge in the Monday Club camp between relative moderates and extremists with links with the Immigration Control Association. It was by no means clear, though, that the Conservative leadership wished to press for repatriation of immigrants as demanded by the extremists. Some local Conservative Associations did become involved at this time with extreme right wing groups on the race issue: in Bradford, for example, the Yorkshire Campaign to Stop Immigration, which had been founded by an ex-councillor Jim Merrick, was seen as having close ties with the mainstream Conservatives locally and its second meeting was held in the premises of the Little Horton Ward Conservative Association.[52] The Parliamentary Conservative party, however, had only a small number of MPs associating themselves with the Monday Club's campaign against the 'race industry', an example being Ronald Bell, who tabled a motion for the repeal of the 1968 Race Relations Act. By 1972, the divisions in the Monday Club resulted in its virtual withdrawal from intra-party lobbying after a counter-attack by activists in its 'Young Members' group against the extremist line of compulsory repatriation which was seen as politically unrealistic.[53]

The militant Monday Club activity of the early 1970s was thus rather unusual, for Conservative Party factions normally relied on general political persuasion through pamphlets and public meetings. The Monday Club, though, began to resemble a political tendency as in the Labour Party by initiating resolutions at Party conference and attempting to influence candidate selection.[54] It was partly in reaction to this that the reorganised Tory 'new right' of the mid-1970s avoided stressing the racial theme and adopted a more overtly intellectual and persuasive stance in intra party political activity. The formation of the Selsdon Group in 1973 to promote monetarist and free market ideas in cooperation with the more academic Institute of Economic affairs illustrated this more careful right wing approach, for the Group's members were kept down to 250 and no branch organisations were established so as to prevent permeation from the National Front.[55] The focus on economic issues also reflected the new right's determination not to get bogged down on racial issues, preferring instead to dwell more upon patriotism and nationalism rather than race *per se*. For a number of the new right Tory intellectuals such as John Biffen, the Heath Government's Immigration Act of 1971 with its patriality provisions was as far as it was politically necessary to go in terms of direct legislation on the issue. Their reaction to support for the National Front (which in 1976 reached some 8% in the local elections and as much as 15% in some areas like Leicester, Sandwell and Bradford) was not to consider political collaboration but to attempt to rebuild a confident middle class through free market policies. The problem was, Biffin wrote in 1976, that 'the very sections of society that have traditionally provided community and business leadership feel defeated' and there was a consequent danger that the Tory party would become 'remote from the problems of immigration as their political base is more concentrated in the suburbs and the shires'.[56] There was a certain nostalgia about this ideal of rebuilding a new middle class local elite with a similar kind of political and ideological hegemony as its Victorian forbears, but clearly the strategy was more concerned with national self confidence than with racial identity. This became clear in the wake of Mrs Thatcher's takeover of the party leadership from Edward Heath in 1975. In 1976 the statement of Conservative Party aims, *The Right Approach*, put forward the notion of a 'British character' discerned by de Tocqueville in the mid nineteenth century in terms of a 'spirit of trade' and self-reliance.[57]

## THATCHERISM AND THE BREAKUP OF CONSENSUS

Thatcherite political ideology nevertheless assumed a somewhat uneasy sway over Conservative party thought at a time of political and economic crisis in the mid-1970s. The downfall of the Heath government in February 1974 in the wake of the miners' strike and the three-day week led to a state of growing unease in dominant Conservative circles at the possibility of nationalism – divorced as it now was from the former grandeur and mystique of empire – to provide adequate ideological continuity and stability in what was seen as a period of rapid economic and industrial change. The mid-1970s were thus a crisis period in the true historical sense of allowing for both continuity and change 'for "crisis" implies the continuity of organic processes but not steady equilibrium, decisive conflict but not "total" revolution'.[58] The awareness of this possible failure of the nationalist model and its appeal to *Sammlungspolitik* (the politics of cohesion) did not escape the more perceptive of Tory politicians. 'We have in prospect and already in being', wrote Biffen:

> a social transformation in England that is as profound and far reaching as the impact of the Industrial Revolution itself. It is a massive change and the very tensions that flow from such a development could tear down the tradition of tolerance and sense of national cohesion that have sustained this country[59]

The appeal to economic neo-liberalism was part of a strategy of rejuvenating the capitalist economy and transforming the system of class relations that had been institutionalised in the corporatist Keynesian consensus of the post war years. Thatcherism is in many respects less a distinct ideology but a range of political creeds that include neo-liberalism, moral authoritarianism and Anglicised Gaullism.[60] At the heart of Conservative political ideology there is the recognition of the basic primacy of politics over economics, for this was so not only in the classical age of the limited state of the nineteenth century but even more the case in the modern era. The significance of Conservative thought thus lies in its crystallisation at moments of political crisis for it is, in essence, 'a situational ideology which appears on the historical scene at critical moments in order to defend cherished institutions in terms of a few abiding principles'.[61] It was this protean quality of modern Conservative ideology which ultimately became clear on the issue of race and immigration.

The interpretation of Conservatism, for example through the mode of Humean scepticism of reason and the appeal to instinctivism, as in Martin Barker's attempt to link modern

Conservative ideology with racism, mistakes the mode of conservative political thought for its actual substance.[62] Hume does not see national character as some unchanging concept that is inherited through successive generations, but believes merely that human groups tend on the whole to be more influenced by the 'nation' they happen to live in than others. Consequently this need not imply the 'racist' exclusion of immigrant minorities from the conception of a British 'nation' and certainly does not lead to the simple conclusion that the 'racism' of British nationalism means repatriation.[63] Conservative thought has therefore been shaped by Hume's conception of the need for national cohesion and it has thus tended to eschew political dogmas since it has needed to perform a brokerage role between different groups and components of a ruling class. This became expecially evident in the course of the debate on the new definition of Conservative policy between 1974 and 1976 when Sir Keith Joseph, the politician most closely identified with the assumptions of the monetarist creed, was careful to point out in a speech at Brighton the need 'to get economics back into perspective, as one aspect of politics, important but never really the main thing'.[64]

It was in this context of the primacy of politics that the debate on the Tory right acquired an unusual degree of sophistication in the late 1970s as a number of intellectuals began a reformulation of Conservative ideology in reaction to the impact of the rising marxism in the Labour party and the left generally. Maurice Cowling, in a collection of *Conservative Essays* he edited in 1978, believed this reformulation was part of a class war that needed to be 'handled with skill and subtlety'.[65] John Casey, one of the more perspicacious intellectuals propounding the new Tory philosophy, saw the issue in terms of Hegel's notion of the owl of Minerva, Goddess of Wisdom, taking flight only at dusk 'for a conservative philosophy complete with a view of its own historical situation takes wing only in a moment of crisis'.[66] In this mood of crisis, the central challenge facing those who wished to reformulate Conservative philosophy was one which required 'the largest imaginative leap' in order to grasp 'the alteration and decay of customs and patterns of behaviour' betokening 'a profound change in the consciousness of the age'.[67] This new model Conservatism adapted to a situation of breakdown of political consensus and the emergence of class and political conflict which erupted in widespread rioting in many of Britain's major cities such as Bristol (St Paul's) in 1980 and

Liverpool (Toxteth) and Brixton in 1981.[68]

In the course of the 1970s and early 1980s, therefore, the Powellite warning of impending racial conflict similar to that of the United States appeared increasingly pertinent to the British political scene. By seeing the 'racial threat' in more generalised international terms, the Tory philosophy of nationalism became divorced from the more overt racism employed in the rhetoric of the National Front, despite evidence of limited contacts forged with some fascist groups by individual Conservative politicians and constituency associations.[69] It is thus an exaggeration to conclude, as Barker has done, that in the 1970s Conservative political ideology manifested an inherent racism through its employment of a political theory of instinctivism drawn from theories of ethology and sociobiology. While some individuals such as Sir Alfred Sherman of the Centre for Policy Studies sometimes voiced such sentiments, it is by no means clear that these theories were at all well understood even in mainstream right wing Conservative circles, let alone amongst the party members at large.[70]

A more dominant political tendency by the new Tory philosophers has been a search for historical roots behind British national identity. This became linked to a change in the political debate on race and immigration in the 1970s following the 1971 Immigration Act. There was a shift in emphasis away from the external 'threat' posed by numbers of new immigrants to the 'threat' presented by ethnic communities and other minority groups in inner cities and to British national homogeneity. By 1982, for example, John Casey saw the issue of ethnic minority settlement as one that challenged what he saw as the impoverished political vocabulary of the Conservative Party. He sought to move the direction of political debate beyond the discourse of free market capitalism, which might ultimately undermine the historical conception of community, and link it to the notion of patriotism as the basis of political authority:

It implies *at least* that there be a degree of continuity, cohesion, community of sentiment that makes the acceptance of this authority both truly general and truly 'immemorial'. The destruction of continuity and community must tend to the destruciton of the constitution itself. There is no way of understanding British and English history that does not take seriously the sentiments of patriotism that go with a continuity of institutions, shared experience, language, customs, kinship. There is no way of understanding English patriotism that averts its eyes from the fact that it has at its centre a feeling for persons of one's own kind. The Germans have the term *Sittlichkeit* to express the moral obligations I have to an historic community of which I find myself a part. The moral life finds its fulfilment only in an actual, historic human community, and above all in a nation state.[71] (emphases in original).

This notion of the historical community of the nation state also went beyond a theory of racial identity. Casey continued, '. . . the state of nationhood is the true state of man, and danger of ignoring the sentiment of nationhood is actually the danger of the destruction of man as a political animal'.[72] It was this centrality of national identity as a *political* state which the new Tory theorists were anxious to assert for to do otherwise would be to wed Conservatism to another determinist dogma for which they pilloried their left wing opponents. As Roger Scruton, editor of *The Salisbury Review*, defined the issue in *The Times*:

Race is at best an influence on behaviour, not the moral source of it. It is the individual alone who acts, and he alone who should bear the benefits and the burdens of moral judgement. In all questions of right and duty, it is both wicked and nonsensical to refer to a person's race whether the purpose be to accuse him [sic], or to exonerate him. To do so is to place the crucial attribute of responsibility where it does not belong – with the abstract totality, rather than with the concrete individual.[73]

The economic neo-liberalism which had gained an important influence in Conservative discourse in the late 1970s thus acted as a considerable ideological brake on the emergence of a full-blown Tory organicism which, allied a theory of racial nationalism, would have taken the party's intellectual right a good way towards a British fascist ideology.[74] Nevertheless, Casey's 1982 paper was notorious for the manner in which he appeared to use the word 'nation' as a euphemism for 'race' and supported repatriation on the grounds that black Englishmen and a multi-racial society were incompatible notions.[75] The arguments propounded by the 'Cambridge conspiracy' centred around *the Salisbury Review* have not had much direct influence on the policy-making at the centre in Downing Street.[76] Their arguments nevertheless have provided a high table buttress for the more populist attacks against multi-racialism which gained a renewed impetus while Parliament was considering the Nationality Bill in 1981. Such Tory MPs as Ivor Stanbrook (Orpington), John Stokes (Halesowen and Stourbridge) and Nicholas Budgen (Wolverhampton South West) have continued the Powellite attack against immigration with little or no respect for political niceties. Stokes, for example, said in Parliament that the 'Great Jew Disraeli' said that 'race was everything, and he was right. But race and racial origin are not mentioned in the Bill, and John Bull becomes a very shadowy figure indeed.'[77]

This was an opportunistic attempt to establish a Conservative historical tradition behind the principle of British nationality and also transform its legal status from the traditional territorial notion of *ius soli* or patriality to the continental conception of *ius sanguinis* or right of 'blood'. 'If we wish to retain our sense of cohesion as a nation', he urged, 'we must refer to the concept of allegience.'[78] In contrast, the arguments of Harvey Proctor, MP for Billericay, against continued black immigration in 1981 were somewhat paradoxically of a more distinctly liberal vintage. Citing John Stuart Mill's statement that 'free institutions are next to impossible in a country made up of different nationalities', Proctor tried to establish a more direct connection between immigration and free market ideology than his idol Enoch Powell had done. Thus New Commonwealth immigration represented not only 'a challenge to our values, traditions, heritage and customs, culminating in the breakdown of law, order and authority' but also led to the growth of quangos such as the Commission for Racial Equality. The CRE was to be particularly condemned, he remarked at a Monday Club Young Members Group meeting in March 1981, for its opposition to recruitment by employers through personal recommendation. Proctor championed this process of 'by word of mouth' as desirable for small family businesses and as an example of a 'personal choice' whose 'individualistic nature need to be contrasted with the "collective concept" of "racial choice" '.[79]

This varying and often contradictory array of arguments from the Conservative right however, failed to make much headway with the Conservative leadership which, by the early 1980s, tried to steer a middle course between the 'populist' and 'progressive' wings of the party on the race issue. Race and immigration had been less important issues in the 1979 election than either the economy and law and order. Indeed, Crewe and Sarlvik concluded on the basis of public opinion surveys that the Thatcher leadership would do better to follow a populist–authoritarian strategy on the law and order issue than on immigration. It was significant that Mrs Thatcher's reference to the electorate's fear of being 'swamped' by coloured immigration in a television interview in 1978 was not emphasised in the run-up to the 1979 election.[80] Nevertheless, the continuing appeal of the racial populists probably contributed to an ambivalence felt by many Tories towards the idea of a multi-racial Britain as envisaged in the Scarman Report in 1981.[81] The race card did not play a significant part in the government's response to the 1980–81 riots and the appointment of the Scarman Commission of Enquiry. It is thus highly unlikely that, as Miles and Phizacklea have suggested, there is an inherent trend in British politics towards a policy of deportation. Indeed the evidence suggests that the early 1980s a more complex strategy has begun to emerge, based on the government trying to establish political links with the Asian community and dividing it from the West Indians, whom it has generally seen as a permanent element of Labour support in inner city areas.

## DIVIDE AND RULE?

A number of observers believe that the growth in Asian immigration to Britain in the 1960s and early 1970s, especially from East Africa, may result in conventional black–white racial politics being replaced by a more complex pattern of inter ethnic alliances. Gordon Lewis, for example, has suggested that an East African colonial situation might be reproduced in the British context in which Asians become a buffer group between black and white 'introducing a secondary divisive element frustrating the growth of a black–brown coalition'.[82]

Certainly the appeal of this to the Conservative government in the 1980s has increased since the Commission for Racial Equality and local Community Relations Councils have declined in influence.[83] Since the late 1960s right wing Conservative spokesmen on race have expressed distrust in the 'race industry' and their suspicions increased during the 1970s as the Labour government enhanced the CRE's powers in the 1976 Race Relations Act. They believed that legislation of this type and the concept of racial 'integration' conflicted with the political objective of re-establishing a cohesive ideology of British nationalism directly. In so far, too, as this nationalism entailed a populist appeal by the government directly to the electorate it precluded the buffering functions exercised by intervening state-run quangos that smacked of the older style neo-corporatist 'consensus'. Though some liberal Conservatives such as David Lane became actively involved in this machinery, it was also criticised for being what Maurice Cowling termed 'an exercise in liberal fascism, dedicating to the improvement of the nation's mind whether the nation's mind wishes to be improved or not'.[84]

The new strategy of the Thatcher government has thus been to ignore both the CRE and local CRCs which have been left in effective political limbo, neither abolished as some populists on the right have long wished, nor given active support and encouragement as the small liberal wing in the Conservative party have somewhat pessimistically hoped.[85] The strategy accorded with Mrs Thatcher's own personal style of leadership whereby use has been made of personnel from outside government and party support mobilised to outflank critics of her policies.[86] One political pundit, T. E. Utley, has described the strategy in terms of a rejuvenated British national mission in which all who wished to be seen as 'British' could be enjoined to follow no matter what their ethnic or racial backgrounds:

> What we have to do is to develop a British nationalism so strong and generous as to enlist the loyalty of all who genuinely wish to be British. The point we have to emphasize is that British citizenship is a commitment, a complete and lifelong commitment, to our laws and customs. We may not agree with Disraeli's belief that race is all, but no Tory can accept the view that the existence within one small and homogeneous island of a huge variety of divergent cultures and religions is in itself a source of strength. The speed with which the ethnic elements are admitted to the community is a proper concern of government. But the positive task is to foster a national feeling strong enough to unite these divergent elements into a common loyalty.[87]

There has thus been an element of the Victorian imperial ideal of 'civis Britannicus sum' in the current Tory ideal of national regeneration. The objective, in fact, has been less a racial than an economic strategy based on the idea of reviving the old middle class in the cities as a source of authority and leadership. As the political consequences of the government's economic policies since 1979 became clear, the prospects of inner city revival and the restoration of pre-1914 values looked increasingly bleak, at least in the short term. Indeed many city councils were captured in the early 1980s by militant Labour machines whose high spending policies the government has now sought directly to control through rate-capping.[88]

Nevertheless, it is unlikely that the government's strategy will be guided solely by the political dogma of national cohesion which has, in its extreme forms, many of the trappings of a 'civil religion' developed to replace the older Tory appeal to a Christian faith that has declined in an increasingly secular age. This decline has occasionally exasperated some of the Tory populists such as John Stokes who has berated the churches for abandoning their missionary roots and avoiding the task of converting the 'heathen immigrants' to Christianity.[89]

The Conservative electoral support in the inner city areas has in fact disastrously slumped and fears have been expressed that, even if the party stays in power through its massive success in the suburbs and in the South, it will be at the expense of the idea of 'One Nation' Conservatism.[90] The longer the government has stayed in office, the more prone it has been to make a number of U-turns and some academic opinion has seen signs of a growing pragmatism, after the earlier years of monetarist dogmatism, and by 1983 there were signs of the economy coming slowly out of recession.[91] Perhaps the most important consideration by 1984, anyway, was a more straightforward one of industrial relations conflict with some of the more militant of the traditional industrial unions. One observer in *The Times*, Ronald Butt, has gone as far as arguing in the context of the strike by the National Union of Mineworkers led by Arthur Scargill that the real essence of Thatcherism is the ideological reaction to the 'revolutionary socialism' visible on the Bennite left of the Labour party and its allies amongst the Militant tendency.[92]

Certainly with the resurgence of more conventional class conflict, there has been less emphasis on race and ethnicity. The strength and cohesion of the Asian family has been a theme that has increasingly appealed to some Conservative politicians for its innate conservatism is seen as an important element in the middle class authority that the government hopes can be re-established in the inner city areas. Mrs Thatcher has on occasions made strong overtures to the Asian community such as by speaking at a rally to commemorate Mrs Gandhi's visit to Britain and visiting Southall in the wake of the Brixton riots in 1981. For the liberal Conservative wing, winning the

Asian vote has become a strong issue and Geoffrey Lawler in the Tory Reform Group's journal *Reformer* has berated the fact that the Conservative share of the Asian vote has increased by only 0.4% from 1979 to a mere 15.4% in 1983. The existence of Anglo-Asian Conservative Associations, he has argued, can be no substitute for active party membership by Asians, especially of the second generation, who he clearly believes can be won over by stressing a common British nationalism.[93] For many Asians, the identification of the Conservatives with tough immigration restrictions ever since the 1971 British Nationality Act led to a refusal to admit fiancées whose marriages have been arranged will continue to dash Conservative political hopes of gaining Asian votes.

If the emergence however of a populist style of government under Mrs Thatcher has to some extent defused the appeal of the Monday Club as the main locale for the racially-minded Tory-right, the decline of the National Front in the 1980s has led to alternative channels of entryism by groups on the far right. The report to the Young Conservatives at the 1983 party conference, despite being attacked by the Party Chairman, John Selwyn Gummer, for making unsubstantiated claims, indicated the emergence of new bridging groups such as WISE, Tory Action, the London Swinton Circle and the Focus Policy Study Group under David Irving. The disparate nature of these groups, however, indicates a less cohesive anti-immigration platform in the wake of the Monday Club's decline, though an area that continues to provoke concern amongst the party's liberals on race.[94]

For the meantime, the Thatcherite divide and rule strategy may be able to capitalise on the strong cultural links within the Anglo–Indian tradition of literature and cultural expression which enhance the possibilities of Asian 'impatriation' into British society in a manner similar to Jewish settlement earlier this century. Unlike the comparatively isolated West Indian community which has tended to be confined more to inner city ghettoes, the media has begun to portray a healthy image of 'Asian communalism' through an historical reassessment of the Raj such as the successful television dramatisation of Paul Scott's *The Raj Quartet* and David Lean's film *A Passage to India*.[95] While reinforcing in part a romantic and nostalgic view of Britain's imperial past, these dramatic portraits of India also contributed to a positive image of Asian ethnic and cultural cohesion. While clearly not pluralist in anything like the American sense, the Thatcherite populist conception of national cohesion has tended to follow a wider climate of opinion on the British national identity which has emerged in recent years. This view can be traced to the debates of the 1970s for, as Sir Keith Joseph argued in 1974 at a time of Conservative reassessment after the secnd general election defeat:

> Our view of ourselves as a national party has always meant basing ourselves on what the nation has in common, notwithstanding the many distinctions which characterise it and which will continue to do so. We do not believe that national unity implies homogeneity.[96]

There was thus a continuing theme of One Nation Conservatism, though one that has tried to accommodate to a diversity of social groupings. This apparent flexibility of Conservative doctrine reflects the fact that, in the last analysis, Conservatism is not simply an autonomous tradition of ideas, nor an aristocratic defence of hierarchy and the status quo but, a 'situational' ideology which employs arguments in defence of institutions. Unlike its American counterpart, though, British Conservatism is more strongly aware of the force of historical tradition in its formulation of arguments in defence of the legitimacy of the society's dominant political institutions anchored around the Centre at Westminster and Whitehall.[97]

The central ideological challenge the Conservative Party thus faces in the next decade, if it remains in government, is its capacity to adapt towards a more pluralist social make up. This means incorporating many essential liberal arguments, based on the rights of groups, as well as individual expression in a common society. These do, though, in some degree undermine the stability of national institutions which since the later Victorian phase of liberal idealism have been seen in mainstream English liberal thought as being to a considerable degree anchored around a cohesive notion of national homogeneity.[98] Given, however, the degree of opportunism of mainstream Conservative discourse, which has traditionally shown a remarkable capacity to adapt and incorporate many of the arguments and assumptions of its political opponents, this should not necessarily prove an impossible task.

## NOTES

1. Donley T. Studlar, 'Political Culture and Racial Policy in Britain' in Richard Rose (ed.), *Studies in British Politics* (The Macmillan Press, 1977) p.110.
2. Cmnd 2739 (HMSO, 1965).
3. Zig Layton-Henry, 'Immigration' in Zig Layton-Henry (ed.), *Conservative Party Politics* (The Macmillan Press, 1980) pp.60–1.
4. Stuart Hall, 'The Great Moving Right Show' in Stuart Hall and Martin Jacques (eds), *The Politics of Thatcherism* (Lawrence & Wishart, 1983).
5. Martin Barker, *The New Racism* (Junction Books, 1981) p.43 and *passim*.
6. Ibid., p.23.
7. Ibid., p.31.
8. Ibid., p.42.
9. Ibid., p.75.
10. Ibid., p.76.
11. David Edgar, 'Bitter Harvest', *New Socialist* 13 (Sept./Oct. 1983) p.22.
12. Errol Lawrence, 'Just Plain Common Sense: the "Roots" of Racism' in CCCR, *The Empire Strikes Back* (Hutchinson, 1982) pp.82–8. For a similar view see the editorial 'Inflation and Democracy: Wanted – "a Leader" ', *Patterns of Prejudice* 85 (Sept.–Oct. 1974) pp.13–16.
13. Robert Miles and Annie Phizacklea, *White Man's Country: Racism in British Politics* (Pluto Press, 1984) p.114.
14. Nicholas Deakin, 'The Immigration Issue in British Politics, 1948–1964', Ph.D. Thesis, University of Sussex, 1978, p.3; Donley T. Studlar, 'Elite Responsiveness or Elite Autonomy: British immigration policy reconsidered', *Ethnic and Racial Studies*, 3, 2 (Apr. 1980) pp.207–23.
15. Paul Foot, *Immigration and Race in British Politics* (Penguin Books, 1965) pp.198–9.
16. National Union of Conservative and Unionist Associations, *80th Annual Conference*, Brighton, Second Session, 11 Oct. 1961, p.27.
17. Ibid., p.28.
18. Ibid., p.30; see also Norman Pannell and Fenner Brockway, *Immigration: What is the Answer?* (Routledge & Kegan Paul, 1965) where Pannell argued in terms similar to Victorian environmentalist theories of race differences for 'the sudden change to the comparative harsh climate imposes a severe strain on the constitution of tropical immigrants', p.19.
19. NCCL Files, University of Hull, DCL 93/7 N. Fisher to M. Ennals 23 June 1961 initially favourable to a programme of opposition to the bill; M. Ennals to N. Fisher 11 Aug. 1961 indicating a meeting of interested parties on 4 Nov. at the NUR hall in Euston Road; N. Fisher to M. Ennals 29 Aug. 1961 declining to be involved.
20. Elspeth Huxley, *Back Street New Worlds* (Chatto & Windus, 1964) p.153.
21. Lord Elton, *Among Others* (National Book Assoc., n.d.) p.276.
22. Lord Elton, *Imperial Commonwealth* (Collins, 1945) p.523.
23. Bernard Porter, *Britain, Europe and the World, 1850–1982: Delusions of Grandeur* (Allen & Unwin, 1983) p.111.
24. Anthony Barnett, *Iron Britannia: Why Parliament Waged Its Falklands War*

(Allison & Busby, 1982) p.58. See also Graham Dawson and Bon West, 'Our Finest Hour?: the Popular Memory of World War II and the Struggle over National Identity' in Geoff Hurd (ed.), *National Fictions* (British Film Institute, 1984) pp.8–13.

25. *Parliamentary Debates*, House of Lords, 20 Nov. 1956, col.297.
26. C. J. W. Parker, 'The Failure of Liberal Racialism: the Racial Ideals of E.A. Freeman', *The Historical Journal*, 24, 4 (1981) pp.825–46.
27. Lord Elton, *The Unarmed Invasion* (Geoffrey Bles, 1965) p.19.
28. Ibid., p.87 citing G. C. L. Bertram, *West Indian Immigration* (The Eugenics Society, 1958) p.21. See also *The Times*, 30 Sept. 1958.
29. Dan Herewitz, 'The British Conservatives and the Racial Issue in the Debate on Decolonization', *Race*, XII, 2 (1970) pp.169–87.
30. Peter Griffiths, *A Question of Colour?* (Leslie Frewin, 1966) p.14.
31. Ibid., pp.17–18, Barker op. cit. has seen Griffiths's assertion as a residue of genetic racism, p.41.
32. Ibid., p.19.
33. Ibid., p.22.
34. For a discussion of this white settler ideology distinguishing town and country see Paul Rich, ' "Milnerism and a Ripping Yarn": Transvaal Land Settlement and John Buchan's novel Prester John, 1901–1910' in Belinda Bozzoli (ed.), *Town and Countryside in the Transvaal* (Ravan Press, 1983) pp.412–33. For the liberal attacks on apartheid in the 1950s see Paul Rich, 'Africa, Apartheid and the emergence of the "colour problem" in British politics, 1945–1960', *New Community* (forthcoming).
35. Ibid., p.226.
36. Cited in Paul Foot, *The Rise of Enoch Powell* (Penguin Books, 1969) p.14.
37. Enoch Powell, Speech at the Royal Society of St George, 22 Apr. 1964 in *A Nation Not Afraid*, (Hodder & Stoughton, 1965) p.144. See also 'The Myth of Empire: ce n'est que l'illusoire qui dure?', *The Round Table*, 240 (Nov. 1970) 435–41.
38. *The Rise of Enoch Powell*, p.59.
39. Diana Spearman, 'Enoch Powell's Postbag', *New Society* (9 May 1968) 667–9.
40. Cited in Bill Smithies and Peter Fiddick, *Enoch Powell on Immigration* (Sphere Books, 1969) p.122.
41. K. Phillips, 'The Nature of Powellism' in Neill Nugent and Roger King (eds), *The British Right* (Saxon House, 1977) pp.99–129.
42. Douglas E. Schoen, *Enoch Powell and the Powellites* (The Macmillan Press, 1977) p.245.
43. Ibid., pp.198–231.
44. Ibid., p.240; Alan Marsh, 'Who hates the blacks?', *New Society* (23 Sept. 1976) p.651; Donley T. Studlar, 'British Public Opinion, Colour Issues and Enoch Powell: a Longitudinal Analysis', *British Journal of Political Science*, 4 (1974) pp.371–81.
45. Hans Jaegar, 'Towards a New Right: Enoch Powell's Appeal to the Left', *Patterns of Prejudice*, 3, 2 (Mar.–Apr. 1969) pp.16–17, 31; Anthony King, 'The Changing Tories', *New Society* (2 May 1968).
46. For the demise of CARD see Benjamin Heinemann, *The Politics of the Powerless* (OUP for the IRR, 1972); see also John Rex and Sally Tomlinson, *Colonial Immigrants in a British City* (Routledge & Kegan Paul, 1979) pp.31–2.

47. Pressure for Economic and Social Toryism, *Immigration and the Commonwealth* (PEST, 1965).
48. William Deedes, *Race Without Rancour* (CPC, 1968) p.26.
49. George K. Young, *Who Goes Home?* (The Monday Club, 1969) p.20.
50. Ibid., pp.10–11.
51. W. K. Hancock, *Country and Calling* (Faber & Faber, 1954); 'I do not think the word euphorious, but it is less question-begging than the expression Race Relations which has recently come into fashion, and is perhaps more precise and flexible than the other fashionable phrase, plural society', p.161.
52. 'Bradford's Main Stream Extremistis', *Race Today* (May 1971) pp.171–2. See also C. Richardson and J. Lethbridge, 'The Anti-Immigrant Vote in Bradford', *Race Today* (Apr. 1972) pp.120–3.
53. Max Hanna, 'Immigration and the Monday Club', *Race Today* (Jan. 1972) p.5.
54. Patrick Seyd, 'Factionalism in the 1970s' in Layton-Henry, op.cit., p.241.
55. Ibid., p.237.
56. John Biffen, *A Nation in Doubt* (CPC, 1976) p.16.
57. *The Right Approach: a Statement of Conservative Aims* (Conservative Central Office, 1976) p.12.
58. Randolph Starn, 'Historians and "Crisis" ', *Past and Present* 52 (Aug. 1971) p.17.
59. *A Nation in Doubt*, pp.13–14.
60. Peter Riddell, *The Thatcher Government* (Martin Robertson, 1983) p.11. See also Arthur Aughey, 'Mrs Thatcher's Philosophy', PSA Conference Paper, University of Newcastle, Apr. 1983.
61. Robert Eccleshall, 'English Conservatism as Ideology', *Political Studies*, XXV, I, p.63. See also Sheldon Wolin, 'Hume and Conservatism', *American Political Science Review* 48 (1954) pp.999–1016 in which it is pointed out that Hume's empirical Conservatism that turned Enlightenment reason against itself was forged in the era of Augustan political calm in Eighteenth Century England and was rather useless in the more revolutionary years after his death in 1776. Empiricism could make no strong political challenge if the central facts of political life were controlled by revolutionaries and by the end of the century Conservatives were driven to transcendental norms to combat the revolutionary appeal to reason, especially via irrationalism, romanticism, religion and history.
62. Barker, op.cit., esp. pp.54–77.
63. Hugh V. McLachlan, 'Hume and the "New Racism": a Comment', *New Community*, XI 3 (Spring 1984).
64. *The Times*, 21 Oct. 1974.
65. Maurice Cowling, 'The Present Position', in Maurice Cowling (ed.), *Conservative Essays* (Cassell, 1978) p.1.
66. John Casey, 'Tradition and Authority' in Cowling, op.cit., p.82.
67. Ibid., p.87.
68. Martin Kettle and Lucy Hodge, *Uprising: the Police, the People and the Riots in Britain's Cities* (Pan Books, 1982). Harris Joshua and Tina Wallace, *To Ride the Storm* (Heinemann, 1983).
69. For the dominance of racism in National Front ideology see Stan Taylor, *The National Front in English Politics* (The Macmillan Press, 1982) esp. pp.53–81. By the early 1980s the NF 'threat' was beginning to recede as the movement began to splinter in the wake of the 1979 Tory election victory. Stan Taylor, 'The Far Right Fragments', *New Society*, 26 Mar. 1981.

70. Barker, op.cit., pp.20–2, 42, 155.
71. John Casey, 'One Nation: the Politics of Race', *The Salisbury Review* 1 (Autumn 1982) p.25.
72. Ibid., p.28.
73. Roger Scruton, 'A Socialist Evil to Rival Racism', *The Times*, 28 Feb. 1984; see also the same author's 'Race Hatred the Antis Ignore', ibid., 3 Apr. 1984; 'The Enemy in the Classroom', ibid., 22 May 1984.
74. For Scruton's indebtedness to Hayekian philosophy see 'Hayek, professor of truth', *The Times*, 16 June 1984.
75. Casey, 'One Nation: the Politics of Race', p.27.
76. Edgar, 'The Bitter Harvest', pp.20–1. Riddell, op.cit., has seen the *Salisbury Review* group as having no real influence and merely providing Mrs Thatcher with the opportunity to have some good arguments, pp.54–5; Geoffrey Smith has stated the same in personal conversation with the author. Scruton's articles in *The Times* indicate a more wide-ranging attempt to change the climate of educated and middle-class opinion rather than directly influence particular policy. See also John Vincent, 'Where Powell is really at fault', *The Times*, 10 Nov. 1982.
77. *Parliamentary Debates*, House of Commons, 28 Jan. 1981, cols 989 and 1004.
78. K. Harvey Proctor and John R. Pinniger, *Immigration, Repatriation and the Commission for Racial Equality* (The Monday Club, 1981) pp.4–5, 7.
79. R. Behrens and J. Edmonds, 'Kippers, Kittens and Kipper Boxes: Conservative Populists and Race Relations', *Political Quarterly* 52 (1981) pp.342–7.
80. Ivor Crewe and Bo Sarlvik, 'Popular Attitudes and Election Strategy', in Layton-Henry, op.cit., pp.259–63. The notion of 'swamping' though has a strong pedigree in terms of British racial discourse stretching back to the segregationist writer William Archer in 1910, see Paul Rich, 'Doctrines of Racial Segregation in Britain, 1900–1944', *New Community*, XII, 1 (Winter 1984–85) p.80.
81. Robert Behrens, 'After the Fire of London: The Conservative Reaction to Scarman', unpublished paper.
82. Gordon K. Lewis, 'Race and Colour in Contemporary Britain: the Return of the Native' in *Slavery, Imperialism and Freedom* (*Monthly Review*, New York and London: 1978) p.337.
83 The buffering argument was especially stated in Ira Katznelson, *Black Men, White Cities* (OUP, 1973). For reservations about the capacity of the CRE and local CRCs to play this role in a highly centralised British race relations structure see Brian Jacobs, 'Black Minority Participation in the USA and Britain', *Journal of Public Policy*, 2, 3 (1982) pp.237–62.
84. Cowling, 'The Present Position', p.13.
85. Zig Layton-Henry, 'Commission in Crisis', *Political Quarterly*, 51, 4 (Oct.–Dec. 1980) pp.441–50.
86. Martin Burch, 'Mrs Thatcher's Approach to Leadership in Government', paper presented to the PSA Conference, University of Newcastle, Apr. 1983.
87. T. E. Utley, *One Nation: 100 Years On* (CPC, 1983).
88. Keith Middlemas, 'The Crisis of the Tory Party', *New Society* (6 Oct. 1983) p.13.
89. *Parliamentary Debates*, House of Commons, 28 Jan. 1981, col 989.
90. Middlemass, op.cit.
91. James Douglas, 'The Conservative Party: from Pragmatism to Ideology – and Back?', *West European Politics*, 6, 4 (1983) pp.71–3.

92. Ronald Butt, 'With Friends Like Scargill . . .', *The Times*, 26 Apr. 1984.
93. Geoff Lawler, 'The Asian Community, *Reformer* (Spring 1984) pp.16–18.
94. Zig Layton-Henry, 'The Conservative Party and the Far Right: Political Aspects – no. 10', *New Community*, XI, 3 (Spring 1984) pp.323–8.
95. Salmon Rushdie however has seen the series as part of a wider strategy to bolster the myth of national grandeur, 'The Raj Revival', *The Observer*, 1 Apr. 1984. For the greater degree of Asian political involvement compared to West Indians see Z. Layton-Henry and D. Studlar, 'The Political Participation of Black and Asian Britons', paper presented to the Fourth Annual Conference of the Council of European Studies, Oct. 1983, Washington D.C.
96. *The Times*, 21 Oct. 1974.
97. S. P. Huntingdon, 'Conservatism as an ideology', *American Political Science Review* (June 1957) pp.454–73. J. Bulpitt, 'Conservatism, Unionism and Territorial Management', in P. Madgwick and R. Rose (eds), *The Territorial Dimension in United Kingdom Politics* (Manchester University press, 1982) pp.139–76.
98. Paul Rich, 'T H Green, Lord Scarman and the Issue of Ethnic Minority Rights in English Liberal Thought', *Ethnic and Racial Studies* (forthcoming).

# 3 Race and the Thatcher Government

## ZIG LAYTON-HENRY

There has been a significant contrast in the way race relations and immigration issues have been managed during the two administrations led by Mrs Thatcher. When the Conservatives were elected to office in May 1979 they were committed to a large number of specific commitments to tighten immigration controls. They had also promised a fundamental reform of the citizenship and nationality laws. These initiatives meant that race and immigration policy would play a major role in the first Thatcher administration. The furious outbursts of anti-police violence in inner-city areas in 1980 and 1981 largely, but not wholly, perpetrated by young blacks meant that race relations, particularly police-community relations would play an even more central role. By the time the second Thatcher administration took office in May 1983 the Conservative leaders seem to have decided to play down race relations and immigration and to avoid allowing them to remain a prominent area of decision-making and conflict.

## PREPARING FOR GOVERNMENT

The election of Margaret Thatcher in February 1975 elevated a tough, self-made individualist to the leadership of the Conservative party. She appeared to have little sympathy with the poor, the unemployed or those who were disadvantaged in any way, including the West Indian and Asian communities.[1] In contrast with her predecessor, she lacked sensitivity on race relations matters. Mr Heath, as party leader, had in many respects an honourable record on race issues. While he had introduced the Immigration Act (1971)

73

with its patriality provisions, he had also forbidden Tory candidates to exploit the race issue in elections, he had sacked Enoch Powell from the Shadow Cabinet after his rivers of blood speech in April 1968, and he had honoured Britain's pledges to the Ugandan Asians.[2] Unlike Powell and some of the intellectuals of the new right, Heath was on record as stating that 'there is no reason why cultural diversity should not be combined with loyalty to this country'.[3]

After the two general elections in 1974, some sections of the party leadership became increasingly aware that the Conservatives should be less preoccupied with questions of immigration control and should be more positive in appealing to the small but growing Afro-Caribbean and Asian section of the electorate. The establishment of an ethnic relations unit in Central Office, the proposals for Anglo-Asian and Anglo-West Indian Conservative Societies, the positive response to a far-reaching race relations Bill and the Party's proposed participation in the Joint Campaign Against Racialism can all be cited as evidence in support of this view. In retrospect it is surprising, for example, that Conservative leaders were prepared to accede to the Race Relations Act (1976), given its very broad definition of racial discrimination and the wide powers given to the new Commission for Racial Equality to conduct strategic investigations. This legislation was opposed by many right wing Conservatives, 43 of whom rebelled against the decision to abstain and voted against the Bill on its Third Reading. It is now less surprising to learn that Mrs Thatcher also had considerable reservations about the legislation, and one author has reported that she was on the verge of ordering total Conservative opposition to the Bill, and was prevented from doing so only by a threatened revolt of liberal Tories.[4] Similarly, she opposed Conservative participation in the Joint Campaign Against Racialism and vetoed the appointment of a party vice-chairman, John Moore, as joint chairperson with the Labour Party nominee, Joan Lestor. In an unprecedented move, the Executive Committee of the National Union insisted on participation in the JCAR and nominated Shelagh Roberts as joint chairperson. Shelagh Roberts, now a Member of the European Parliament, had been a member of the Race Relations Board.

Opposition to the liberal policies fostered by Hailsham and Whitelaw grew in the Conservative party during 1976 and 1977. The Malawi Asian scare in May 1976 brought immediate electoral benefits to the National Front in the local elections. Powell exploited the leaking of the Hawley Report with its concern over continuing immigration from the Indian sub-continent later the same month, and there was considerable unease in the Conservative Party over the Race Relations Bill. In July, the Government was bending to pressure and Roy Jenkins, the Home Secretary, announced the establishment of the Franks Committee to examine the feasibility of a register of dependants.[5] In October both *The Right Approach* (the Conservative proto-manifesto) and Whitelaw's speech at the party conference indicated that the party was again considering ways in which immigration controls might be strengthened.[6] In 1977 Whitelaw asked Keith Speed, his new junior spokesman for Home Affairs, to investigate immigration controls with a view to drawing up new proposals.

This undercurrent of opinion surfaced decisively on 30 January 1978, shortly after the leaks to the press about Keith Speed's brief to prepare new proposals to curb immigration. In an interview on Granada Television, Mrs Thatcher publicly committed herself to a populist approach, and thus seized from the party's liberals the initiative in determining Conservative immigration policy. She claimed that people were rather afraid that this country and the British character might be swamped by people with a different culture, that people had the right to be reassured about numbers, and that the Conservative Party should hold out the prospect of an end to immigration, except in compassionate cases. She stated that neglect of the immigration issue was driving some people to support the National Front, and that she wished to attract to the Conservative Party voters who had been supporting the National Front. She said, 'we are not in politics to ignore people's worries but to deal with them'.[7]

The response to this interview appeared to confirm Mrs Thatcher's view that the majority of people felt as she did. The Conservative Party shot ahead in the polls, she received a deluge of mail supporting her,[8] and the party comfortably won the Ilford North by-election.[9] In her January interview Mrs Thatcher said 'If you want good race relations, you have got to allay people's fears on numbers', but she must have known very well that immigration policy could make only a very minor impact on the numbers of the black community and that she was raising expectations which could not be fulfilled. Not all Conservatives were pleased by her performance and, as Bernard Levin[10] wrote in *The Times*:

You cannot by promising to remove the cause of fear and resentment fail to increase both. If you talk and behave as though black men were some kind of virus that must be kept out of the body politic then it is the shabbiest hypocrisy to preach racial harmony at the same time.

However, this calculated use of the race issue was regarded with approval by right-wing backbenchers who felt it would generate widespread popular support. More surprisingly, it was greeted with acquiescence by Conservative liberals – only Peter Walker and Edward Heath spoke out. Walker attacked her emotive language and argued that the principles of a multi-racial society are more important than winning votes: '. . . if you exploit people's worries in a way which shows hostility to minorities, you will do immense damage to racial harmony'. Heath interpreted Mrs Thatcher's remarks as being partly a criticism of his administration. He castigated her in the House of Commons, arguing that the issue had not been ignored, that the Immigration Act (1971) gave the Government full control over immigration, and that she was deliberately misleading people by suggesting that significant reductions could be made. He was disdainful of the way she had callously exploited such a sensitive issue for electoral purposes.[11]

The tough new proposals prepared by Mr Speed were outlined to the Central Council of the Conservative Party on 7 April by Mr Whitelaw and were approved. They were later incorporated in the party manifesto, and in 1979, the Conservative Party entered the general election campaign with a manifesto which contained a list of specific commitments to reduce immigration. These were:

(i)    We shall introduce a new British Nationality Act to define entitlement to British citizenship and the right of abode in this country. It will not adversely affect the rights of anyone now permanently settled here.

(ii)   We shall end the practice of allowing permanent settlement for those who came here for a temporary stay.

(iii)  We shall limit entry of parents, grandparents and children over 18 to a small number of urgent compassionate cases.

(iv)   We shall end the concession introduced by the Labour Government in 1974 to husbands and male fiancés.

(v)    We shall severely restrict the issue of work permits.

(vi)   We shall introduce a Register of those Commonwealth

wives and children entitled to entry for settlement under the
1971 Immigration Act.

(vii)    We shall then introduce a quota system, covering everyone
outside the European Community, to control all entry for
settlement.

(viii)   We shall take firm action against illegal immigrants and
over-stayers and help those immigrants who genuinely wish
to leave this country – but there can be no question of
compulsory repatriation.

The Manifesto went on to justify these tough proposals by
claiming that racial harmony within Britain was dependent on
effective control of immigration, saying:

The rights of all British citizens legally settled here are equal
before the law whatever their race, colour or creed, and their
opportunities ought to be equal too. The ethnic minorities have
already made a valuable contribution to the life of our nation, but
firm immigration control for the future is essential if we are to
achieve good community relations. It will end persistent fears
about levels of immigration and will remove from those settled,
and in many cases born here, the label of immigrant.[12]

## IMPLEMENTING MANIFESTO COMMITMENTS

The election of the Thatcher Government in May 1979 brought an
immediate clash between the populist authoritarian promises on
immigration in the Manifesto and Whitehall pragmatism. Home
Office advisers, following the Franks recommendations, warned that
a register of dependants was impracticable, would greatly inflate the
numbers likely to come and would outrage Commonwealth
governments, particularly that of India. Similar arguments were put
forward against the proposed quota covering everyone outside the
EEC who wished to come to settle in Britain. Moreover, efforts to
devise simple and effective ways of reducing immigration ran into
unexpected opposition when it became clear that stricter regulations
would threaten the rights of entry of white Britons as well as of New
Commonwealth citizens. For example, the Conservative commitment 'to end the concession to allow husbands and male fiancés the
right to enter the United Kingdom for settlement'[13] would have an

adverse effect on white British women who were engaged or married to foreign nationals and who might wish to return to the United Kingdom to settle with their husbands. Some Conservative spokesmen argued that it was normal for wives to settle in their husband's place of residence and assume his nationality. In a number of countries, including Egypt and the USA, British wives organised themselves into groups to lobby the Government. Womens' groups within Britain protested at the unequal treatment of the sexes, and MPs were lobbied by large numbers of constituents with children and grandchildren settled overseas. A significant number of MPs visited the Home Secretary to express the anxieties of their constituents. This unexpected resistance to changes in the rules delayed publication of the Government's proposals until November, when a White Paper was laid before Parliament.[14]

The new immigration rules proposed that husbands of women settled in Britain would need an entry certificate to be admitted to the United Kingdom, and this would be refused if the entry clearance officer had reason to believe that (1) the marriage was arranged solely to gain admission to the United Kingdom, (2) the husband and wife did not intend living together, or (3) the couple had not met. An entry certificate could be issued if the wife was born in the United Kingdom.[15] Similar conditions would apply if applications from fiancés were made. Elderly dependants would only be admitted if wholly or mainly dependent on sons and daughters in Britain and 'they must also be without relatives in their own country and have a standard of living substantially below that of their own country'.[16] These conditions would effectively disqualify elderly dependants from third world countries, as remittances from their children in Britain would inevitably raise their standard of living significantly. The regulations governing change of category for people entering the United Kingdom as visitors or students were tightened to prevent such a change resulting in a right to settlement, and their ability to seek employment was restricted. The new provisions relating to 'au pair' girls would be restricted to nationals of West European countries.

In the debate on the new rules, held on 4 December 1979, the Opposition declined to support them on the grounds that they violated the principle that the rights of all British citizens legally settled here are equal before the law whatever their race, colour or creed.[17] The Opposition's case was weakened by the fact that the Labour Government had restricted the right of entry of husbands and male fiancés in 1969, and Merlyn Rees apologised to the House for his involvement in introducing these earlier restrictions, admitting that he had been wrong.[18] The Government was also criticised by some of its own backbenchers who argued that the provision for elderly dependent relatives was very mean, and that the rules discriminated against British women not born in the United Kingdom. Although the Government had a majority of 42 and thus easily won the debate, 19 Conservative MPs abstained.

The Government clearly felt the need to modify its new rules to appease its critics, and the final statement of changes in the immigration rules was published and laid before Parliament on 20 February 1980. The right of entry was extended to husbands and fiancés whose wives or fiancées were born or who had one parent born in the United Kingdom, providing the primary purpose of the marriage was not settlement. Furthermore, elderly dependants would be allowed to enter the UK providing they were wholly maintained by their children or grandchildren. These final provisions were debated and approved on 10 March when the government had a majority of 52, and this time there were only 5 Conservative abstentions.

The Government thus experienced considerable difficulties in fulfilling its manifesto promises. Its efforts to change the immigration rules were opposed by many of its own supporters as well as the opposition parties. It was forced to drop two of its most widely publicised commitments, the register of dependants and the quota. The government proved to be highly sensitive to the criticisms from the left that it was racist and from the right that it was failing to keep its promises, but it could not find a 'non-racist' formula for stopping New Commonwealth immigration. The way out of these difficulties seemed to be to link the right of entry and permanent abode in the United Kingdom to citizenship. Discrimination by sovereign states in favour of their own citizens was an internationally accepted principle which would absolve the government from accusations of operating racist immigration laws. Moreover a new British Nationality Act would fulfil a major manifesto commitment. A Conservative party policy document published on 16 March confirmed that the common citizenship of the UK and Colonies and the status of Commonwealth citizens would soon be ended and that immigration policies would be linked to citizenship. It stated:

Future immigration policies, if they are to be sensible, realistic and fair, must be founded on a separate citizenship of the U.K., and it is therefore essential that a reformed law of nationality should, for the first time, make clear just who are the 'citizens of the U.K'.[19]

## REFORMING THE 'SUS' LAWS

While the government had been concentrating on the problems of immigration control, a number of events in the spring of 1980 drew attention to the suspicion and hostility which had been building up between many young black people and the police. In April the Report of the Unofficial Committee of Enquiry into the events surrounding the death of Blair Peach was published,[20] and in the same month the disturbances in the St. Paul's area of Bristol received widespread publicity. On 29 June more than 100 delegates from over 40 immigrant organisations met at the Afro-Asian Caribbean Convention to establish a national council of black organisations. A motion by the conference calling for Afro-Caribbean and Asian people not to cooperate with the police caused a furore in the press.[21] Further concern about police–black relations was expressed in the second report from the Home Affairs Committee on Race Relations and the 'sus' law.[22] The Select Committee was very concerned at the inconsistent use made of the suspected persons provision of Section 4 of the 1824 Vagrancy Act by the police, and especially by the fact that it was used to any extent only by the Metropolitan Police and the forces in Merseyside and Greater Manchester. While the Committee did not feel that the Metropolitan Police used the law with a deliberate racial bias they reported that they were 'confident that there will be a gain to society in the improvement of Police/black relations if the law was repealed'. The Committee also felt that there were strong general reasons for the abolition of 'sus', arguing the 'The most powerful argument against "sus" is that it is a fundamentally unsatisfactory offence in principle. It is not generally acceptable in English law to exact penalities for forming a criminal intention. The intending criminal has usually to carry out some act as an attempt to implement his intention.'[23]

The report was widely welcomed, especially by those who had given evidence to the Select Committee about the damage the law was doing to police–black relations and also by the Labour opposition which had slowly come to support repeal. On the other hand, the Police Federation, in a letter to all MPs, stated its opposition to repeal, arguing that 'we find the principle of tailoring the criminal law of the country to the alleged requirements of sections of the population somewhat offensive'. Sir David McNee, the Commissioner of the Metropolitan Police, said that 'repeal would leave an unacceptable gap in the law and would encourage further street crime'.[24]

It quickly became clear that the Government was not prepared to accept the recommendation of the Select Committee. On 5 June Mr Merlyn Rees on behalf of the Opposition moved a motion noting with approval the Second report from the Home Affairs Committee. Mr Whitelaw for the Government moved an amendment which 'welcomes the important contributions made by the Report of the Home Affairs Committee relating to Section 4 of the Vagrancy Act of 1824, accepts the need for a change in the law, and looks forward to the imminent publication of the Law Commission's Report on Attempt and to the public response to these reports, as providing the basis for an early decision as to the best way of reforming the law while ensuring adequate protection for the public'.[25] In spite of strong appeals by Conservative members of the Select Committee, the amendment proposed by the Government was carried, though all Conservative members of the Committee, except Mrs Jill Knight who was absent, voted with the Opposition.

The Law Commission published its Report on Attempt on 25 June, but the Home Secretary made no commitment to repeal the 'sus' law and both Mr Whitelaw and his junior minister at the Home Office, Mr Timothy Raison, made it clear that if 'sus' was abolished it would be replaced by a similar Act. The members of the Select Committee were so concerned that they published a second report on the 'sus' law on 5 August, criticising the Government for failing to respond to its earlier report, deploring the continuing delay and concluding:

> No Committee of this House can escape its continuing responsibility for the recommendations it has made. It therefore follows that, if there is no measure to repeal 'sus' foreshadowed in the recent Queen's Speech, members of the Committee will themselves place such a bill before the House.[26]

Although many Conservative MPs were clearly lukewarm about the Select Committee's recommendations, which may have contributed to the reluctance of the Government to act, there was a commitment in the Queen's Speech to repeal the 'sus' provisions. The Government thus avoided a further confrontation with the Select Committee and forestalled the Committee's threatened action which would have provoked an interesting constitutional crisis.

## RIGHT-WING PRESSURE

The first eighteen months of Mrs Thatcher's Government saw some pressure on the Government from Conservatives on the far right of the party who demanded that the commitments in the Manifesto should be implemented in full. A motion on immigration control was voted on to the agenda of the 1979 party conference by delegates and there was ugly heckling of non-white speakers. Powell continued to return to the issue from time to time, and in July 1980 warned the Surrey Branch of the Monday Club that 'citadels of urban terrorism were being established among the black population'.[27] At the end of July there was a furious row in the Commons when three backbench Conservative MPs called for tougher controls on immigration, the abolition of the CRE, the repeal of the 1976 Race Relations Act and consideration of voluntary repatriation.[28]

At the 1980 Party Conference, party managers established a firm grip over the immigration issue. An innocuous motion, untypical of the majority submitted, was selected for debate at the end of a busy day dominated by debates on unemployment and industrial relations. However, outside the Conference hall, the Monday Club continued to focus its attention on immigration and, at their fringe meeting, Ronald Bell demanded the end to the flow of 'tropical people' to Britain and a massive repatriation programme backed by a system of resettlement grants to encourage people to leave. He called for the immediate abolition of the CRE and repeal of the Race Relations Act which, he said, had continued to make free speech impossible for ordinary people, restricted employers and victimised the police. The machinery set up to protect immigrants from unfair discrimination, he described as 'a most oppressive and outrageous system of law'.[29] Mr Bell's views were repudiated by the Government but they served as a warning that race relations

remained an emotive issue and that views even within the party
were extremely diverse.

## THE BRITISH NATIONALITY BILL

Perhaps the most wide-reaching commitment made by the Conservatives in their election manifesto was the promise to introduce a
new British Nationality Act. It was widely agreed among politicians
that the law relating to citizenship and nationality had become
increasingly anachronistic as Britain's imperial rule had declined,
and especially as the succession of immigration laws meant that the
status of 'citizen of the United Kingdom and Colonies' no longer
carried with it the automatic right of entry and abode in the United
Kingdom. This was the main reason why the Labour Party was also
committed to a review of the Nationality Law and had published its
Green Paper in 1977 which discussed a variety of possible changes.[30]
The Green Paper had argued that a new scheme of citizenship
should reflect the strength of the connection which various groups of
people had with the United Kingdom. It proposed two categories of
citizenship, namely British citizens and British Overseas citizens.
This latter group was to consist mainly of people connected with
existing dependencies and those who had retained their British
citizenship when the colonies or dependencies in which they lived
became independent.

The Government published a White Paper on its proposed
nationality legislation in July 1980.[31] There was enormous concern
about the implications of the proposed Bill and considerable
representations were made to both the Government and opposition
parties from ethnic minority organisations, the churches, the
Commission for Racial Equality and groups concerned with civil
rights. The Government, however, was totally committed to the
legislation and published the Bill in January 1981.[32]

The Bill set out three major categories of citizenship: British
citizenship, citizenship of the British Dependent Territories, and
British Overseas citizenship. British citizens would be those citizens
of the UK and colonies who had a close personal connection with
the UK either because their parents or grandparents were born,
adopted, naturalised, or registered as citizens of the UK or through
permanent settlement in the UK. One controversial proposal was
that, as a general rule, British citizenship should descend only to the

first generation of children born abroad to British citizens born in the UK. This caused consternation to expatriate Britons spread around the world and also to Britons working abroad, some of whom had not themselves been born in Britain. The Bill also proposed that children born in Britain of foreign parents or whose parents were of uncertain status – because of illegal immigration or overstaying their period of residence, for example – should not automatically be entitled to citizenship. Mr Whitelaw was to tell the House that 'The Government sees no reason why a child should ever have citizenship simply because his parents happen to be in the United Kingdom when he is born'.[33] Persons marrying a British citizen could apply for citizenship after three years' residence. Citizenship of the British Dependent Territories would be acquired by those citizens of the UK and Colonies who had that citizenship by reason of their own or their parents' or grandparents' birth, naturalisation or registration in an existing dependency or associated state. The third category, British Overseas citizenship, was essentially a residual one with virtually no rights. It was intended for those citizens of the UK and colonies who did not qualify for either of the first two categories and related mainly to holders of dual citizenship who lived in Malaysia.[34] British Overseas citizens would not be able to pass on this citizenship, nor would they have the right of abode in any British territory. In reality, it was an invitation to those British subjects permanently settled abroad and with no close connection with the UK to acquire full local citizenship as quickly as possible. This was a further indication that the British Government wished to divest itself of overseas imperial obligations. Problems might arise with British Overseas citizenship if the children of these citizens were refused citizenship by their country of birth. They would then be born stateless.

Mr Whitelaw, the Home Secretary, introduced the Bill for its Second Reading on 28 January 1981. He declared that under the immigration laws it would not adversely affect the position of anyone lawfully settled in the UK. He claimed that it did not discriminate on racial or sexual grounds, and that it provided the comprehensive and logical overhaul of citizenship legislation that had so long been required and which it had long been the duty of the UK Government to introduce.[35]

The opposition attack on the Bill was more ritualistic than usual as the opposition itself was committed to a revision of the citizenship laws and as the Conservative proposals owed much to the Green Paper of the previous Labour Government. Conservative back-benchers spent much of the debate making representations on behalf of dependencies such as Gibraltar, the Falkland Islands and Hong Kong. Some of them also argued that it was unjust to distinguish between children born abroad to British citizens by birth and those parents who were British by naturalisation or registration. There was also considerable support for the view, put forward by Mr Hattersley for the opposition, that each colony should have its own citizenship rather than the cumbersome common citizenship proposed in the Bill for the British Dependant Territories. The government had a comfortable majority of 50 on the Second Reading.

Shortly after the debate the Home Secretary announced two major amendments to the Bill: firstly, that any child born in the UK who did not acquire British citizenship at birth might acquire citizenship after ten years continuous residence, irrespective of the status of the parents; and secondly that citizens by naturalisation or registration would be allowed to transmit citizenship to children born overseas in the same way as British-born citizens. These amendments were reassuring to members of the ethnic minority communities and were even welcomed in the Rajya Subha by the Indian Foreign Minister, Shri Navasimha Rao. They were not, however, welcomed by some members of the Conservative right wing who were annoyed at the concessions made by the government. Ivor Stanbrook, a member of the standing committee examining the bill, said they showed a contempt for back bench opinion and were a betrayal of government pledges on immigration.[36]

After considerable discussion in Committee and on the floor of the House, the Bill received its Third Reading on 4 June. It then went to the Lords and returned to the Commons with 90 amendments, all except one of which were accepted by the government, including the controversial Gibraltar amendment. This gave Gilbraltarians special access to British citizenship, a concession which was later extended to the Falkland Islanders after the war with Argentina. The Nationality Bill was enacted and came into force on 1 January 1983.

The Home Secretary published a White Paper on 25 October 1982 setting out proposals for changes in the immigration rules made necessary by the Nationality Act. Mr Whitelaw argued that the Act now defined those belonging to the UK and that all women who were British citizens should have the right to be joined by their husbands or fiancés. In future, all British citizens would be able to bring their husbands or wives or their fiancé(e)s into Britain.[37]

The Labour opposition amendment, while accepting the need for immigration control, declined to support the new rules on the grounds that they were based on the racially and sexually discriminatory principles of the 1981 Nationality Act. The Opposition was particularly concerned that some children born in Britain would not have the right of free entry, that women legally resident in Britain but without British citizenship would not have the right to be united with their husbands in Britain and that some dependent relatives would also be excluded from entry to the UK.[38]

A substantial group of MPs on the right of the Conservative party also opposed this relaxation in the rules but on very different grounds. They claimed that the changes were in direct contradiction of pledges in the Conservative Manifesto to reduce immigration and were also a reversal of the immigration rules agreed by Parliament in 1980. They would increase primary immigration at a time of heavy unemployment and would encourage abuse of the immigration law by means of the arranged marriage. Fifty Conservative MPs supported a reasoned amendment tabled by Ivor Stanbrook opposing the revision of the rules on these grounds.[39]

During the debate, John Wheeler emphasized that primary immigration from the Indian sub-continent was over and that the immigration of dependants was declining rapidly as families were reunited. Immigrants to the UK from all parts of the world in 1981 totalled 153 000, while 233 000 emigrated. He argued that all British citizens should be treated equally. He also suggested, anticipating a request by the Home Affairs Select Committee, that the quota for UK passport holders in India be raised, but the Government was to turn down this proposal.[40] In the vote on the Opposition's amendment, the Government had a majority of 81. The new rules were finally approved by Parliament on 15 February 1983.

The new British Nationality Act passed by the Conservatives in 1981 was yet another milestone in the decline of Britain from the status of a great imperial power with world-wide commitments to an insular European nation-state. It was also a major retreat from the Commonwealth ideal that had been such an important part of British foreign policy in the 1950s and 1960s. The days were long gone when a Conservative Minister could say 'In a world in which restrictions on personal movement and immigration have increased we can still take pride in the fact that a man can say *civis Britannicus sum* whatever his colour may be, and we take pride in the fact that he wants and can come to the Mother Country'.[41] Successive immigration Acts since 1962 had eroded the rights of Commonwealth and colonial citizens to enter and settle in the UK. The new Nationality Act brought British citizenship laws into line with those of other states and abandoned the increasingly untenable notion of Commonwealth citizenship. The citizenship of the Dependent Territories and British Overseas citizenship were transitional categories which were clearly meant to be temporary and to be phased out as quickly as possible.

## THE RIOTS, RACIAL DISADVANTAGE AND THE SCARMAN ENQUIRY

It has been one of the major ironies of Mrs Thatcher's Britain that lawlessness and public disorder have been greater under her administration than at any period since the war. This is in spite of the fact that Mrs Thatcher has made law and order an even more central part of her programme than have previous Conservative leaders. The pay and strength of the police has been greatly enhanced, police powers have been extended under the Police and Criminal Evidence Bill, and a major prison building programme has been initiated. Despite this strong support for law and order and for the police, the crime rate has continued to rise. Moreover, the role of the police has been so openly criticised and so much more controversial that, on occasion, the police have vigorously responded by joining publicly in essentially political debates.

The critical events which revealed the appalling state of relations between young people, especially young black people in inner city areas, and the police were the riots in Brixton in April and in Toxteth in July 1981. The Brixton riots lasted three days, during which period 226 people were injured, including 150 policemen, and 200 arrests were made. There was extensive damage to property and 26 buildings and 20 vehicles were burnt by rioters. The riots in Liverpool were even more serious with greater damage to property and larger numbers injured. In Toxteth, for the first time in Britain, CS gas was used to quell rioters. The events at Brixton and Toxteth were made more serious by the previous year's riot in St. Paul's,

Bristol, and the outbreak of lesser disturbances elsewhere in urban
England in 1981.

The Government's immediate response to the riots was to
condemn the rioters and support the police. Mrs Thatcher stated
that there was absolutely no justification for riots in a democracy
and that her Government would ensure that law and order was
upheld, that law breakers would be punished and that all citizens
would be protected.[42] Mr Whitelaw, mindful of his role as a Tory
Home Secretary, was fulsome in his praise of the police. When he
made his statement to the House of Commons on 13 April, after the
Brixton riots, he said:

> Whatever questions may arise in people's minds about the reasons
> why this outbreak of violence occurred, there is no doubt in my
> mind, nor should there be in the mind of any member of this
> House, that Metropolitan Police officers of all ranks carried out
> their duty with great bravery and professionalism.[43]

He announced that an inquiry would be set up into the Brixton
disorders under the terms of the Police Act 1964, to establish what
happened and to investigate the role of the police. The inquiry
would be undertaken by Lord Scarman.

Before the Scarman Inquiry was complete, an important and well-
publicised report on 'Racial Disadvantage' was published in August
by the Parliamentary Select Committee on Home Affairs.[44]
Liverpool was one of the areas to which the Select Committee had
given particular attention, and the members had visited Toxteth in
the course of their investigations. The report provided further
evidence of continuing discrimination and disadvantage among
Liverpool's black population, despite the fact that most were British
born and not immigrants. The Committee reported that:

> The situation of Liverpool's ethnic minority population is,
> however, of particular interest because of the way in which
> patterns of disadvantage in employment, education and housing,
> so far from disappearing with the passage of time have, if
> anything, been reinforced over the years to the extent that
> Chinese or Asian 'newcomers' are in a better position than
> Liverpool's indigenous blacks. If we cannot combat racial
> disadvantage in our other cities now, we will soon have a dozen
> Liverpools but on a far greater scale.

The Liverpool Black Organisation warned the sub-committee that 'What you see in Liverpool is a sign of things to come.' The Select Committee added 'We echo that warning.'[45]

The Select Committee, worried that their report would be sceptically received as just another report on racial disadvantage, urged the Government to react positively to its many recommendations. In the event, the Government's response to it, as the Committee feared, was profoundly disappointing, especially as it had been warmly commended by Lord Scarman and used by him as a major source. Most of the recommendations were rejected, notably the recommendations that the Home Office should play a more active coordinating role and that special race monitoring units should be set up in some government departments. Also rejected were recommendations to establish a body in the Home Office to oversee research into race relations, to found a central programme of teacher training on multi-cultural education and to consider positive discrimination in police recruitment or in education as a worthwhile means of redressing racial disadvantage. The acceptance of recommendations to reform Section 11 of the Local Government Act (1966) under which local authorities can claim grant aid to meet staff costs for providing special services for ethnic minority populations, and to monitor, on an experimental basis, the number of black people recruited into the Civil Service, did not compensate for the overwhelmingly negative response to this major report.[46]

However, the seriousness of the riots, particularly those in Liverpool, forced a positive response from the Government. A major coordinated attempt to combat racial disadvantage in the inner cities was recommended by Michael Heseltine, Environment Secretary, in a confidential report 'It Took a Riot' prepared for the Prime Minister. This was reinforced by Lord Scarman who made a similar recommendation in his report.[47] Inner-city policy was transformed by the riots from a minor item on the Cabinet Agenda to a matter of urgent and substantial importance.[48] Michael Heseltine was quickly appointed Minister with special responsibility for Merseyside, for one year, backed by a special Merseyside Task Force consisting of civil servants from the Departments of the Environment and Industry, the Manpower Services Commission and managers from Merseyside companies. More generally the Government expanded the number of ethnic minority projects under the Partnership Schemes and the Urban Programmes. Funding for voluntary sector schemes to combat racial disadvantage was more than doubled between 1981/82 and 1984/5, rising from £7 million to £15 million. More substantially, spending under the Urban Programme rose from £202 million in 1981/2 to £338 million in 1984/5. Also in 1985/6 some £127 million is being spent in Partnership areas.[49] A variety of other initiatives to combat racial disadvantage have also been undertaken, for example, under the Youth Training Scheme run by the Manpower Services Commission. The scale of the problems, however, caused by inner city decline and the massive concentrated unemployment in these areas, especially among young blacks, is so high that even substantial spending can have only a marginal impact. The Government was nervous in 1982 that the riots might be repeated and was greatly relieved when these fears proved to be unfounded.

A crucial factor contributing to the riots and more generally to tension in inner city areas is the relationship between the local community, particularly the black community, and the police. Most of the Scarman Report was concerned with the role of the police rather than with underlying social causes of the riots. In order to improve police relations with the ethnic minorities, Scarman recommended reforms in police recruitment, training, supervision and methods of policing. The Home Secretary accepted the recommendations on police training, liaison arrangements with local committees of community representatives and the need to reform police complaints procedures.[50] The police, however, have been less than wholehearted in showing a willingness to respond to criticisms of their methods or to suggestions for reform, and the Government has been reluctant to push through reforms. The Police Federation and the Police Superintendents' Association opposed the introduction of a specifically disciplinary offence of racially prejudiced conduct on the grounds that it was already covered by the Police Disciplinary Code. They were not prepared, in the interests of improving relations with the black community, to allow the offence to be specifically mentioned in the Code. The Association of Chief Police Officers told the Home Affairs Select Committee that they were opposed to statutory liaison committees. The chairman of the Police federation attacked Lord Scarman's criticism of saturation policing to stop street crime and argued that operations like 'Swamp 81' in Brixton were necessary. The police counter-attack against Lord Scarman's criticisms continued in 1982 when London crime statistics for 1981 were published purporting to show that black people were disproportionately involved in street crime. In September 1984 crime statistics were published suggesting that crime in Brixton was soaring and that the police were being forced to treat black criminals leniently.[51] The establishment of trust and respect between the police and the ethnic minorities, and particularly between the police and young black people, is of vital importance if alienation and future conflicts are to be avoided. It is therefore urgent that politicians and senior police officers make this a high priority.

Another area of law enforcement which needs to be considered in assessing government and police performance in relation to the ethnic minorities is their reaction to racially motivated attacks. There is considerable evidence that violence and harassment, particularly against members of the Asian communities, is continuing at a horrifying level, especially in the East End of London. The Home Office study of Racial Attacks estimated that some 7 000 racially motivated incidents would be reported in 1982 and that this estimate was likely to be on the low side.[52] A majority of West Indians and a large minority of Asians felt that they definitely or probably could not rely on the police for protection against racial violence.[53]

## THE ENFORCEMENT OF THE IMMIGRATION LAWS

The determination of the Conservatives 'to end immigration as we have known it in the post-war years'[54] depended not only on legislation to control immigration but also on strict enforcement of the immigration laws. Firm action against those who broke or evaded the immigration rules was promised in the 1979 general election manifesto. However, tough enforcement of the rules involves personal misery, not only for those trying to evade the rules but also for many innocent people. Families are separated while applications for vouchers are processed. Businessmen, tourists and students are delayed entry, sometimes in detention, while investigations are made to determine whether they are genuine. Aliens and Commonwealth citizens whose marriages to British citizens have broken down may be liable to deportation. As millions of people enter and leave the UK each week it is inevitable that immigration officers focus most attention on people from those countries where pressure to migrate is highest. The operation of the immigration rules inevitably involves some discrimination. The government has been determined to reduce the numbers of New Commonwealth immigrants accepted for settlement but this has been hard to achieve. A variety of administrative means have been used to reduce the numbers, for example by requiring higher standards of documentation and proof of family relationships, delays in processing applications and higher refusal rates. Refusal rates, for example, for applications for family reunification in the Indian subcontinent rose from 29.8% in 1981 to 44% in 1983. New Commonwealth immigration has fallen consistently since 1976.

TABLE 3.1   *Total acceptances for settlement, 1973–82 (000s)*

|  | 1973 | 1976 | 1979 | 1980 | 1981 | 1982 | 1983 | 1984 |
|---|---|---|---|---|---|---|---|---|
| Citizens of New Commonwealth and Pakistan | 30.3 | 55.1 | 37.2 | 33.7 | 31.4 | 30.4 | 27.5 | 24.8 |
| Total | 55.2 | 80.7 | 70.7 | 69.7 | 58.1 | 53.8 | 53.5 | 51.0 |

SOURCE: *Home Office Control of Immigration Statistics UK* (1983 and 1984).

Tough immigration controls command widespread popular support but strict enforcement of the immigration laws may generate opposition firstly from organisations, pressure groups and politicians concerned with protecting civil liberties and, in addition, from the press and public opinion who may be concerned with the treatment of individuals on compassionate grounds.

The political hazards of tough enforcement were made dramatically apparent by the 'virginity test' scandal in 1979. In February, before the Conservatives took office, an intending immigrant was subjected to a vaginal examination at the request of an immigration officer who wished to know if she had had any children. The subsequent scandal seriously embarrassed the Government and led to the Commission for Racial Equality deciding to conduct a formal investigation into the immigration control procedures to determine whether they were racially discriminatory. The power of the CRE to conduct such an investigation was contested by the Home Office in the High Court where they argued that it could never have been the intention of Parliament that the CRE should have the power to embark on such an investigation. They argued that 'immigration controls do not affect the equality of opportunity of those established here and are not concerned with the interaction of different racial groups'.[55] Interestingly the High Court upheld the right of the CRE to proceed with its formal investigation.

Inside Britain the Government at first adopted a vigorous strategy against illegal entrants, overstayers and people who were working in breach of their conditions of entry. In May and June 1980, for example, there were highly publicised raids on Bestways warehouse, the Hilton Hotel in Park Lane and the Main Gas factory in North London by police and immigration officials. These resulted in a storm of protest by opposition MPs, unions and civil liberties groups against what appeared to be random raids for illegal immigrants. On 29 July the Home Office minister responsible for immigration, Mr Timothy Raison, reaffirmed that it was not government policy to carry out random raids. Also in 1980 it was discovered that some 400 Filipino women, recruited to work as resident domestic workers, were in danger of deportation as illegal entrants. This was because the agencies which had recruited them had supplied false information when applying for employment permits, often claiming, for example, that married women were single women without dependants. After a vigorous campaign by the Migrants Action Group most of the women under threat of deportation were allowed to stay. Table 3.2 gives the figures for illegal entrants detected and removed from 1976–83.

TABLE 3.2  *Illegal entrants detected and removed, 1976–83*

| | Commonwealth Citizens | | Aliens | | Total | |
|---|---|---|---|---|---|---|
| | Detected | Removed or left voluntarily | Detected | Removed or left voluntarily | Detected | Removed or left voluntarily |
| 1976 | 213 | 156 | 181 | 130 | 394 | 286 |
| 1977 | 510 | 340 | 299 | 201 | 809 | 541 |
| 1978 | 439 | 313 | 495 | 357 | 934 | 670 |
| 1979 | 394 | 420 | 596 | 486 | 990 | 906 |
| 1980 | 583 | 462 | 1,040 | 809 | 1,623 | 1,271 |
| 1981 | 431 | 351 | 563 | 523 | 994 | 874 |
| 1982 | 607 | 481 | 650 | 331 | 1,257 | 812 |
| 1983 | 426 | 281 | 404 | 269 | 830 | 551 |

SOURCE: *Home Office, Control of Immigration Statistics, UK* (1983).

These figures suggest that the numbers of illegal entrants is relatively small and is as much a problem of illegal alien entrants and overstayers as of Commonwealth citizens.

However, while illegal immigration and the enforcement of the immigration rules are not major issues in Britain at the present time, there are signs that it could become more important in the future. This is first because pressure to migrate from the Third World is likely to remain high for the foreseeable future, and as opportunities to migrate legally are reduced, potential migrants may resort to other means. Secondly, as the rules have become stricter, more potential migrants have been allowed into Britain for temporary periods or under specific conditions and, when they are discovered to have broken their conditions, they may be able to mobilise local support to oppose their deportation. Thirdly, there are a significant number of people who are liable to deportation through no fault of their own, but because their marriage has broken down, or because their spouse has broken the immigration rules, and they have no established rights of residence themselves. There has thus been a growing number of local and even national campaigns in support of people like the Pereiras, the Hasbuduks, Vinod Chauhan, Afia Begum, Manjit Kaur and Muhammed Idrish. These campaigns have gained the support of local people, churches, local MPs, unions, and even local authorities. Interestingly, while most people support tough immigration controls and are presumably very opposed to evasion of the immigration rules in general, in specific cases of individuals whom they know, people are in favour of generosity and compassion. Particular individuals and families threatened by deportation have gained considerable support from the local communities where they have lived and worked. This has been true for the Pereiras, Vinod Chauhan, and Muhammed Idrish. In the case of Muhammed Idrish, his union, NALGO, organised a major national campaign to support his case to stay. In May 1980, over a hundred MPs signed a Commons early day motion appealing to the Home Secretary not to deport Verhese and Meena Varkki. On 16 August 1984, Manchester City Council advertised in *The Guardian* against the deportation of three people threatened with deportation because their marriages to British citizens had broken down.

The administration of the immigration rules and of Government policy to restrict Third-World immigration as far as possible puts a heavy burden on those ministers who have to deal with a large number of appeals and with pressure from MPs and public campaigns for them to exercise their discretion to allow people under threat of deportation to stay. This pressure is clearly resented. On 28 March 1984, speaking in the House of Commons to the Monday Club, the Home Secretary, Mr Leon Brittan, drew attention to what he called pernicious attempts by unscrupulous politicians and others to erode the basis of our present immigration controls, through agitation and allegations based on highly selective and biased accounts of individual cases.[56] Earlier, in July 1983, Mr David Waddington, the Home Office minister responsible for race and immigration, announced that he intended to restrict the opportunities for MPs to intervene in immigration cases as he claimed that he was concerned about the suffering caused by delays. The longer the delay, of course, the harsher the eventual decision to deport, and consequently the more unfavourable the publicity. The announcement by Mr Waddington can thus be seen as part of a trend to reduce the opportunities for political discretion and to deal with these matters administratively and quietly, so that the public is not confronted with the personal individual misery caused by the general policy.

## CONCLUSION

The general election of 1983 appeared to herald a major change in the Government's management of immigration and race relations issues. The Conservative poster 'Labour Says He's Black, Tories Say He's British' held out the hope that the Conservative leadership realised that immigration control was no longer a major issue and that the acceptance, security and involvement of black Britons in a multi-racial society was the major priority. In the period before the 1979 election the Conservatives had made New Commonwealth immigration a major issue. The newly elected Conservative Government had been determined to reduce immigration, to tie rights and benefits of all kinds (to entry, settlement, welfare, housing and health services) to citizenship, and to restrict British citizenship to those who had close ties with the United Kingdom. The inner city riots of 1980 and 1981 also forced the government to give a high priority to programmes designed to alleviate racial disadvantage and the heavy unemployment among young blacks.

Immigration as a politically exploitable issue has declined in importance for Conservative leaders. All practicable controls have been introduced and the Nationality Act has been passed. Any further controls would be inhuman and would contravene Britain's obligations under the European Convention on Human Rights. The nature of the immigration debate has thus moved from the political to the administrative arena. Mrs Thatcher now has the status quo to defend and can only realistically raise the issue to contrast her policies with those of the opposition parties. It is remarkable how united the Conservative party is behind the present controls and even liberal Tories support them and believe they are the only way to preserve harmonious race relations.[57] There are signs that interest in immigration as an issue is also declining at grass roots level in the Conservative party but this decline is dependent on restraint by politicians who have frequently shown in the past how easy it is to stir up popular prejudices.

There is some realisation among leading Conservatives such as Francis Pym and Peter Walker that 'we cannot allow racial minorities to become alienated from national life',[58] but there is no positive Conservative strategy to combat disadvantage and aid integration. Such a strategy would be opposed by those in the party who espouse individual responsibility and also by those opposed to positive discrimination. Pym opposes positive discrimination, arguing 'preferential treatment for any minority will justifiably anger those who suffer and are not preferred'.[59] However, the anxiety and insecurity of members of the ethnic minorities is very evident. The introduction of the Nationality Act in 1981 precipitated something like a stampede for British citizenship among members of the ethnic minorities in spite of the fact that since 1975 the costs of registration and naturalisation have risen considerably. In 1982–83 there were 95,897 applications for British citizenship and the income to the Home Office was £10.95 millions. This was estimated as a profit to the government of £6.45 millions.[60] This led to an investigation into Nationality Fees by the Home Affairs Select Committee and a recommendation for substantial reductions.[61] These were partially agreed by the Government.

The Conservative Government has been willing to intervene strongly to control immigration and to reform the nationality laws. It has been more reluctant to take strong action to combat racial disadvantage, except in the aftermath of the riots. Generally the work of combatting racial disadvantage has been left to the agencies most closely involved such as the Manpower Services Commission, the schools, the social services and the CRE. The Greater London Council which has recently made a major effort to combat racism, attack racial disadvantage and fund ethnic minority projects is to be abolished. The White Paper describing how the functions of the GLC would be carried out after abolition made no mention of this aspect of its work.[62]

It is hard to agree with the argument that successive British governments and particularly the Thatcher government have cleverly used their powers of statecraft to minimise the political impact of race and immigration.[63] These matters have had a substantial impact on post-war politics. Racial prejudices have been cynically exploited for electoral purposes and the frustration and resentments of unemployment and police pressure have welled up into serious violence. At the present time these issues have been allowed to subside after playing a major role in the first Thatcher administration. However, the deeply held prejudices remain among the majority population and in a political crisis the temptation to exploit them once again might prove irresistable and the impression of statecraft would then evaporate.

## NOTES

1. T. Russell, *The Tory Party* (Penguin, 1978), p.117 states Mrs Thatcher had a hard line and unsympathetic attitude towards the coloured community.
2. Z. Layton-Henry, 'Powell and the Heath Government', ch.6, in *The Politics of Race in Britain* (Allen & Unwin, 1984).
3. Letter to Bexley Community Relations Council, June 1970. In contrast see J. Casey, 'One Nation: the Politics of Race', *The Salisbury Review*, No. 1, Autumn 1982.
4. T. Russell, op.cit., p.119.
5. Parliamentary Debates (Commons), vol. 914, col. 985–6 (5 July 1976).
6. *The Right Approach*, Conservative Central Office, London, Oct. 1976. *Annual Conference Report* (1976) Conservative Central Office (1976) pp.40–7.
7. Verbatim Report of an interview by Gordon Burns with Mrs Thatcher, 'World in Action', *Granada*, 30 Jan. 1978.
8. N. Wapshott and G. Brock report that Mrs Thatcher received 10 000 letters after her interview, many from Labour supporters and most of which supported her views. N. Wapshott and G. Brock, *Thatcher* (Futura Books, 1983) p.156.
9. This was held on 2 Mar. 1978. The Conservatives captured the seat from Labour. By-election polls indicated the immigration issue contributed significantly to the Tory victory.
10. *The Times*, 14 Feb. 1978.
11. T. Russell, op.cit., pp.117–18.

12. *Conservative Party Manifesto* (1979) (Conservative Central Office, 1979).
13. On 27 June 1974, Mr Roy Jenkins, then Home Secretary, relaxed the rules of entry to allow foreign husbands automatic entry to the UK. In 1973 the number of foreign husbands entering the UK was 2400 and in 1976 it was 11,061. The proportion of New Commonwealth husbands rose from 5% in 1973 to 57% in 1976. The number of fiancés accepted for settlement was 1010 in 1975 and 2190 in 1976, almost all from India and Pakistan. On 22 Mar. 1977, immediate settlement ceased to be granted automatically.
14. *Proposals for Revision of the Immigration Rules*, Cmnd. 7750 (HMSO, Nov. 1979).
15. Ibid., paras 50–3, pp.116–17.
16. Ibid., para. 48.
17. Parliamentary Debates (Commons), vol.974, cols 265–6 (4 Dec. 1979).
18. Ibid.
19. *'Who Do We Think We Are?'* (Conservative Political Centre, Mar. 1980).
20. *Southall, 23 April, 1979*, Report of the Unofficial Committee of Enquiry (National Council for Civil Liberties, 1980).
21. *The Times*, 30 June 1980; *Guardian*, 1 July 1980; *'West Indian World'*, 4 July 1980; M. Phillips, *New Statesman*, 25 July 1980.
22. *Race Relations and the "SUS" Law*, Second Report from the Home Affairs Committee, Session 1979–80, HC.559 (HMSO, 26 Apr. 1980).
23. Ibid., pp.4–41.
24. *Runnymede Trust Bulletin*, no.122 (July 1980).
25. Parliamentary Debates (Commons), vol. 985, col. 1768–9 (6 June 1980).
26. Fourth Report from the Home Affairs Committee, *Race Relations and the "SUS" Law*, Session 1979–80, HC.744 (5 Aug. 1980), p.iv, clause 8.
27. *The Guardian*, 8 Oct. 1970.
28. Parliamentary Debates (Commons), vol. 987, no. 225, cols 1714–18 (31 July 1980).
29. *The Guardian*, 8 Oct. 1980.
30. *British Nationality Law: Discussion of Possible Changes*, Cmnd 6795 (HMSO, Apr. 1977).
31. *British Nationality Law: Outline of Proposed Legislation*, Cmnd.7987 (HMSO, 31 July 1980).
32. *'British Nationality Bill'*: Session 1980/81' (HMSO, 13 Jan. 1981).
33. Parliamentary Debates (Commons), vo. 31, col.697 (11 Nov. 1982).
34. But also to East African Asian UK passport holders, e.g. those resident in India who were being allowed to enter the UK under a quota system.
35. Parliamentary Debates (Commons), vol.997, cols 931–41 (28 Jan. 1981).
36. *The Guardian*, 5 Feb. 1981.
37. Parliamentary Debates (Commons), vol. 31, col.692–9 (11 Nov. 1982).
38. Ibid., col. 699.
39. *The Guardian*, 11 Nov. 1982.
40. Parliamentary Debates (Commons) vol.31, col.727–30 (11 Nov. 1982).
41. Henry Hopkinson, Minister of State for the Colonies, Parliamentary Debates (Commons), vol.532, col.827 (5 Nov. 1954).
42. BBC, Radio 4, 3 May 1981.
43. Parliamentary Debates (Commons) vol.3, col.21 (13 Apr. 1981).
44. Fifth Report from the Home Affairs Committee 1980–81, *Racial Disadvantage*,

House of Commons 424–1 (HMSO, 1981).
45. Ibid.
46. The Government Reply to the Fifth Report from the Home Affairs Committee, 1981–2, Racial Disadvantage (HMSO, 1982).
47. *The Brixton Disorders 10–12 April 1981*, Report of an Inquiry by the Rt. Hon. The Lord Scarman, Cmnd. 8427 (HMSO, 1981).
48. P. Lindley, 'The Merseyside Task Force', paper presented at the Annual Conference of the Political Studies Association, Oxford, Aug. 1983.
49. D. Walker, 'Defusing the Time-Bombs in Britain's Inner Cities', *The Times* 14 May 1985.
50. Parliamentary Debates (Commons), vol.14, cols 1001–8 (10 Dec. 1981).
51. *The Times*, 8 Sept. 1984; *The Observer*, 9 Sept. 1984; *The Times*, 10 Sept. 1984.
52. Home Office, *Racial Attacks*, Nov. 1981.
53. C. Brown, *Black and White Britain: The Third PSI Survey* (Policy Studies Institute and Heinemann Books, 1984).
54. W. Whitelaw, Speech to annual Conservative Party Conference, Conference Report 1974, 40–7.
55. Commission for Racial Equality, *Immigration Control Procedures: Report of a Formal Investigation* (Feb. 1985).
56. Conservative Party News Service, 28 Mar. 1984, cited in *Legalised Abduction The struggle of Vinod Chauhan*, Vinod Chauhan Defence Campaign, 1984.
57. C. Patten, *The Tory Case* (Longman, 1983) p.53.
58. F. Pym, *The Politics of Consent* (Hamish Hamilton, 1984).
59. Ibid., p.120.
60. *Annual Report*, Joint Council for the Welfare of Immigrants, 1981–82 (London, 1983).
61. House of Commons, *Nationality Fees*, Report of the Home Affairs Select Committee (HMSO, Apr. 1983).
62. Department of the Environment, *Streamlining the Cities*, Cmnd 9063 (HMSO, Oct. 1983).
63. J. Bulpitt, *Continuity, Autonomy and Peripheralisation: The Anatomy of the Centre's Race Statecraft in England*, ch. 1.

# 4 Opposition Parties and Race Policies, 1979–83

## MARIAN FITZGERALD and ZIG LAYTON-HENRY

## INTRODUCTION

If issues of 'race' had previously been consigned to the periphery of politics,[1] they returned to the centre of the political stage during the parliament of 1979 to 1983, and the opposition parties were more than happy to keep them there.

The Conservatives took office facing immediate pressure for an inquiry into events in Southall during the General Election campaign which had resulted in the death of Blair Peach and nearly 350 arrests. There followed vigorous opposition to changes in the Immigration Rules in the autumn and winter of the first session, to Nationality legislation introduced in the second and to further changes in Immigration Rules in the winter of 1982/83. For a full year, beginning in May 1980, the Race Relations and Immigration Subcommittee of the Select Committee on Home Affairs devoted itself to an extensive investigation of racial disadvantage. The impact of its report in July 1981 was heightened considerably by the rioting in Brixton, Liverpool and elsewhere at around the same time which had been foreshadowed by similar events in Bristol the previous year. Subsequently Lord Scarman's inquiry into the disorders (and the fear of any further recurrence) maintained the political salience of 'race' issues. Meanwhile, in the background, a plethora of other issues, events and policies with a 'race' dimension continued to claim the attention of a government whose election manifesto had gone little beyond a commitment to firm immigration control. These matters included a constant flow of reports from the Race Relations and Immigration Subcommittee, the controversy over the inclusion of an ethnic question in the 1981 Census, and the Commission for Racial Equality's investigation into the Immigration Service. There were also campaigns against deportation cases (particularly those concerning Filipino domestics), the decision over whether to adopt the CRE Code of Practice on Employment, and the report of the Rampton Committee on the education of West Indian children.

On most of these issues the Government was under constant pressure from the opposition parties and from individual Members of Parliament. Opposition MPs tabled Parliamentary Questions and demanded Adjournment and Supply Day debates. They challenged the Conservatives on the floor of the House, in the Lords, in committees, in ministers' offices and on public platforms. To a degree the level of their activity was determined by the Government's own legislative agenda and by external events. But it was invigorated by factors at work within the opposition parties themselves and by developments which had taken place outside Parliament during the period of office of the previous Labour government.

In the mid-1970s, racist reaction to the arrival of Malawi Asians and the subsequent rise in the electoral fortunes of the National Front and other far-right groups sparked off a vigorous upsurge in anti-racist activity, epitomised in the rallies and demonstrations of the Anti-Nazi League. The opposition parties were forced to stand by their principles and to declare themselves as full-blooded anti-racists. Perhaps the majority of young party activists were already caught up in the anti-racist movement and those whose commitment to racial equality had previously been channelled outwards – for example as their party's representatives on local Community Relations Councils – became more vigorously introspective. Certainly in the Labour and Liberal parties the rising political generation were no longer prepared to accede to a 'softly, softly' approach to matters of racial equality and they, in turn, strengthened the hands of older party members whose commitment in this area had generally been the exception rather than the rule. Where either or both had access to political power in local authorities, they began to take action in pursuit of their ideals.

Meanwhile, black people themselves were becoming more politically demanding. Asians in particular achieved greater impact than ever before in campaigning against repressive immigration controls under the umbrella of the Action Group on Immigration and Nationality, while the Afro-Caribbean led 'Scrap Sus Campaign' attracted considerable publicity and succeeded in capturing the political imagination of many. In the 1979 general election campaign a series of demands were made of the political parties in the form of a 'Black People's Manifesto'.[2]

Important too was the rise of the belief, which began to circulate after the Community Relations Commission published its report on the 1974 election,[3] that there was a 'black vote' the parties could bid for and that it could influence election results in strategic seats. Crewe[4] has argued that this belief is 'a myth, albeit a benevolent one' and suggests that there are, anyway, more racist votes in the British electorate than Afro-Caribbean and Asian combined. However, by 1979, the Labour and Liberal parties with their newly polished anti-racist image had irrevocably committed themselves to a policy of appealing to black voters. Undeservedly, perhaps, Labour was seen as 'soft' on immigration but, in any case, immigration as such was ceasing to be the primary concern of the racists. The speeches of Enoch Powell, the publications of the Monday Club and those of the even less respectable far 'Right' were increasingly preoccupied with the notion of 'the enemy within', that is, with the rate of natural increase of those who had already been allowed to immigrate and with the problems alleged to stem from the established fact of Britain as a multi-racial society.

It was no coincidence then that in 1979 a black journalist was able to write that this was 'the first British election in which race issues escaped from under the carpet'. In the succeeding parliament, opposition members might well have taken a strong stand on immigration and nationality. They had few further racist votes to lose and an increasingly articulate black electorate to satisfy. As for the riots – which were claimed by the prophets of doom to vindicate their warning about 'the enemy within' – opposition parties were at pains to point out that these were not 'race' riots. While acknowledging the particular disadvantage experienced by black people, their role in these events had been primarily, in Elizabeth Burney's classic phrase, as 'the barium meal' in British society.[5] The riots had been about wider issues which affected white people as well as black. They had been about policing and urban renewal and, above all, they had been about unemployment and the emasculation of local authorities. These added up to a strong indictment of central government policies.

## THE LABOUR PARTY: THE AFTERMATH OF DEFEAT

The general election of 1979 was a major defeat for the Labour party. The Conservatives returned to office with an overall majority of 43 and the Labour party's parliamentary representation was reduced by 50. However, the tough stand taken by Mrs Thatcher on immigration control had a much more devastating effect on the National Front. Despite a major electoral effort, fielding 303 candidates, and the free publicity provided by the party political broadcasts on radio and television, the National Front's share of the vote fell everywhere and it lost all of its deposits. There were high swings to the Conservatives in erstwhile National Front strongholds such as North-East London and the East End where the National Front had traditionally a significant presence and much support.

The analysis of the election results showed that black and Asian voters were the most loyal part of the Labour electorate. It was noticeable that the Labour party did well in constituencies with substantial Asian electorates. There were two party swings to Labour in Bradford West (–2.9%) and Leicester South (–2.8%) and Southall produced the lowest swing (0.8%) in the South East. All these constituencies had substantial Asian electorates. Curtice and Steed[6] drew attention to a double racial effect with Labour doing well in constituencies with high proportions of non-white voters and badly in white working class constituencies near areas of immigrant settlement. This was most noticeable in four Birmingham constituencies, where the 1971 population contained more than one-sixth born in the New Commonwealth. There were very low swings to the Conservatives (mean 3%) whilst the remaining eight (all with less than 10% New Commonwealth born in 1971) had much higher swings (9%).[7]

The erosion of Labour's support among the white working class has meant that black constituents have assumed greater electoral importance for those inner city MPs who were returned to Parliament in 1979. There were also many in the party who felt that the loyalty of black voters should not be assumed, otherwise they might be tempted to defect to other parties or abstain. In October 1979 the Labour Party Race Action Group emphasized this by circulating a leaflet to all Constituency Labour Parties entitled 'Don't take Black Votes for Granted'.[8] The National Executive Committee was also keen to pursue a more positive stance on race issues and included in its Human Rights Committee a number of new people critical of the party's record on race and immigration issues.

In February 1980, the National Executive circulated its own Advice Note to all Constituency Labour Parties 'Labour and the Black Electorate'.[9] This had been prepared by the Human Rights Commitee and finalised in conjunction with the Organisation Commiteee. The document was notable for its self-critical approach towards urging greater black involvement in the party. It was also highly critical of the Labour government which it said had:

> failed to deliver the promised changes in the living and working conditions of Britain's ethnic minorities. We failed to replace the racist immigration laws; or to make immigration laws more flexible in operation; or to end the harassment of blacks by the police – by, for example, repealing 'sus' and disbanding the Special Patrol Group; or to take adequate steps to tackle racial disadvantage and give a clear lead in the promotion of equal opportunity policies especially in employment.[10]

The Labour party was not only polishing up its racial credentials now that it was in opposition. There was a realisation of the growing importance of the black electorate in the Parliamentary Labour Party. Many of the new English Labour MPs represented constituencies with significant proportions of black voters. In fact, of those newly elected in England, replacing retiring MPs or those who had left the party, nearly half represented constituencies with populations of 10% or more born in the New Commonwealth and Pakistan and of these two-thirds had ethnic minority populations of 20% or more. The influence of black voters on the Labour Party was thus bound to rise.

Initially the Home Office team of Merlyn Rees and Shirley Summerskill retained their portfolios in opposition but they could not be expected to give a radical lead on race and immigration issues. Neither represented constituencies with sizeable non-white electorates and both had been cautious in office. In fact the Green Paper on nationality[11] introduced by Rees in 1977, despite all the subsequent disclaimers, bore an embarrassing resemblance to the Nationality Bill later introduced by the Conservatives. Thus, in December 1979 there was a certain ambivalence in Rees' attack on the changes in the immigration rules. Labour, he said, opposed them not only on principle but also because they were 'unnecessary'. For in practice the numbers allowed in for settlement would *only* be reduced by between 2000–3000 per year.[12]

In the autumn of 1980 a new front-bench team on Home Affairs was appointed to lead the attack on the Nationality Bill. Roy Hattersley became Shadow Home Secretary and John Tilley opposition spokesman with special responsibility for race, immigration and nationality matters. These two MPs both represented inner city constituencies with substantial numbers of immigrant electors. Hattersley had represented Birmingham Sparkbrook for 15 years and had considerable experience, from his constituency surgeries, of the problems facing immigrant families. He carried the stigma of having supported the Commonwealth Immigrants Act (1968) but instead of trying to gloss over this he adopted the bolder strategy of publicly admitting and apologising for this error whenever appropriate. Hattersley determined to launch a strong offensive against the government on all issues relating to race and immigration. It was clear that the Nationality Bill would provide him with a major platform as this Bill was certain to take up considerable Parliamentary time. This strategy had a number of attractions. As a right-winger with ambitions to become Party Leader, he felt his opposition to the Bill would give a boost to his standing with the left of the party within and outside Parliament. It would thus strengthen his position within the party and there was the additional bonus that this stand would be highly popular with his constituents. John Tilley had been leader of Lambeth Council. His Lambeth Central constituency included Brixton and he naturally had a special interest in race relations. Tilley had risen rapidly in the Parliamentary Labour Party since being elected at a by-election in 1978. As a backbencher he tabled numerous questions on race issues as well as an Early Day Motion in 1979 on the repeal of the 'sus' law. He had previously been national chairman of the Labour Party Race Action Group.

## THE BRITISH NATIONALITY BILL

The government published its British Nationality Bill on 13 January 1981 and it was debated and received its second reading on 28 January. Hattersley seized this parliamentary opportunity to give the Bill a very hostile reception. He argued that the Bill was racist and sexist and in reality an immigration control Bill dressed up as a Nationality Bill. He argued:

> What we need is a positive statement of nationality based on objectively defined principles, clear of all racial considerations. From that statement of nationality a non-discriminatory immigration policy should then flow.[13]

Mr Tilley summing up for the opposition argued that the Bill would be improved out of all recognition if six major changes were made: (1) preservation for their lifetime of the entitlement of many Commonwealth citizens to register as British citizens; (2) objective criteria for granting nationality and the right of appeal against refusal; (3) a guarantee that no child should be born stateless as a result of the Bill; (4) a commitment to continue the existing civic rights of Commonwealth and Irish citizens resident here; (5) a citizen's right to a passport, which no one has at present; and (6) that all children born in Britain should automatically be British.[14] Mr Raison defended the Bill for the Government which passed its Second Reading with a majority of 50.

The campaign which Mr Hattersley wished to launch against the Bill was weakened by two major amendments announced by the Home Secretary on 6 February. These were that any child born in the UK who did not acquire British citizenship at birth might acquire citizenship after ten years continuous residence, irrespective of the status of the parents and, secondly, that citizens by naturalisation or registration would be allowed to transmit citizenship to children born overseas in the same way as British born citizens. These amendments went some way towards allaying the anxiety of members of the ethnic minorities.

## THE RIOTS

The riots of 1980 and 1981 had particular significance for the Parliamentary Labour Party as most of the violence took place in constituencies with Labour MPs. The immediate response of some opposition MPs was anger that their warnings had not been heeded. Thus Robert Parry, MP for Liverpool Scolland Exchange said:

> I was not surprised by the riots in Toxteth. Over the last couple of

years I have raised on the Floor of this house at Question Time and in debates – it is recorded in the Official Report – the whole problem of the danger of riots in Liverpool. . . . it is unfortunate that my warnings were ignored.[15]

Many other Labour MPs representing riot areas spoke with feeling about the plight of young black people. But the general emphasis of the opposition's response was not on the particular problems of young blacks but to insist that the riots were not 'racial'. This was the major theme the Labour party emphasised in the debate on 16 July. Hattersley, leading for the opposition, identified the root cause of the riots as lying in the conditions of deprivation and despair in the decaying areas of our old cities. He noted four features common to these areas: 'The first is housing that is decaying and inadequate . . . , secondly, these areas have a woeful lack of amenities, thirdly there is inadequate provision of remedial education for deprived families and the nursery places that can give poor children a head start. Fourthly, and most important, unemployment in the inner cities is monstrously high'.[16]

Indeed in the debate setting up the inquiry into the Brixton riots on 13 April the opposition had demanded wider terms of reference to allow Lord Scarman to investigate the underlying causes of the riots which Hattersley suggested were youth unemployment, poor housing and the relations between the Brixton police and the Brixton public.[17]

Thus although opposition spokesmen acknowledged that black people were worse hit than most, it was primarily their experience as inhabitants of Britain's inner cities and victims of government economic, employment and local government policies which had encouraged them to resort to rioting alongside young whites who shared the same problem. Summing up the Labour party's view Stuart Holland said:

Unless we attack the economic and social problems of deprivation in such areas on a massively greater scale than the government has so far proposed, events such as those that occurred in Brixton will be likely to occur again.[18]

The publication of the Scarman Report with its detailed recommendations on police actions and training enabled the opposition to take up the issue of police accountability. They pressed for the implementation of the recommendations on monitoring the Criminal Attempts Act in case it became another 'sus' law; the introduction of a system of lay visitors to police stations; the reform of the police complaints procedure; the revision of section 3 of the Public Order Act to enable selective bans to be placed on marches; and the inclusion in the police disciplinary code of an offence of racially prejudiced behaviour.

## LABOUR BACKBENCH ACTIVITY

The growing importance of race issues for members of the Parliamentary Labour Party can be seen in the extremely large number of matters raised in the House by opposition MPs. These ranged from immigration controls and the 'sus' law to the treatment of Rastafarians in prison, the need for racially mixed juries and the use made of section 11 funds. Some MPs had long campaigned on these issues; for example, Jo Richardson was particularly active in criticising the Home Office over the 'virginity test' scandal and Alex Lyon played a prominent role on the Select Committee on Race and Immigration. Newly elected MPs from areas of immigrant settlement were active in taking up race issues. A good example of such an MP was Alf Dubs from Battersea South. As a local government officer in Lewisham he had been responsible for some pioneering work in the area of local authority equal opportunity policies. He was also one of the founder members of the Labour Party Race Action Group. Amongst the issues raised by Dubs were government policy on 'fishing raids' for illegal immigrants and the plight of Filipino women threatened by deportation. When the government refused to collect information on the operation of its newly introduced health service charges for overseas visitors, Dubs announced that he, personally, would undertake his own monitoring of the system.

## THE LACK OF A COHERENT POLICY

The strong stance by the Labour Front Bench on race issues and the activity of backbenchers concealed the failure of the opposition to develop coherent alternative policies to those of the government.

Despite promising to introduce 'a non-racist, non-sexist Nationality Act' when they were returned to power, the Parliamentary Labour Party were unable to coordinate their opposition to the Government's proposals as was clearly shown during the committee stage of the Bill. Similarly the Front Bench demand for a ban on National Front marches was contradicted by the minority report tabled by the three Labour members of the Home Affairs Select Committee when it presented its recommendations on the Public Order Act in September 1980. The Labour members had argued that 'bans were wrong in principle and unnecessary in practice'.[19]

Another striking example of opposition confusion was the division over the matter of an ethnic question in the 1981 census. The government at first decided to include such a question in the census but after considerable controversy and the failure of a piloting experiment in Haringey which attempted to test public reaction, decided to drop it. The Commission for Racial Equality was strongly in favour of such a question, arguing that it was an indispensable tool for measuring racial disadvantage and for assessing whether government policies were succeeding in combating it. Other groups, however, felt it was discriminatory to attempt to identify people by race, that the data would be inherently inaccurate and that the information would provide ammunition for those who favoured tighter immigration controls. Alex Lyon, who was a strong supporter of the CRE's position, tabled an amendment to the Census Order to insert a question on ethnic origin. However, he was only supported by 15 MPs in the division and the official position of the opposition was that the government were right not to insert the ethnic question as a suitable question had not yet been devised.

Labour Party policy between 1979–83 largely consisted of 'ad hoc' initiatives by the Shadow Home Secretary and individual backbenchers. Most of these consisted of simply opposing government initiatives even at the risk of creating public confusion about their position. Thus the Parliamentary Labour Party welcomed the Scarman Report enthusiastically and unequivocally but voted against the government motion accepting the report 'to show our concern lest the government should not implement it with the determination and enthusiasm that we believe it deserves'.[20] In July 1981 Roy Hattersley proposed that a legal obligation should be placed on all employers to use their best endeavours to ensure that black people were properly represented in every workforce. This

initiative, taken without prior consultation with colleagues, provoked a hostile reaction even from left-wingers who might have
been expected to support positive action. Norman Atkinson warned
that the unions would not accept a 'black draft' and Judith Hart
warned of the dangers of 'feeding fascism'.[21]

Such, indeed, was the absence of policy that the Party was still
wrangling over a statement on nationality to be presented at the Party
Conference a month after the Tory Nationality Bill had completed
its Committee stage. The proposed Immigration Policy did not go to
conference until October 1982 and at the time of writing (May 1985)
the official policy on promoting racial equality consists in a hastily
written outline drafted for 'Labour's Programme 1982'.

## POLICY-MAKING IN OPPOSITION

The transition from government to opposition may have a dramatic
effect on policy, particularly in the case of the Labour party. Gone
are the practical constraints on policy implementation, such as the
need to maintain a parliamentary majority, win the cooperation of
interested groups at home and abroad, provide financial resources
and gain public consent. In opposition, the mass party and
especially the Annual Conference and the National Executive
Commitee no longer have to compete with civil servants for the
major influence on frontbench policy. It is probably also true to say
that the more prominent role they normally play in this situation
was enhanced during 1979–83 by the heightened sensitivity of the
party at all levels to the need both to close ranks and heal divisions
after the general election defeat and to ensure greater accountability
by the party leadership. However, one of the penalties of opposition
is that the leadership's resources for *detailed* policy-making are
severely depleted. In government it has access to the expertise of an
army of civil servants in every department, in opposition when it
comes to putting flesh on the bones of party conference decisions it
is thrown back on a limited number of staff at party headquarters
and the voluntary contributions of party members.

Thus, the Human Rights Committee of the NEC was serviced by
a single hard pressed researcher who had responsibility for a wide
range of issues such as the police, penal policy, freedom of
information, womens' rights and gay rights. At one stage she also
had to cover transport policy. The committee, therefore, was

heavily dependent on voluntary experts to help with policy development by preparing draft papers and proposals for the committee. Inevitably their first task was to formulate new policies on nationality in response to the government's Bill.

In April 1980 the NEC issued a discussion paper 'Citizenship and Immigration' which had been prepared before the general election but which differed significantly from the Labour Government's Green paper. Both papers retained the 'jus soli' (the automatic right to British citizenship by birth in Britain) and both agreed to keep the commitment to admitting United Kingdom passport holders from East Africa. The major difference lay in the proposals for the remaining UK passport holders abroad who were permanent residents of other countries. These were mainly residents of Malaysia who had retained their British citizenship on independence. The Green Paper had proposed these should have British Overseas citizenship together with citizens of colonies and British Protected Persons. The idea was taken up in a modified form by the Conservatives in the British Nationality Act. However, the discussion document proposed giving UK citizens in the colonies a new citizenship specific to their colony of residence. The fate of other UK citizens, British Protected Persons and British Subjects without citizenship who were non-patrial and living overseas would be agreed at a proposed Commonwealth conference. It stated 'our hope would be to negotiate citizenship with the countries where they live permanently'.[22]

The NEC working group on Race Relations which was then given responsibility for producing a detailed nationality policy had by February 1981 proposed that, if such a conference failed to reach agreement, the Labour party would restore to these groups their rights of entry which had been lost by the Commonwealth Immigrants Act 1968 and automatically give them all full British citizenship. However, the Home Affairs Committee – frightened by the numbers this might involve – modified the proposal so that the NEC's statement to conference (issued in July) read 'we would, *where necessary*, restore their rights lost in 1968 and admit them to the new UK citizenship. We are determined that, if these individuals have no legal right to live anywhere *and if* their children will be stateless, they should be granted full British citizenship with rights of entry.'[23]

Members of the working party then threatened to dissociate themselves from the statement and, as a compromise, the version finally approved by the conference stated:

We are determined that if these individuals have no legal right to live anywhere they should have access to full British citizenship with rights of entry.

During 1981 and 1982 the working party went on to produce proposals as the basis for new legislation to replace the 1971 Immigration Act. The new policy started from an affirmation of the right of free entry to all British citizens, and established the principles under which others could qualify for admission. These would include respect for family life, the right to study and travel and the recognition of international obligations towards refugees through the incorporation into UK law of the 1951 Convention and the 1967 protocol relating to the status of refugees.[24] Other provisions included the liberalisation of rules for admission of dependants, the elimination of race and sex discrimination over the admission of husbands and fiancés, the right of appeal prior to deportation or removal, the improvement of the appeals procedure, the publication of instructions to immigration officers and the discontinuation of medical examinations for administrative purposes.[25] This time the working party's recommendations had the full support of the NEC and Roy Hattersley, the Shadow Home Secretary, and were unanimously passed by conference.

Between 1979 and 1982 the Labour party gave priority to revising nationality and immigration policy because of the need to respond to Government initiatives in this area and the desire to repudiate the embarrassing legacies of previous Labour governments. Even so the commitments to repeal the 1971 Immigration Act and the 1981 Nationality Act were not so radical as they sounded. Both these Acts were to be replaced by legislation which was broadly similar to the legislation which was to be repealed.

The new immigration policy started from the premise that Britain could not unilaterally abandon all control of immigration and in the near future it would not be possible for the economy to provide jobs for significant numbers of workers from overseas. The main innovation in the new nationality policy was to reclassify the citizens of the British Dependent Territories as citizens of their colonies of residence and thus to legitimise their continued exclusion from Britain under international law by confining their right of abode to their colony of residence.

## POSITIVE ACTION

The preoccupation with nationality and immigration policy led to the relative neglect of positive action policies aimed at ensuring equality for black people settled and, in increasing numbers born, in Britain. Many constituency Labour parties and Labour local authorities were supporting positive action programmes in employment, housing and education. The Greater London Council most notably was attempting to lead the way with a firm anti-racist stance. After completing the policy statement on immigration the NEC's working party on race relations hastily prepared an outline of positive action policies for inclusion in Labour's Programme 1982. This programme was intended as a comprehensive statement of party policy and the basis for the party's campaign leading to the general election.

The major initiative proposed by the working party was the appointment of a senior minister in the Department of the Environment with special responsibility to lead the offensive against racial inequality. The minister would chair a Cabinet committee whose work would be supported by specialised racial disadvantage units in the major government departments. Positive action programmes would be encouraged, alongside a major public education initiative aimed at changing the racial prejudices of white people. There would be increased resources under section 11 of the Local Government Act and the Urban Programme. The working party proposed changes in legislation to deal more effectively with racial incitement and provocative marches. It also supported ethnic record keeping and monitoring but shied away from the controversial issue of an ethnic question in the census.[26]

Members of the working party also insisted that the goal of racial equality could not be pursued in isolation, but should be recognised as a dimension of other areas of domestic policy. In principle, they agreed, it was as important to ensure that this was reflected in other relevant chapters of Labour's Programme. The problems of voluntarism, though, were well illustrated by the fact that only two members of the group regularly attended meetings subsequently organised to review the sections on employment, education, housing and the social services.

All the proposals of the working party were approved by the annual conference and formed the basis of the proposals included in the 1983 general election manifesto, *The New Hope for Britain*. However the detail of these policies was never worked out for the NEC declared a moratorium on policy development in the run up to the general election and this continued in the wake of the catastrophic electoral defeat. By the time the working party was reconvened, the efforts to develop more detailed positive action policies were overshadowed by the campaign for black sections in the party. Thus the working party on positive action policies was replaced by a working party on positive discrimination within the party itself. The wider issues were forgotten and bitter divisions sprang up around what to many outsiders seemed a mere constitutional nicety. Party activists – many of them black – became involved in bitter attacks on the leadership in a fresh outburst of the mutually destructive recriminations which seem perennially to beset the party but which rarely since 1968 had been associated with race.

## THE ALLIANCE PARTIES

By contrast with Labour, the Liberal party – particularly in terms of its parliamentary representation – had very weak links with the deprived inner city constituencies in which most black people are concentrated. According to the CRE, in 1979 they received even less support from black voters than the Conservatives – the figures being 5% and 8% respectively.[27] Further, it has been noted that, with a high proportion of its electoral support being a 'protest' vote, Liberal candidates at election times sometimes gain the support of very illiberal electors.[28] This is particularly ironic since the Liberals claim with some justification that, compared with the other two major parties, they have an outstanding record on race and immigration issues. They have remained faithful to the central tenets of nineteenth century liberalism, of which one was freedom of movement across national boundaries in order to promote economic and cultural exchange. As a consequence the party has generally been opposed to immigration controls or, more recently, has argued that controls should be linked to the availability of jobs and not to the country of origin of intending migrants. The Liberal party has thus strongly opposed the immigration control measures introduced since 1962 by Tory and Labour administrations. Most notably, they led the opposition to the 1968 Commonwealth Immigrants Act which was supported by both the major parties.

On issues of racial equality they have also taken a lead. In 1977, they were founder members of the Joint Committee Against Racialism which Labour joined once it had been set up and which the Conservatives also joined with the support of the National Union against the expressed wishes of Mrs Thatcher. In the 1979 general election, they issued a 'Special Manifesto' on race and were even then, only three years after the 1976 Race Relations Act had been passed, promising an even more comprehensive law and proposing to enforce legislation against race, sex and political discrimination through a single Anti-Discrimination Board.[29]

In the House of Commons, inevitably because of their lack of numbers, their impact had been relatively slight. But in the House of Lords, Lord Avebury, the Liberal peer and former MP Eric Lubbock, made full use of his position to promote the causes he had tirelessly championed throughout his political career. Not only did he take up individual immigration cases and work closely with campaigning organisations in this field, but he also repeatedly tabled motions, called debates and even introduced Bills in the Lords to ensure that issues were raised publicly and that pressure was put on the Commons, in turn, to take them up.

Between 1979 and 1983, the Liberals in the Commons were strengthened in the input they were able to make on race and immigration matters. After a by-election in March 1979, they were joined by David Alton, representing Liverpool Edge Hill, and in 1981, Bill Pitt won Croydon North-West, a constituency with a New Commonwealth and Pakistan population of 22%. Pitt himself brought to the parliamentary party a strong personal commitment based on years of work, as he put it 'in Brixton, at the sharp end'.[30] The formation of the Social Democratic Party then brought into the Alliance a significant number of inner city MPs with experience of representing New Commonwealth constituents. These included two further Liverpool MPs, Eric Ogden (West Derby) and Richard Crawshaw (Toxteth) and Edward Lyons who for years had been taking up cases for his Asian constituents in Bradford West. Neville Sandelson, John Cartwright and Tom Bradley had similar constituency experience. Though not inner city MPs, Shirley Williams and Roy Jenkins, who were elected as SDP members at by-elections during the course of the same parliament, also brought to the Alliance their personal reputations as outstanding former members of the liberal wing of the Labour party as far as race issues were concerned.

## THE ALLIANCE IN PARLIAMENT

The Liberals in Parliament strongly opposed the 1981 Nationality Act. David Steel described it as the latest in a long line of shabby measures reducing basic rights and discriminating against the ethnic minorities.[31] They also opposed both sets of changes in the immigration rules – their contribution being strengthened on the second occasion by the addition of SDP MPs. Indeed, it was Roy Jenkins who successfully moved the motion on 15 December 1982 to disapprove the changes to the immigration rules and no less than ten other Alliance MPs made contributions to the debate.

In the various debates on the riots, the Alliance, with its contingent of inner city MPs, three of whom represented Liverpool constituencies, was also better placed to catch the Speaker's eye than the pre-1979 Liberal party would have been.

Beyond some strong speeches on the floor of the House, however, the Alliance impact on race and immigration policy between 1979 and 1983 was limited and rather lacking in distinctiveness. There were no Liberal MPs on the Committee on the Nationality Bill and the Alliance was never represented on the Race and Immigration Subcommittee of the Select Committee on Home Affairs. Almost without exception, they joined Labour in the division lobbies, opposing both the inclusion of an ethnic question in the Census, and the Scarman Report. Speeches made by Alliance MPs on the riots were in many respects indistinguishable from those made by Labour members. Thus, Richard Crawshaw listed the main reasons for the riots as unemployment, the physical environment and the breakdown of police–community relations.[32] In the debate on the Scarman Report, Bill Pitt emphasized the need 'for a moral commitment from the Government to a multi-racial society'[33] as one of the most important prerequisites for avoiding a repetition. But, like Labour, the main thrust of the Alliance in response was that race had *not* been a significant factor in the riots. Richard Crawshaw stressed:

> With regard to the breakdown of relationships between the police and the community, it should be understood that in the area of Toxteth where the trouble occurred it is not just a matter of blacks versus the police; it is the whites versus the police as well.[34]

David Alton went so far as to claim that race had not been a factor

> particularly in the case of the riots in Liverpool, which is a city prized for its racial tolerance and successful integration and assimilation of ethnic communities.[35]

At the same time, however, the Alliance was anxious to be seen to take an independent line from Labour and, while opposing the Conservatives, to score points off Labour wherever possible. For SDP members who had formerly been Labour MPs, this was not always easy. In the debate on the changes in the Immigration Rules of 15 December 1982, for example, the Home Secretary, William Whitelaw, took evident relish in discomfiting his chief protagonist, Roy Jenkins, thus:

> The right honourable member for Hillhead arrived with a great flourish of trumpets in 1974. He said that there were great difficulties and that he would consider them, and he wondered whether there might not be abuse if he made changes. He thought about the matter for some time and then decided to make the changes. Of course, it was not long – perhaps three years – before he moved to other pastures and his right honourable friend, the Member for Leeds South (Mr Rees), his successor, decided that his proposals had to be restricted, and they were. So let no Home Secretary live in a white sheet. It is an extremely difficult matter and we all know it. I shall put only one point to the right honourable member for Hillhead. For him, of all people, to talk about lack of courage and the line of least resistance, in view of what he did when he was deputy leader of the Labour Party on many matters . . .and for him to lecture me about that is the height of hypocrisy.[36]

Consistently, however, in the debates on the riots, Alliance MPs – while calling for greater police accountability and a more satisfactory complaints procedure – tried to paint the Labour party as being anti-law and order. Richard Crawshaw implied that Labour members would deny the police the wherewithal to deal with a riot:

> In cases of civil disorder, the priority should be to protect law

abiding citizens and to restore order. I sometimes wonder whether we in the House live in a real world. We say that we must not do this and that we must not do that in case a rioter gets hurt . . .[37]

The right honourable and learned Member for Dulwich (Mr Silkin) said that the consent of the Home Secretary should be sought in such cases. I wonder whether the right honourable and learned gentleman has ever seen a riot, where the situation changes from minute to minute, and where the police line can be driven back 100 yards down the road. How is it possible to get the consent of the Home Secretary to use CS gas in such circumstances?[38]

His colleague, David Alton, then took the offensive and blamed left-wing agitation for much of the trouble, specifically naming the Young Socialists. On the night of the riots, he said:

a leaflet was delivered by the Labour Party Young Socialists which says that they defend 'all those arrested during these events, and call for their immediate release and the dropping of all charges against them.'

The leaflet was printed and published at 70 Victoria Street, which is the headquarters of the Labour Party in Liverpool and bore the telephone number of a prospective Labour Party candidate . . . . . . those wolves in sheeps clothing who distributed that sort of wicked literature . . . deliberately incited people in that area to go on looting, burning and pillaging in the expectation that all charges against them would be dropped, whatever the nature of their offences.[39]

Similar tactics were used on the question of the Nationality Bill after the Liberal party had failed to be represented on the committee. While they were still trying to decide who would represent them on it, Enoch Powell asserted his right as a Privy Counsellor to the one remaining place and was automatically accepted by Labour and Conservative members of the committee. The Liberals were discomfited by their unexpected exclusion and tended to blame the Labour party for keeping them off the committee in favour of Enoch Powell.

POLICY-MAKING IN ALLIANCE

The Alliance parties not only shared Labour's problems of lack of resources when it came to formulating detailed policy, they had additional problems of their own.

The Liberal party, although desperately short of finance and full-time staff, did, in fact, have a well-established Community Relations Policy Panel which met regularly. It was chaired by Lord Avebury and several of its members were closely associated with the Commission for Racial Equality. During the period in question, it was serviced by the party's campaigns officer who had himself immediately previously been secretary of the Joint Committee Against Racialism. For many of its members, the alliance with the SDP proved frustrating in that, for the Liberal side of the partnership, it put a brake on policy development.

The SDP only came into existence in the second year of the 1979 Parliament and set out to develop policy according to its founding principles of party democracy. Policy was first prepared in the draft form of a 'green paper' which was then circulated throughout the party for consultation. Only after this process was completed was policy finalised in a 'white paper'. There were two major green papers which covered race and immigration policy the first on Citizen Rights and the second on Urban Policy. The green paper on Citizen Rights argued that major and urgent reforms were needed in the immigration and nationality laws. It proposed that British citizenship should, as before the Nationality Act of 1981, apply automatically to all those born within British territory, and that East African Asian passport holders should be made full British citizens with automatic rights of entry to the UK. Citizens of the British Dependent Territories should become citizens of their own territories with the exception of the people of Hong Kong, whose status would, presumably, have to be negotiated with the People's Republic of China. Meanwhile their status would remain unchanged. The costs and procedures for registration and naturalisation would be reduced and simplified. Immigration controls would not be based on grounds of race, colour or religion. They would comply with the United Kingdom's obligations under the European Convention on Human Rights and give a high priority to family unity. The procedures would be speeded up by the appointment of more staff and an independent Judicial Officer would be appointed to expedite the appeals procedure. The Green Paper also suggested merging the Equal Opportunities Commission and the Commission for Racial Equality into a new Human Rights Commission and strengthening its powers and resources. The most far reaching recommendation was the proposal that the British Parliament should enact a Bill of Rights guaranteeing the rights and freedoms covered by the European Convention on Human Rights. These rights and freedoms would be enforceable in the courts with a final right of appeal to the European Court at Strasbourg.[40]

The Green Paper on urban policy[41] emphasised the crisis in the inner cities highlighted by the riots of 1980 and 1981. It proposed a range of programmes to combat urban decay, improve police–community relations and combat racial discrimination in housing, employment and education. These included requiring public contractors and other employers in receipt of public contracts to prove they were pursuing equal opportunity policies. More recently, David Owen has reaffirmed the Social Democratic Party's commitment to racial justice and in particular to committing more resources to positive action to deal with disadvantage and discrimination.[42]

The inhibitions the SDP's policy making process imposed on the Liberals and the frustrations it caused are well illustrated in the thwarting of a Community Relations Panel initiative after the riots in 1981. By September of that year, the panel had produced a 'Report on Inner City Disturbances' which recommended, inter alia, that:

> the Assembly call upon the Standing Committee to set up a working party with the SDP to include representatives of ethnic minorities to examine further the remedies that are necessary to ensure that the breakdown of law and order in our inner cities does not become more widespread; and to develop an agreed programme for action by the next Government in the field of immigration and race relations; and to report to their respective parties.[43]

The working party, however, was never set up because the SDP said it could not participate until it had been through the democratic process of determining its own policy in the area.

Most frustrating of all for the Liberals, perhaps, was the joint Alliance manifesto commitment on nationality which referred only to 'amending' the Tory Act, thereby pulling back from the Liberal policy which was to repeal it. To underline the point, delegates to the Liberal Party annual conference that autumn unanimously passed a resolution calling for the repeal of the Act and its replacement by a new law.

## 1983 GENERAL ELECTION

Labour and the Alliance went into the 1983 general election campaign with manifesto commitments on race and immigration which closely resembled each other. Both parties promised full repeal of the Nationality Act and the Alliance proposed introducing a Bill of Rights and the establishment of a UK Commission on Human Rights to cover both race and sex discrimination. Both made far more specific promises to black voters than the Conservatives and there was considerable interest in seeing whether the Alliance would be able to make inroads into the high level of ethnic minority support for the Labour party. Critics of the Labour party had been warning for years that black voters were becoming disillusioned with the party and were questioning whether their support for it would be maintained, but until 1983 black voters had little choice as the Conservative party was perceived as so hostile to their interests. In 1983, it looked as though the rise of the Alliance might change everything by offering black voters a *real* alternative to the Labour party for the first time.

Alliance support among black voters did, indeed, rise in 1983. According to the CRE figures it rose to 11% compared to the 5% which went to the Liberals in 1979.[44] It still fell considerably below the 25% which the Alliance received from the electorate at large. By the same token, black voters remained by far the most loyal element in Labour party support: Labour lost 25% of its 1979 support among voters in general but only 5% among black voters.[45]

To add to their discomfiture, the Alliance lost many of the MPs who represented inner city constituencies. These included Bill Pitt, Edward Lyons, Richard Crawshaw, and Eric Ogden, all of whom were defeated. Also unlike Labour and Conservative black candidates who, with two notable exceptions, fared much the same as their white colleagues, the six black Alliance candidates all did worse than average for their party.[46]

The parliamentary record of the Alliance, the stand taken by their

MPs, their manifesto promises and the black candidates they put up in areas with large black electorates – none, it seems swayed any significant number of black voters. For race plays very much less a part in shaping the party loyalties of black voters than has been claimed. This is illustrated by a survey of political attitudes conducted by the Greater London Council in the summer of 1984 among 304 Afro-Caribbean, 277 Asian and 424 white Londoners.[47] It included an open question on respondents' perception of the three main parties. Of those who evaluated the parties on specific issues rather than in very general terms, only 15 (2%) of all black respondents mentioned the Conservatives' race policies, 30 (4%) mentioned race policies in connection with Labour but none mentioned race in connection with the Alliance.

The 1983 general election, then, conclusively demonstrated that the 'black vote' argument had been massively overstated and the predictable response of the parties might be to revert to their previous low profile on 'race' issues. But the momentum which has been generated within the parties, the increasing political awareness and activity of black people – both within the parties and outside them – and, above all, the riots of 1981, reinforced by those of 1985, have put them squarely on the political agenda. Even if they wanted to, politicians of any party would find it difficult to be sure of keeping race on the 'back burner' again.[48]

## NOTES

1. J. Bulpitt, *Continuity, Autonomy and Peripheralisation: the Anatomy of the Centre's Race Statecraft in England*, ch.1.
2. *West Indian World*, 24 Apr. 1979.
3. Community Relations Commission, *Participation by the Ethnic Minorities in the General Election, October 1974, CRC*, 1975.
4. I. Crewe, 'The Black, Brown and Green Votes', *New Society*, 12 Apr. 1979.
5. E. Burney, *Housing on Trial: a Study of Immigrants and Local Government* (Institute of Race Relations/Oxford University Press, 1967) p.4.
6. J. Curtice and M. Steed, 'An Analysis of the Voting' in D. Butler and D. Kavanagh, *The British General Election of 1979* (Macmillan, 1980).
7. Ibid.
8. Labour Party Race Action Group, *Don't Take Black Votes for Granted* (LPRAG, 1979).
9. Labour Party, *Labour and the Black Electorate* (Labour Party, 1980).
10. Ibid.
11. Home Office, *British Nationality Law: Discussion of Possible Changes* Cmnd

6795 (HMSO, 1977).

12. Parliamentary Debates (Commons) Session 1979–80, vol.975, cols 265–6 (4 Dec. 1979).

13. Parliamentary Debates (Commons), Session 1980–81, vol.977, col.946 (28 Jan. 1981).

14. Ibid., col.1033.

15. Parliamentary Debates (Commons) Session 1981–82, vol.14, col.1046 (10 Dec. 1981).

16. Parliamentary Debates (Commons) Session 1980–81, vol.8, col.1408, (16 July 1981).

17. Parliamentary Debates (Commons) Session 1980–81, vol.3, col.21–2 (13 Apr. 1981).

18. Parliamentary Debates (Commons) Session 1980–81, vol.14, col.1056 (10 Dec. 1981).

19. House of Commons, Fifth Report from the Home Affairs Committee, Session 1979–80, *The Law Relating to Public Order* (HMSO, 1980).

20. Parliamentary Debates (Commons) Session 1981–82, vol.14, col.1009 (10 Dec. 1981).

21. *The Times*, 1 Aug. 1981.

22. Labour Party, *Citizenship and Immigration* (Labour Party, 1980).

23. Labour Party, *British Nationality Law: Our Alternative to Tory Legislation* (Labour Party Research Department, Sept. 1981).

24. Labour Party, *Immigration: Labour's Approach*, Statement to Conference by the NEC, Annual Conference Report 1982, 144–50.

25. Ibid.

26. *Labour's Programme* (Labour Party, 1982) pp.188–91.

27. M. Anwar, *Votes and Policies: Ethnic Minorities and the General Election 1979* (Commission for Racial Equality, 1980).

28. M. Steed, 'The National Front Vote', *Parliamentary Affairs*, 31, 3 (1978) pp.282–93.

29. Liberal Party, *The Real Fight is for Britain*, Liberal Party Election Manifesto (1970). For a further discussion of the Nationality Bill, see Chapter 3.

30. Parliamentary Debates (Commons) Session 1981–82, vol.14, col.1062 (10 Dec. 1981).

31. Parliamentary Debates (Commons) Session 1980–81, vol.997, col.954 (28 Jan. 1981).

32. Parliamentary Debates (Commons) Session 1980–81, vol.8, col.1437–9 (16 July 1981).

33. Parliamentary Debates (Commons) Session 1981–82, vol.14, col.1063 (10 Dec. 1981).

34. Parliamentary Debates (Commons) Session 1980–81, vol.8, col.1439 (16 July 1981).

35. Ibid., col.1465.

36. Parliamentary Debates (Commons) Session 1982–83, vol.34, col.358–9 (15 Dec. 1982).

37. Parliamentary Debates (Commons) Session 1980–81, vol.8, col.1437 (16 July 1981).

38. Ibid.

39. Ibid., col.1468.

40. Social Democratic Party, *Citizen Rights, Policies to Safeguard and Enhance Individual Freedoms*, Green Paper no.10 (Aug. 1982).
41. Social Democratic Party, *Britain's Urban Crisis*, Green Paper no.9 (1984).
42. D. Owen, *Britain's Black Communities*, Speech to mark 4th Anniversary of the Limehouse Declaration, Social Democratic Party (24 Jan.1985).
43. Liberal Party Community Relations Panel, Report on Inner City Disturbances, Liberal Party (Sept. 1981).
44. M. Anwar, *Ethnic Minorities and the 1983 General Election*, Commission for Racial Equality (1984).
45. Z. Layton-Henry and D.T. Studlar, 'The Electoral Participation of Black and Asian Britons: Integration or Alienation', *Parliamentary Affairs*, vol.38, no.3 (Summer 1984) pp.307–18.
46. J. Curtice and M. Steed, 'An Analysis of the Voting' in D. Butler and D. Kavanagh, *The British General Election of 1983* (Macmillan 1984) p.350.
47. Reports to the GLC Ethnic Minorities Committee, numbers 847, 908 and 1138.
48. K. Young and N. Connelly, *Policy and Practice in the Multi-Racial City* (Policy Studies Institute, 1981) p.154.

# 5 The House of Commons Home Affairs Sub-Committee and Government Policy on Race Relations

JAQI NIXON

## INTRODUCTION

A number of commentators have suggested that during 1979–83 the Conservative Government, whilst taking steps to control immigration and to tackle law and order problems, devoted little attention to policies which might improve race relations. Indeed, where there have been specific measures to improve race relations, such as the appointment of a Minister with special responsibility for race relations within the Department of Environment or the review of Section 11 funding, these are generally regarded as having been responses to external pressures or crises, for example the street riots of 1981.[1] Alternatively, they have been viewed either as a means of deflecting attention from the main issues or peripheralising the management of a controversial and complex policy to local authority or non-government agencies.[2]

During the same period, however, considerable interest in race relations was evinced and much activity undertaken by one particular group operating within the precincts of Westminster itself, namely the Home Affairs Sub-Committee on Race Relations and Immigration (HASC). And it is the contrast between the apparent lack of Government interest in race relations and the considerable activity of HASC which leads us to consider the extent to which

125

HASC may have been effective in influencing Government policy and practice during this period.

Three measures of effectiveness would seem to be relevant to an assessment of HASC's influence. Firstly, it is possible to suggest that such Government interest and activity as there was would have been less but for the work of HASC. Secondly, though having a direct or immediate impact on government policy and practice is important, it is no less important to assess the influence of HASC in terms of its capacity to permeate a wider audience which may contribute, in more indirect ways, to the formulation of policy. Ideally, such an assessment should embrace a number of key 'stakeholders' including those beyond the boundaries of Parliament and central government departments who have responsibility for implementing policies.[3] The present chapter, however, will confine its analysis of HASC influence to those parts of the race relations policy environment which are in close proximity to the centre. Thirdly, it may be argued that HASC could itself have had a more direct effect on policy if certain procedures governing the operations of Select Committees in general or of HASC in particular had been modified.

Each of these possibilities will be taken into account in this assessment of HASC but, first, we must set the Sub-Committee in context by providing a brief outline of the development and role of Select Committees in general. This will enable us to identify their main objectives and to appreciate their operational constraints and their limitations. In addition, we will highlight certain features which are peculiar to HASC and which may have some bearing on the degree to which it has been successful in meeting the objectives which it has set for itself. The ensuing analysis relates to events which occurred between 1979, when the reformed Select Committee procedures were introduced, and the dissolution of Select Committees, following the General Election of June 1983.

## THE REFORMED SELECT COMMITTEE SYSTEM

The Home Affairs Committee (HAC) is one of fourteen all-party Committees approved by Parliament in 1979. These Committees were designed to replace the existing Select Committees which had evolved piecemeal, mainly during the 1960s and 1970s, and which tended to be either departmentally based or subject oriented. In contrast, the reformed Select Committee system, introduced in 1979, was to provide a comprehensive, departmentally-related organisation capable of undertaking a 'continuous and systematic' scrutiny of public service activities.[4] Thus, each Select Committee was to be related to a particular department of government and provided with the following broad and most challenging remit: 'to examine the expenditure, administration and policy of the principal government departments, and associated bodies . . .' (para. 1 of the Standing Order approved 25 June 1979).

Moreover, the reformed Select Committees were to enjoy more autonomy and continuity than their predecessors. Unlike previous Committees, which had been sessional and which could be disbanded if they incurred the displeasure of the government, the reformed Committees were appointed under Standing Order for the term of a Parliament. In addition, the powers and scope of Committee enquiries were considerably strengthened and extended, especially with regard to the provision of information, the attendance of witnesses and the production of records and papers.

## THE HOME AFFAIRS COMMITTEE AND ITS SUB-COMMITTEE

HAC has the responsibility of examining the expenditure, administration and policy of the Home Office and associated public bodies. Moreover, it is one of only three Committees granted the power to appoint a Sub-Committee.[5] At their first meeting in December, 1979, members of HAC agreed unanimously that the Sub-Committee should concern itself exclusively with race relations and immigration. Their decision only met existing expectations of House of Commons members since, until 1979, a Select Committee had been solely concerned with the same subject.

The Home Affairs Sub-Committee, in only a short space of time, succeeded in establishing for itself an identity distinct from that of the main Committee. During the period under study it has achieved a sound reputation not only for the quantity, but also for the quality of its work. Moreover, all Sub-Committee members have been prepared to invest a great deal of time and energy in the HASC enquiries, even though the combined responsibility of both main Committee and Sub-Committee work places a considerable extra burden on their already numerous Parliamentary duties. Although statistics denoting attendance rates should be viewed with caution, since a member has only to put in an appearance at a Committee session to be registered as present, HASC has, to date, the highest average attendance record of all Select Committees.[6] As evidence of the extent of Sub-Committee work, we may note that between 1979 and 1983, HASC undertook three substantive enquiries, received over 60 memoranda from the Home Office and other Departments, innumerable written submissions from organisations and individuals outside the government, held 65 evidence sessions in public and attended 45 sessions for private deliberations. It published twelve separate reports, eight of which required a formal Government reply.[7]

## THE CHAIRMAN

Most commentators and participators of committee systems stress the importance of chairmanship in determining the success of a committee in terms of both how it operates and its final output.[8] And the reformed Select Committees provide a further exemplar of this class of general observation. In view of the fact that the chairman's role is crucial to the effective functioning of Committees, it is important to recount the specific events which led to the selection of chairman for HAC and its Sub-Committee.

It was a decision of the Whip's office, following a decision of the House of Commons, that HAC, together with seven other Committees, should have a Conservative member appointed as chairman. It was then left in principle to Committee members to select their own chairman. In practice, their choice was not a little influenced by the Party Whips. In the case of HAC, Labour members disagreed with the Conservative members' initial choice of chairman and it was only after a vote had been taken that Sir Graham Page was appointed to chair the main Committee. In the absence of any clear directive about the appointment of Sub-Committee chairmen, members of HAC then voted that Alex Lyon, Labour Member, should become chairman.[9] He was, arguably, the most obvious candidate on account of his considerable previous experience in race relations matters, not least his former experience as Minister of State at the Home Office. Subsequently, however, the Whips' Office made clear its original intention that the Sub-Committee as well as the main Committee should be chaired by a

Conservative member. Lyon undoubtedly would have refused to relinquish the chair but Conservative complaints made to members of the Shadow Cabinet about breaking agreements, followed in turn by Party pressure on Labour members of HASC to withdraw their support, ensured, finally, that Lyon was removed from the chair. John Wheeler, though elected to Westminister for the first time in 1979, was appointed to replace him. In spite of his lack of Parliamentary experience, Wheeler, it appears, was the only Conservative member of HASC who was acceptable to Labour as well as Conservative members of the main Committee.

These initial problems over selection did not ease the Sub-Committee's passage from birth to infancy. However, HASC's early difficulties proved short-lived as it rapidly adjusted to working under a new chairman. No member of HASC, it seems, has had reason to regret the choice of Wheeler as chairman of the Sub-Committee.

## SUB-COMMITTEE PROCEDURES

In assessing how HASC operates and the processes whereby the chairman, in common with other Select Committee chairmen, seeks to secure a unanimous report,[10] it is necessary to examine briefly how the Sub-Committee relate to the main Committee. Both HAC and HASC operate in exactly the same way in respect of taking evidence from witnesses in public session, inviting written submissions, preparing the chairman's draft report and holding private sessions in which the draft report is considered and, on occasion, amended. The procedures for the Sub-Committee differ, however, in one important respect. The chairman's draft, once agreed upon by the HASC members, has then to be submitted to the main Committee where, once again, the report is discussed, paragraph by paragraph, and members are entitled to put down amendments. It is, in fact, rare for members of the main Committee to seek further amendments, since it is generally accepted that only HASC members have seen the evidence and it is really for them to produce their own report. Accordingly, as the Sub-Committee chairman explains:

It is, to say the least, unfortunate that five MPs should devote a great deal of their time to an enquiry and to a careful assessment of papers etc., agree to a report, and after all that, to have to submit that report to another group of MPs the majority of whom have not assessed the evidence, nor read the papers, who then have to agree or disagree with the findings of the Sub-Committee.

Not surprisingly, therefore, HASC members, on the whole, find this arrangement 'cumbersome, inefficient and incompetent'. Yet under existing Parliamentary procedures the arrangement must be retained and HASC reports may only be published as main Committee reports. However, given the present arrangement, it may be argued that some advantage accrues to minority Labour members of HASC who, having been overruled on an amendment in the Sub-Committee, have a second chance to seek an amendment tabled at the main Committee. More importantly, it is only in the case of HAC that the proceedings of the Committee are published. It is thus only at main Committee sessions that members are able to place on public record their opposition, either to certain sections of a report, or, if the amendment takes the form of a minority report (which to date, has happened only once in HASC),[11] to the Committee's report as a whole.

## PROBLEMS OF EVALUATION

Before attempting to assess the contribution made by HASC to Government policy on race relations, we must identify the apparent objectives of Select Committees in general, against which any achievements of HASC may be measured.

The primary aim of the reformed Committee structure, according to St John Stevas, was 'to strengthen the accountability of Ministers to the House for the discharge of their responsibilities'.[12] This perception of the main fuction of Select Committees is one shared by John Wheeler, chairman of HASC: 'They are there to restore to backbench MPs the ability to fulfil Parliament's historic role as the monitor of the Executive, and to look at how policies are arrived at and to measure their effectiveness.'

Other Sub-Committee members, however, see Select Committees as performing the rather separate function of influencing the development and content of government policy rather than monitoring it. Lyon argues, for example, that the basic role of Select Committees is 'to try and improve the policy-making decisions of the Executive'. Indeed, a brief review of HASC's enquiries since 1979 does suggest that the Sub-Committee has, on occasion, sought to change in a very direct way, either the content of policies or certain practices relating to race relations. In addition, this more interventionist function was endorsed by the chairman of HAC in his own report to the Liaison Committee: 'our purpose has been . . . to influence Ministers in the formation of policy'.[13]

A third function identified for Select Committees is that of providing the House and the public at large with factual information elicited from Committee witnesses and written memoranda, the interpretation of which may be, or, as some would argue, should be, a political matter. Select Committee enquiries have made available to interested groups both within and outside Westminister voluminous amounts of official and other information much of which would have remained, but for the Committees' powers to send for persons and papers, untapped. Indeed, according to some Select Committee members, it is the ability of members to engage in a non-partisan fashion, in drawing together and analysing the evidence, and presenting recommendations emanating from the evidence, which is the real strength of the Select Committee system. Certainly at least one Conservative member of HASC, John Hunt, stressed the importance of the Sub-Committee's information gathering and disseminating function: 'it is probably rather more important than keeping an eye on the Executive which can be done in other ways'.

Thus, it would appear that HASC members not only perceived Select Committees as fulfilling different functions but also tend to accord rather different weight to the significance of each of these. Given, then, the prevailing disparate views on Select Committee objectives and functions, any attempt to evaluate the possible impact of HASC will be that much more difficult.

A second factor to be borne in mind is the need for caution in attributing results on policy changes solely to the deliberations, or more particularly, the reports, of HASC. Select Committee reports are usually only one of a number of pressures brought to bear on government in respect of a particular policy issue. Moreover, much may depend upon the timeliness of a report's publication, whether it can be appropriately linked with other current issues or events either inside on outside Parliament and, most significantly perhaps, its capacity for attracting media attention. In short, issues and events beyond the work of HASC may be no less important determinants of policy change or modification than the Sub-

Committee's report. It is difficult, furthermore, to establish at which point in time one should assess a Committee's impact or effectiveness. Influencing the climate of opinion on a particular issue may be a lengthy process, but no less important for that.

## ASSESSING HASC'S CONTRIBUTION

The Sub-Committee's decision to concern itself solely with issues pertaining to race relations and immigration may be interpreted as a declaration of Parliament's own intention to continue giving priority to these subjects. Although, as has already been indicated, the House assumed that HASC would take over responsibilities from the previous Select Committee on Race Relations and Immigration, an understanding which, interestingly, was not extended to the previous Select Committee on Nationalised Industries, there is no reason, procedurally, why it should do so. Indeed, as the chairman of HASC notes in his report to the Liaison Committee: 'We reserve the right to use the Sub-Committee for some other purpose in the future if this should seem desirable.'[14] To date, members of HASC have managed to persuade the full Committee of the continuing need to give priority to race relations and immigration issues.

The most widely reported success of HASC in terms of its direct and speedy impact on Government policy was undoubtedly its report on *Race Relations and the 'Sus' Law*, which was followed by a second report on 'sus' a mere two months later. Together, these reports finally ensured that a commitment to abolishing the 'sus' Law was included in the Queen's Speech in November 1980. Members of HASC, including Conservative members who had voted with the Opposition in the Commons Debate on the Sub-Committee's second report on 'sus',[15] were clearly of the opinion that the 'sus' enquiry represented their major success. They believed that it provided a measure of the influence they are able to exert on a Government which might otherwise be reluctant to make any changes.

A similar assessment of the impact of the 'sus' enquiry has been presented by both academic and press commentators. Davies, for example, in illustrating the importance of debating Select Committee reports on the floor of the House, notes that 'The "sus" debate and the threat of legislation confounds those who were doubtful that the new Committees would sustain an independent position' and helps to persuade 'other members outside the Committees to behave more like lions and less like lambs'.[16] In similar vein, Layton-Henry comments upon how, reluctantly, Government was prepared to accept, under threat of the introduction of a private member's bill, the Sub-Committee's recommendation for the repeal of 'sus'.[17] The press were likewise impressed with HASC's forthright style. The *Guardian*, for instance, in its editorial, suggested that the 'Committee should be congratulated for the manner in which it has pursued this necessary reform'.[18]

It does not belittle the very real influence exerted on Government by HASC to add that the weight of informed opinion, reflected so clearly in the oral evidence presented to the Sub-Committee, already pointed in the direction of repeal of 'sus'. Reasons for the unpopularity of the 'sus' Law varied, and so, too, did the proposals for replacing it but, by and large, as one member of HASC readily acknowledged, the Sub-Committee was already 'pushing at an open door'. Even so, there seems little doubt that without HASC's sustained demand for action, the 'door' leading to the repeal of 'sus' may have remained ajar rather than being pushed wide open.

'sus' represented the sort of enquiry which, according to some members, the Sub-Committee is best equipped to carry out: a limited investigation on a specific topic, the boundaries of which are clearly delineated. As Alex Lyon explained in interview: 'a restricted issue which is capable of making a big impact when you produce a report, is more likely to get government assent than a major report which contains a lot of background material'.

The latter part of Lyon's description certainly applies to one of HASC's more substantive reports, *Racial Disadvantage*, which appeared in August 1981, together with two volumes of published minutes of evidence and memoranda. However, before subscribing to the view expressed by Lyon, we must first distinguish between different types of enquiry: those which have a short-term rather than a longer-term influence; those which require government responses to limited, discrete recommendations rather than to more general wide-ranging ones, and those with recommendations directed specifically at a Government department rather than ones which fall outside the province of government responsibility. In other words, since both the nature and content of a *major* Committee report are more complex, so, too, is the business of assessing its possible impact. Yet almost without exception, commentators have suggested that, in terms of provoking a direct Government response, the *Racial Disadvantage* report was disappointing.[19] This assessment will be examined in more detail below, but it is perhaps worth noting at this juncture John Wheeler's own view that the report was important precisely because it helped to change attitudes in the longer term.

With regard to particular recommendations, the Department of Environment's (DOE) response to the Sub-Committee's proposal that a special race relations unit be established within each major service department, was to appoint a Minister with special responsibility for race relations. In addition, it allocated official responsibility for race relations specifically within the Inner Cities Directorate. These measures received most media attention at the time, though editorial comments naturally differed as to their efficacy.[20] A more 'objective' assessment of the DOE's response was later to be provided by Glazer and Young: 'the casual visitor to the cities in later 1982 can hardly fail to collect anecdotes testifying to the willingness of Department of Environment officials to look favourably on projects which directly benefit the riot areas'.[21]

Of the 36 recommendations included in the *Racial Disadvantage* report which were directed at Government departments, another 13 may be considered to have received a positive response in the Government's Reply (Cmnd 8476)[22] or to have been implemented already. HASC members welcomed such responses as evidence that Government was concerned. These included: the monitoring of the MSC's special programmes to assess rates of ethnic minority participation (rec. 19); the acceptance in principle of the need for monitoring in the Civil Service and the intention to set up a pilot project this end (rec. 34); and the DHSS's intention to keep under review the position of elderly members of ethnic minorities (rec. 29). Nevertheless, members were undoubtedly disappointed with other responses which were either non-committal or even negative. For example, the Home Office rejected the recommendation that it should adopt a more rigorous coordinating role in respect of race relations (rec. 2) and, for its part, the Department of Education and Science (DES) was only prepared to 'note' the Sub-Committee's proposals concerning education and training, without making a commitment to implement any of these.

That Government departments, particularly the DOE, were prepared to pay attention to and, to some extent, implement the Sub-Committee's recommendations was undoubtedly aided by external events.[23] The street riots of April 1981 injected the HASC deliberations with a greater sense of urgency. Moreover, Lord Scarman, in preparing his own report, was able to take advantage of the wealth of evidence submitted to HASC. Thus the timeliness of Select Committee reports, the extent to which they may add fuel to a politically potent issue, though not always a matter over which Committee members have any choice or control, may be a significant factor in ensuring that a report's recommendations elicit a positive Government response.

To reduce the possibility of their recommendations being only nugatory, both Conservative and Labour members of HASC agreed upon the importance of undertaking follow-up enquiries. As Lyon has suggested: 'Every couple of years you ought to be chasing the Department and finding out what they've done about things you've recommended'. Following up departmental action may take two forms. Firstly, and to date the more common procedure, are Select Committees' public scrutiny or evidence-taking sessions with Ministers and their officials. Secondly, a Committee may decide to undertake a further enquiry on a particular subject and to produce a separate report. HASC adopted the former strategy on about four occasions during the period under study. The importance of scrutiny sessions for reviewing departmental progress on Select Committee recommendations, and for giving further consideration to negative Government responses, has not yet been greatly appreciated by research commentators on the Select Committee system. Yet a brief analysis of a series of separate meetings with four different Ministers following the Government Reply to *Racial Disadvantage* helps to illustrate how a Committee can use such sessions to keep up to date on developments and is able to press for further action to be taken.

## SCRUTINY SESSIONS

In a short period of just six weeks in 1982, HASC took evidence on five occasions from either the Secretary of State or Minister at the Home Office, DES, DOE and DHSS.[24] The chairman and members at each of these sought to obtain comments when recommendations had elicited a negative response or when members remained uncertain about what progress had been made, rather than concentrating on areas in which positive action had been taken. One notable example of HASC's success in obtaining information during a scrutiny session was the Home Office's preparation of guidelines on new arrangements for Section 11 funding. The HASC also learnt for the first time that, following the Home Secretary's own initiative in setting up an enquiry into racial attacks, the Home Office was to improve procedures for the collection of data, ensure better liaison between police and communities and hold discussions with the DES about racial attacks in schools. The DHSS, for its part, informed HASC that it was in the process of gathering information on what opportunities existed for ethnic communities to provide social services for their elderly members who might wish to receive separate provision. The Department also informed HASC that it had set up a sub-group of the Inter-departmental Consultative Group on provision for the under-fives, specifically to consider the needs of ethnic minorities.[25] Furthermore, it had appointed, as an adviser, the Director of the 'Stop Rickets Campaign' to assist the Department on 'wider aspects of the health problems of ethnic minorities'.[26] The Sub-Committee also heard from the DoE that it had funded two new projects. One was designed to identify ways in which the needs of ethnic minorities could be recognised and responded to in the Urban Programme,[27] the other to identify difficulties experienced by black groups in dealing with local authorities and other public agencies. Furthermore, this scrutiny session allowed Sir George Young, the newly-appointed DOE Minister with special responsibility for ethnic minorities, to make the following comment: 'The Department is making progress in the right direction, partly as a result of your report. We would like to make faster progress but I think we are on the right lines'. This acknowledged the influence HASC's report had had on the Department.[28]

The scrutiny session with the Secretary of State for Education was, however, to prove less illuminating. This was primarily because the DES, awaiting the deliberations of the Swann Committee on the education of West Indian children, felt unable, at least for the time being, to move ahead in directions suggested in HASC's report. Yet, even from this generally disappointing session, one or two interesting offerings emerged. Contrary to an earlier negative response in the White Paper, which had been widely reported in the press,[29] the Department now declared its readiness to make a more positive attempt to improve teacher-training on race relations issues. In addition, the Secretary of State was prepared to offer, on the spot, as it were, a reassurance to the Sub-Committee that he would make certain that liaison between the Home Office and DES in respect of Section 11 applications, 'works quickly'.[30] Such impromptu responses by a Secretary of State are always most welcome to Committee members, who probably feel they have scored a minor victory when such a promise is committed to public record.

All members of HASC considered the evidence presented by the Home Secretary to be especially disappointing. In part, they were dissatisfied with the inflexible way in which he continued to consider that a more formal coordinating machinery based within the Home Office was neither necessary nor, indeed, appropriate for his role as departmental coordinator on race relations matters. Yet, despite his continuing difference of opinion on a fundamental issue of organisation, the Home Secretary did inform the Sub-Committee that some small developments had taken place. Extra staff had been appointed to deal with the new arrangements for Section 11 funding and, to encourage a greater appreciation of race relations issues, staff engaged in race relations research had been transferred to the Equal Opportunities and Community Programme sections of the Home Office.

Thus, in undertaking an evaluation of the impact of Select Committees it is not sufficient simply to analyse the official Government Reply. As an examination of evidence presented in a scrutiny session indicates, whilst Government, and more particularly the Home Office, remained obdurate on a number of essential points, some of the departments concerned had begun to act upon the HASC recommendations and had made some progress in specific areas. There are grounds, therefore, for concurring with the chairman's prescient comment at the time of the Government's Reply: 'I think that the impact of this report is going to be much greater than this response implies'.[31]

## FOLLOW-UP ENQUIRIES

A second means of securing a more satisfactory Government response is for a Select Committee to indicate its intention to undertake a follow-up to one of its substantive enquiries. HASC and, indeed, most Select Committees, have tended not to pursue this strategy. The one exception has been the Social Services Committee's enquiry into infant mortality. A second report published by the Committee concluded that inequalities in perinatal mortality had, in some Health Authority areas, and for some groups, including ethnic minorities, actually increased since the Committee had first reported on the subject in 1980.[32] In its follow-up report the Social Services Committee noted with some satisfaction:

> This is the first time that one of the departmentally-related Select Committees has mounted a follow-up of a major Committee report. We have found it to be a valuable exercise and commend it to our fellow Committees.[33]

HASC's closest approximation to a follow-up was its enquiry into *Ethnic and Racial Questions in the Census*. A recommendation had already been made in its *Racial Disadvantage* report (rec. 36) to the effect that an ethnic question should be included in the census.

Booth, in her analysis of the Sub-Committee's Census report correctly notes that members already favoured the use of an ethnic question in the census before they embarked upon their enquiry.[34] Lyon, for example, who admits to having spent a good deal of his time arguing for ethnic monitoring generally, saw the issue of an ethnic origin question as crucial in helping to break down existing entrenched positions on monitoring of ethnic origin. In order to present as effective a case as possible for the inclusion of an ethnic question, the Sub-Committee made 'judicious' use of the evidence submitted to it and made a careful selection of written memoranda for publication in its minutes of evidence. It was thus a disappointment for HASC when the Government decided, for reasons of economy, to cancel the mid-term census in 1986 for which an ethnic question might have been adopted. Despite Booth's stricture that HASC's report had been too 'optimistic'[35] and had failed to dispel concern about possible adverse reactions to an ethnic question, nevertheless HASC members themselves believed that they were beginning to gain ground on the issue of ethnic monitoring generally and, similarly, that there was increasing support for an ethnic question in the census. Moreover, the publication of the Government's Reply, in which it acknowledges the need to consider having an ethnic question in the census, has since demonstrated that the Sub-Committee's optimism was not unjustified.[36]

In respect of HASC's final report before the General Election, *British Nationality Fees*, the Government published its official reply in March 1984. This stated: 'Most of the proposals made in the report have been accepted in full and many have already been implemented'.[37] Having already suggested that the formal Government Reply by no means provides complete evidence of a report's impact, it is also necessary to caution against uncritical acceptance of Government's pronouncements. *The British Nationality Fees* enquiry had been prompted by a Commons debate in December 1982 on proposed levels of nationality fees and delays in processing applications. Though HASC members were satisfied that the administrative changes referred to in the Government's Reply[38] would improve the processing of applications and might help to reduce queues, and though they welcomed proposals for a better information service, they were disappointed with the response on a number of counts. Government had rejected first the recommendation that entitlement registrations should be free, second that applicants in receipt of Supplementary Benefit or Family Income Supplement should have their fees waived and, finally, that a maximum fee for a family applying for citizenship should be the same as for a single applicant. However, Government did accept the case for reducing fees for future, though not for existing, applicants, and that unsuccessful applicants should no longer forfeit the whole of their fee. Even so, some Conservative and Labour members of HASC believe that the subject of nationality fees warrants a follow-up enquiry. If there is continued evidence of long delays in processing applications and of financial hardship for applicants, even a Conservative Sub-Committee chairman, reluctant to embarrass the government, which currently makes a profit of over £6 million from citizenship fees,[39] may be persuaded of the need for a second enquiry. This, in turn, may mean that Government's initial negative responses to HASC's report will have to be re-assessed.

## HASC FAILURES

The emphasis, so far, has been on the more 'successful' HASC reports, or, at least, on particular recommendations which have had some influence on Government policy or practice affecting race relations. Instead of distilling from these examples general explanations for the influence of Select Committees, we may, by juxtaposing these with examples of less influential reports, be able to throw more light upon which factors best account for the apparent success or failure of Select Committee reports.

There is little doubt that the least successful of the enquiries undertaken by HASC were its first enquiry into the *Proposed New Immigration Rules*, and its *British Overseas Citizens* enquiry, published in March 1981. Both enquiries were set in train at a time when Government was also dealing with the subject, and neither resulted in recommendations being presented in the Sub-Committee's final reports. To take the first enquiry as an example, this was intended to be brief so that HASC could report before the proposed New Immigration Rules were debated in the House. Initially, at least, this made the enquiry especially attractive to members since it was both topical and timely, and it was hoped that the Sub-Committee's deliberations and presentation of evidence would have an immediate and direct influence on the shape of Government policy.

Having presented its finding, however, the Sub-Committee's report concluded: 'We do not think it possible or desirable for us to form any judgement.'[40] It was, in fact, the impossibility of reaching agreement, rather than the propriety of making judgements, which resulted in the report being published without any recommendations for Government policy-makers. With the benefit of hindsight the chairman of HASC was to acknowledge: 'there is a learning process in Committee work and between colleagues. We have made some mistakes on the Sub-Committee but I think we have benefited from those experiences'. What were these mistakes in respect of HASC's first enquiry, and what lessons have Sub-Committee members been able to derive from them?

In view of the fact that the proposed Immigration Rules were about to be debated by the House, HASC members viewed the subject, though clearly a politically potent one, as deserving their consideration so that they could present the House with the relevant facts about immigration, and so contribute to an informed debate. But, as John Wheeler was later to admit: 'This was a classic example of the Committee beginning an enquiry and knowing that it would not agree on the outcome of a politically motivated enquiry, with strong feelings on both sides. It is a "no win" situation and the report was quite worthless and achieved precisely nothing.' Similar sentiments were echoed by other HASC members. Hunt, for example, who also recognised that useful lessons had been learnt, explained that their first enquiry had presented problems because it was too timely, too much 'an issue of the moment' which, because of pressures placed upon them by their Party Whips, merely encouraged members to take up publicly political postures rather than to seek agreement on specific points emanating from the evidence submitted to them. In the event, members failed to reach any sort of negotiated consensus which could provide a basis for the chairman's draft report.

The first HASC enquiry, therefore, was ill-suited to a bi-partisan approach, not only because of traditional Conservative–Labour public positions on the issue of immigration, but also because, included in the proposed rules, were particular elements of especial concern to Labour members. Indeed, both Conservative and Labour members agreed that one of the most controversial subjects they had to deal with during their first Parliament was the treatment of male fiancés of British citizens born abroad, primarily those from the Indian Sub-Continent wishing to participate in an arranged marriage. Following publication of the Government's White Paper,[41] and recognising the improbability of their ever obtaining a unanimous report, the Sub-Committee decided to hold a scrutiny session with the Minister of State at the Home Office.[42] This at least ensured that HASC could question the Minister closely on the subject of fiancés and that, furthermore, the evidence would be published and made available to the House and the public at large. It is clear from the published evidence that the chairman permitted Alex Lyon to dominate the proceedings on this occasion and to accord prominence to three contentious issues which seemed to undermine the Home Office case for differential treatment of male fiancés. The first was that the number of persons thought to be involved had apparently been over-estimated. The second under-lined the fact that men settled in Britain, but not British citizens, were allowed to bring their fiancées, thereby making clear that the decision to exclude male fiancés was directly related to the question of employment. And the third referred to the fact that British women who choose to have an arranged marriage with a man they have not met are excluded from the 'equality of treatment for citizens', referred to in the Government's White Paper. This public 'record' of both factual information gleaned from the evidence, together with the close questioning of the Minister and his officials on a controversial topic during a scrutiny session, in part prevented the Sub-Committee's first enquiry from being a complete waste of time. However, members' inability to achieve consensus on the interpretation of the evidence meant that, on their own terms, the enquiry must be deemed a failure.

Unlike the *Proposed New Immigration Rules*, the Sub-Committee's investigation into the *Commission for Racial Equality* (CRE) represented a substantive enquiry which resulted in the publication of a unanimous report. Yet it, too, may be more appropriately classified as a failure. In contrast to their conflicting perspectives on immigration rules, both Conservative and Labour members unanimously agreed, before embarking upon their enquiry, that the CRE was in need of reform. Lyon, for instance, had made clear his own view in Parliament: 'We have made a mistake in giving to the CRE powers in addition to the law enforcement role, with which it should be preoccupied. Is not the CRE being diverted into channels that it was never intended to deal with?'[43]

Although, in its formal response, the Government accepted certain of the Sub-Committee's recommendations, it nevertheless disagreed with two of HASC's fundamental proposals. The first had underlined the need to stress the CRE's role of law enforcement and allow its promotional role to develop only in relation to its anti-discriminatory work, which was itself subject to far too much delay. The other major recommendation concerned the need for a more streamlined executive and more competent staff for CRE. Since HASC had presented a unanimous report, which, though no guarantee, generally increases the likelihood of a report being taken seriously by governments,[44] it is useful to consider why the Sub-Commitee might have failed to secure Government support on these points.

First, though *not* perceived as a controversial subject by HASC members, the enquiry did appear to be levelling criticism directly at senior personnel working within the CRE, and it is not surprising, therefore, that the CRE viewed the outcome of the Sub-Committee's deliberations with some alarm. They, in turn, stole a march on HASC by arranging a counter-attack: they ensured that the press would at least present the CRE's own case sympathetically before the Sub-Committee's findings and recommendations had been published.[45] The Home Office, for its part, would have had the unenviable and delicate task of dealing with the resentment and unease felt by CRE staff had the recommendations made by HASC been implemented. In the event, the Department was able to use the appointment of a new CRE chairman, Peter Newsam, both to justify continuity at senior management levels and to press behind the scenes for greater efficiency in CRE work, particularly in relation to long delays in specific investigations, referred to in the HASC report.

Second, though HASC appreciate that the CRE was, on occasions, hampered in its own work by a less than supportive Government department,[46] its report was, nevertheless, forthright in its criticisms of CRE. The evidence selected for publication and the very style of presentation left no doubt about members' views. Para. 28, for example, noted: 'the fact that the Commission has only one part-time legal adviser, but an information service of 12 headed by a principal, does give a clear idea and alarming indication of the Commission's assessment of priorities'. Concerning the CRE's management structure and its relationship with Commissioners: 'This arrangement has caused a measure of confusion both inside and outside the Commission as to who is in effective control of the Commission' (para. 20). Again, in its criticism of delays in investigations, the Sub-Committee is quite unambiguous: 'the Commission recognises that they may have initiated too many investigations, and we cannot but be highly critical of their track record to date. We are convinced that most of the causes of delay in completing investigations rest firmly with the Commission' (para. 60).

It could be suggested, with the benefit of hindsight, that had the report's findings and recommendations been expressed in more moderate terms, the CRE, and subsequently the Home Office, might have been more positive in their response. As it was, the absence of compromise in the report's expressed dissatisfaction with the CRE probably strengthened the Commission's resolve to counter any criticisms made of it. In HASC, as in a number of other Committees,[47] it is common practice for the clerk to the Committee, working with the chairman, to prepare the chairman's draft. On this occasion, however, it appears that the chairman himself played a more than usually prominent role in drafting the report. Moreover, despite some attempt by other members to tone down the language,[48] the chairman's draft was to remain largely unchanged.

A related, but separate, explanation of Government's lukewarm response to the report is that the report was associated incorrectly, though perhaps understandably, with one particular Labour member, Alex Lyon. Even though HASC had presented a unanimous report and even though, as one member explained, it was the Conservative chairman who was really 'out to lambast the CRE', this misconception about Lyon's role would not have encouraged Government to accept the Sub-Committee's report.

## ACCOUNTING FOR SUCCESS AND FAILURE

It has been shown that specific HASC enquiries have been relatively successful in influencing Government policy or practice whereas others have been somewhat disappointing in this respect. It should now be possible to extract from these two sets of examples, general factors which help to explain why some Committee enquiries or, rather, their published reports, have been more successful than others in meeting this particular objective.

First, HASC members, and, indeed, Select Committee members in general, share the view that if an enquiry is to be successful then the subject itself must above all be of intrinsic interest and appear to merit examination. An interesting topic at least ensures that members themselves are prepared to make a worthwhile contribution to the Committee's deliberations. Moreover, it increases the likelihood of maximum media coverage both for the investigatory activities of the Committee and its final recommendations. On occasion, members' interest has been heightened and media attention secured if a subject is also currently under review by Government or if external events suddenly draw attention to a particular issue.

Secondly, whilst controversy may render an enquiry interesting to members, a subject must not be so politically contentious as to nullify a Committee's attempt to undertake a non-partisan investigation or, equally important, to prevent a Committee from formulating agreed recommendations for action. Yet, the chairman of the main Home Affairs Committee was undoubtedly pleased to be able to report to the Liaison Committee: 'We have deliberately avoided confining ourselves to 'safe' or uncontroversial subjects.'[49] Moreover, according to commentaries on the new Select Committee system, HASC may be deemed a success precisely because it has been prepared to deal with contentious issues.[50] But, in fact, when its choice of a controversial topic is also one on which legislation is either before the House (Immigration Rules, British Overseas Citizens) or under consideration by the Home Secretary or other Minister (NHS charges for overseas visitors), HASC has been singularly unsuccessful at producing a report which includes recommendations, and, hence, which may have some chance of influencing Government policy. The evidence suggests, therefore, that HASC is least effective when a subject for enquiry is characterised by both controversy *and* topicality, that is, when it undertakes an enquiry at the same time as government or Parliamentary activity. Whether this applies only to HASC, with its particular combination of Conservative and Labour backbenchers, or whether it applies in the case of other Committees is, in the absence of detailed studies of the individual Committees, difficult to determine. Certainly, as far as HASC is concerned, at least one member stressed the need to avoid 'issues of the moment' which encourage members to 'take up public postures as a result of public pressure or opinions'. Instead, he would choose enquiries not necessarily in the public eye at any one time.

Thirdly, the timely appearance of a Select Committee's report undoubtedly ensures a more positive response from Government. Any Committee report, as has already been suggested, is only one factor amongst many which may have some influence on Departmental policy. Yet the impact of HASC reports has been, on occasion, aided by external events and the publication of other reports, the Scarman report being a case in point. It is, of course, a moot point as to which of the reports is the more significant in terms of Government response. What is possible, however, is for a Select Committee to choose for an enquiry, a topic which is also under investigation by another agency or organisation or even by a Departmental group. Through benign collusion, it should be possible for each to present similar recommendations and arrange approximate dates for the publication of their separate reports in order to ensure maximum impact. Indeed, the Education, Science and Arts Committee collaborated with the Foreign Affairs Sub-Committee on just such a joint approach in an enquiry into overseas student fees. This example well illustrates the possibility of such an approach[51] and there is no reason why informal collaboration between, say, a Select Committee and an outside body or Department should not also take place.

Fourthly, the chairman's report should be drafted in such a way as to secure unanimity among members, but unanimity should not be achieved merely by presenting either an anodyne analysis of the evidence or a series of diluted recommendations. Rather, a report should be capable of indicating where reform is necessary without outraging key witnesses or blatantly contradicting a Government or Party view. A carefully drafted 'sus' report, it seems, helped to secure the support of both Conservative backbenchers and Conservative lawyers, who were persuaded by the evidence presented to

HASC, not that 'Sus' was simply bad for race relations, but that the law itself was unfair.

Finally, and perhaps of most importance, a positive Government reply is more likely in the longer term if a Select Committee holds a scrutiny session, when it is both accepted and expected that majority members will put pressure on Ministers or their officials. Alternatively, a Committee may undertake a follow-up enquiry to ensure that Government has actually carried out what it has promised to do, and to monitor progress since the publication of a particular report. One HASC member suggested in interview that the CRE enquiry was one well-suited to such a follow-up, more especially since the appointment of a new chairman of the CRE, so that HASC could learn about recent developments.

## INFLUENCING THE CLIMATE OF OPINION

We have so far attempted to assess the effectiveness of HASC activities on the basis of evidence derived from formal Government Replies and ministerial statements given in evidence to the Sub-Committee. Yet it is no less important to appreciate that the work of Select Committees has some impact in both Westminster and Whitehall which, because it extends beyond official responses, is less readily discernible. It is to these less tangible areas of influence which we now turn.

The Select Committee system has brought civil servants into much closer contact with backbenchers, especially Opposition MPs. As a result officials have come to understand better the views of individual members on particular issues. In turn, Committee members are provided with the opportunity to 'meet, listen, investigate and seek interpretations about the attitudes of individual civil servants'.[52] Moreover, the very fact that civil servants may be called as witnesses and examined by a Select Committee is sufficient for Departmental officials to be prepared to justify policy decisions. As one civil servant has observed: 'No matter how careful and thorough one thinks one is, no matter how carefully all the angles are examined, it is always beneficial to the decision-making process to know there is an "audit" to follow, and in public too.'[53] Committee members, likewise, appreciate the indirect influence they can exert on Departments. John Hunt, for example, believes that a number of the Sub-Committee's enquiries have prompted a variety of initiatives within different Departments: 'The very fact that we are looking into the matter means that a Department has to look into the matter and begin to think of the sort of case they can present to a Select Committee, so that alone is an advantage.'

Beyond the theatre of public sessions, Select Committees may also influence Departmental policy-making in less obvious ways. Individual civil servants may, for example, be anxious to promote a particular policy or practice and are able to use a Committee's recommendations to prompt their Department into taking action. Thus, it is likely that DHSS officials, rather than the Minister, instigated a series of developments in their Department intended to deal with racial disadvantage and concerning which HASC received information in a follow-up scrutiny session, held ten months after the publication of its *Racial Disadvantage* report.

The extent to which individual Select Committee members can influence backbench opinion in the House of Commons is more difficult to ascertain. Nevertheless, there are a number of different ways in which members of HASC have been able to assert some influence by proffering information or advice on issues relating to race relations and immigration. The most commonly applied, and certainly the most readily quantifiable, indicator of Select Committee influence is the number of debates on the Floor of the House devoted either to Committee reports or to subjects upon which a Committee has held an enquiry. During 1979–83 HASC fared rather better than most Committees in that its first report on *Race Relations and the 'sus' Law* was debated on 5 June, 1980. Merlyn Rees, formerly Home Secretary and an opponent of the repeal of 'sus', presented the motion for debate: 'That this House notes with approval the Second Report from the Home Affairs Committee.' Clearly the Sub-Committee's report was a significant factor in persuading Rees to press for the repeal of 'sus'. As he explained to the House: 'The report reflected almost unanimously the views of honourable members from both sides of the House. No Select Committee report should be ignored, but one as powerfully supported as this one must be given more weight than usual.'[54]

Apart from the handful of Committee reports which have succeeded in securing a full debate in the House, the voluminous evidence published by the Select Committees is increasingly being used to inform and enrich debates on a wider range of topics. As one Committee member has observed: 'It is encouraging to find that Committee proceedings and papers are increasingly being quoted by

MPS during debates on the Floor of the House.'[55] In addition, Select Committee members have increasingly availed themselves of the opportunity to participate in debates relevant to their Committee's remit. For instance, in the spirited debate on the proposed new immigration rules, HASC members used the occasion to reiterate their views on the controversial issue of male fiancés, views which were not without supporters on the Government backbenches.

Membership of other Parliamentary committees or backbench groups is a further potentially useful channel through which Select Committee members may seek to influence opinion in the House. John Wheeler, for example, as Joint Secretary of the Conservative Home Affairs Committee since 1980, has been well placed to relay HASC interests or concerns to a wider backbench audience. Similarly, Alex Lyon, as chairman of the Parliamentary Labour Party Home Affairs Committee until the General Election in 1983, was in a position to influence his Party's policy on race relations and immigration. Certainly there were occasions when Lyon was able to provide his colleagues with detailed information on a particular subject whhich had been supplied in evidence to the Sub-Committee. However, as Lyon himself admits, the current of Party opinion during the period under question, together with intra-party allegiances, his own personality and style of chairmanship, prevented him from having as much impact upon Party policymaking as his membership of HAC and his own ambitions might have implied.

Finally, by disseminating information in less formal ways, HASC members are able to influence backbench opinion. As one member explained: 'It isn't so much the final report, as the way in which the evidence, particularly spectacular evidence, is fed into the thinking of other MPs, so that they can see things in a different way because of the bits of evidence that come along.' One Conservative member of HASC attributes members' influence at this more informal level to their reputation in the House as 'specialists'. In the Conservative Party, at least, colleagues who specialise in a particular area are regarded by others as an 'authority' and, if they are 'reasonable', they will be relied upon as a valuable source of information and as a sounding board against which to assess acceptable Conservative opinion on race relations issues. It is conceivable, for example, that the Government's recent volte-face on the issue of an ethnic question in the census was not a little influenced by the informed opinion of John Wheeler himself, who has sought to win over not only his colleagues on the backbenches but also his friends in the Cabinet.

## CONSTRAINTS UPON HASC EFFECTIVENESS

The reformed Select Committee system has been in operation since 1979. This is a sufficiently lengthy period for both initial supporters and detractors of the new system to reassess their positions. Some academic commentators remain sceptical about the extent to which the 1979 Committees are in any sense innovatory, regarding them as essentially 'the same species of institution they were more than a century ago'.[56] Others caution against too high expectations of what Select Committees can actually achieve.[57] Those who advocate an enhanced Select Committee system argue that there remain a number of weaknesses which prevent the Committees playing a more important role in relation to Parliament.[58] Moreover, individual Committee members have themselves had the opportunity to form their own judgement, based upon practical experience of Committee work, about the sort of improvements which are necessary to increase Select Committee effectiveness. And so, in considering whether HASC might have had more impact upon Westminster and Whitehall during this period, it is useful to bear in mind these various perspectives.

HAC is one of only three Select Committees formally granted the power to set up a sub-committee,[59] and HAC members agreed from the outset that its Sub-Committee should continue the work of the previous Select Committee on Race Relations and Immigration. Whilst this decision was clearly welcome to those both inside and outside Parliament who wished to accord priority to race relations, nevertheless, in practice, it has presented difficulties for MPs who wanted actively to pursue their interests both in the main Committee, which deals with Home Affairs issues generally, and in the Sub-Committee. Unlike other Committees, where informal sub-committees were established almost from their inception and where members devote their energies at any one time to either the main Committee or Sub-Committee enquiry, HASC members remain actively engaged in both, thereby greatly increasing their Select Committee commitments.[60] As one member acknowledged: 'The trouble with HASC work is that it takes at least two afternoons a week and that often interferes with your capacity to take part in debates or other parts of House business.' Yet despite the problems of work load, the Committee, to date, has not taken advantage of an option to appoint a Temporary Committee Assistant to ease the burden of work.

One way of reducing the work load is for Select Committees to make use of specialist advisers. In its First Report, published in 1979, the Select Committee on Procedure recommended that 'all Select Committees should be free to appoint whatever advisers they wish for the purposes of their work'.[61] We have commented elsewhere on the contribution of specialist advisers to the effective performance of Select Committee tasks.[62] And yet HASC has made only one specialist adviser appointment[63] and even the main Committee only two. This contrasts with, for example, the Social Services Committee which, during the same period, appointed as many as fifteen advisers. It is possible to suggest, therefore, that HASC might not only have reduced the burden of members' work but also improved the quality of its output, and, hence, had greater influence either directly or indirectly in Parliament or elsewhere, if it had had recourse to more specialist advice.

Two factors help to explain the reluctance of HASC members to appoint specialist advisers. First, despite a wide range of expertise available in the race relations field, suitable advisers are considered to be hard to find. Members are of the opinion that an expert in race relations would merely 'go down the road which is most familiar to them' so that members themselves would be 'funnelled' in certain directions and hence would lose their 'independence'. Whilst there may be no agreement about what constitutes the ideal adviser, one senses that the major concern for HASC members is the difficulty of finding someone who is sufficiently non-partisan and yet who can, at the same time, demonstrate to the satisfaction of both sides, a sensitivity for the political dimension of the Sub-Committee's work. Secondly, some members believe that they have no need for the services of specialised advisers, partly because of the ability of the Clerks Department and research facilities in the House of Commons are such as to render specialist advice unnecessary, and partly because the Sub-Committee itself comprises members whose own knowledge is so extensive that 'between us, we don't feel we would gain from a specialist adviser'.

Alex Lyon, however, believes that a small pool of researchers, rather than subject specialists, should be retained on a quasi-permanent basis, as in the American Congressional system. These should be people who are good at finding out where the evidence is, and at drawing it to the attention of the Committee. But one must be wary of drawing comparisons between the Select Committee system and the Congressional system. As Giles Radice has commented: 'Those who claim that the Committees are not working . . . want us to develop a mirror image of the United States Congress. But in the United States there is a separation of powers. We do not have that system of government here. We cannot expect to establish the same kind of animal that operates in the United States.'[64] Thus, a more realistic proposal would be for HASC to make more use of specialist advice, at least for a factually complex and politically controversial topic, such as the British Overseas Citizens enquiry, where the contribution of an independent expert might have enabled members to reach agreement on recommendations for the Government.

Of greater concern to HASC members themselves is the requirement that Sub-Committee work has to be referred to the main Committee for formal approval. Both Labour and Conservative members would prefer to have the Sub-Committee elevated to the status of a main Committee, and all members would at least wish to see HASC given the authority to publish its own reports, rather than have to submit these for consideration to the main Committee.

Another cause for concern has been highlighted by the Liaison Committee: 'The connection between Select Committee work and the Floor of the House is of cardinal importance. If committee work is isolated, it is stunted. Its essence is that it is something done on behalf of the House, and committees need to know if the House supports them in what they do.'[65] Most commentators on Select Committees endorse the Liaison Committee's view and, in consequence, agree that too little time is made available for debates on Select Committee reports. Whilst HASC has been more fortunate than other departmentally-related Committees in having its 'Sus' report the subject of a substantive debate, nevertheless members believe that the impact of HASC is diminished by an inability to command more time on the Floor of the House. As one member explained: 'I don't think you can say that every time you produce a report there must be a debate on it, there are so many reports produced there isn't time. But I do think that if any Select Committee thinks it has not been properly treated by the Government in its report, then it ought to be able to command a debate.' An example of such an occasion was, in this member's view, the Sub-Committee's report on *Racial Disadvantage*.

A further reason why Committee members regard debates on their reports as essential is because they are a means of securing wider public recognition for their own hard work as well as for their Committee's recommendations. With evident satisfaction that 'Sus' had been chosen for debate, Sir Graham Page, formerly chairman of HAC, nevertheless took the opportunity in debate to highlight members' concern: 'I think this dispels some of the fears that we had that the Select Committees might be toiling away in vain because time would not be found to debate their reports in the House.'[66] Given that the Liaison Committee's request, made in 1982, for an 'undertaking from the Government that more days will be made available for these debates in the future'[67] continued to be ignored by Government, it is perhaps not surprising that one Conservative member of HASC, who also acknowledged in interview that Ministers occasionally take credit for proposals on ideas which have originated from a Committee enquiry, commented upon members' continuing sense of frustration in the following terms: 'Sometimes you feel you do a lot of work and prepare the report, and to all intents and purposes, it tends to be forgotten.'

## CONCLUSION

In attempting to assess the contribution made by HASC to securing Government interest in race relations, we would counsel against having unjustifiably high expectations of what the Sub-Committee can achieve. Whatever the perceived objectives of Select Committees, these can only be goals to be aimed for, never fully attained. Thus the most likely outcome is improving or modifying aspects of race relations policy rather than effecting radical change. Moreover, our analysis suggests that measuring the impact of HASC upon Government decision-making presents particular problems. Unlike many policies which fall clearly within the domain of one department, race relations policy, though the special responsibility of the Home Office, is one that concerns all Government departments.[68] Thus the diffusion of Departmental responsibility and the range of issues which warrant a race relations dimension compound the problem of evaluating the Sub-Committee's impact on Government, since the exact locus of its potential influence is difficult to determine.

The most important function of a Select Committee, or at least the one which gains most favour with participants and outside commentators alike, is to monitor departmental performance and so provide an effective scrutiny of the Executive. In John Wheeler's words: 'Select Committees are there to probe, to expose, to enquire, to challenge', so that greater accountability of the Executive to Parliament is ensured. In this respect HASC has been generally successful in that it has succeeded in identifying the weaknesses of Home Office or other Departmental policy or strategies in respect of race relations, and exposed Government inaction on a number of important issues. Of especial value in respect of this prime function are the scrutiny sessions with Ministers. These have succeeded on a number of occasions in clarifying the Government's current position on changes that have taken place, and in identifying continuing problems or deficiencies in race relations policy and practice. In addition, HASC members have been able to take advantage of such sessions to wring from the Minister a promise that something would be done, or would be looked into. There remains, however, scope for a more effective monitoring system which would require HASC to undertake more substantive follow-up enquiries which might result in the publication of separate reports. The British Overseas Citizens issue and the CRE would seem to be prime candidates for such an enquiry.

In terms of the more ambitious role for Select Committees, namely that of contributing directly to the shape and content of Government policy, HASC has achieved two notable successes, 'Sus' and the ethnic question. In addition, there is some evidence to suggest that its influence on Departments has been significant in respect of urban aid, health and social services issues, civil service monitoring, training and Section 11 funding. Since, however, HASC members themselves remain divided on the question of whether Committees should act as instigators, rather than simply as monitors, of public policy, then limited achievements are to be expected. None the less the Sub-Committee has been able to influence in less tangible forms, the climate of opinion in which decisions relating to race relations are both made and implemented.

The third function of Select Committees, that of facilitating the process of open government and of providing information for the public at large is no less important. In this respect HASC has made a major contribution to race relations. Its *Racial Disadvantage* report alone included two volumes of published memoranda and minutes of evidence. Such a wealth of information, some of which, but for the deliberations of the Sub-Committee, would not have been made available, is of immense value not only to interested backbenchers, but particularly to outside bodies which may, in turn, try to improve policies and practice by means of external group activity. Allied to this third function is the fact that HASC has helped to stimulate interest and to improve communications in the field of race relations by inviting written and oral evidence from individuals or organisations outside Whitehall. In doing so, HASC has provided a public platform for a whole variety of views and perspectives on race relations. As one member explained: 'The enormous amount of evidence submitted is an indication of the great value that these groups attach to the Select Committees. If you're a group working in a particular field and you suddenly find a Select Committee is taking up your subject, then it's a marvellous opportunity to bring your views to Parliament. And with the press and broadcasting services present, you have a unique opportunity to expound your views in public.'

In summary, therefore, we would suggest that the work of HASC has prevented race relations from being of only marginal interest to either Parliament or Government during the period in question. In spite of apparent countervailing tendencies,[69] the Sub-Committee has helped to secure for race relations a continuing place on the political agenda. Whilst it would be unreasonable to expect any single policy area to be accorded priority for the duration of a Parliament, nevertheless issues relevant to race relations have featured regularly both in the business of the House and, more importantly, in the internal affairs of Government departments. This sustained interest cannot be explained solely in terms of external crises or pressures, important though these were. In addition, significant changes have taken place as a result of continued pressure from HASC and at times when no obvious external event provided an impetus for reform. The Government's decision to accept, in principle, the need for an ethnic question in the census, taken 18 months after the publication of the Sub-Committee's report, is just such an example. It illustrates, moreover, the wisdom of judging the impact of HASC from a longer-term perspective.

## APPENDIX

**Home Affairs Sub-Committee on Race Relations and Immigration Reports, 1979–83**

*Session 1979–80*

First Report. *Proposed New Immigration Rules and the European Convention on Human Rights*, HC 434 (11 Feb. 1980).
Second Report. *Race Relations and the 'Sus' Law*, HC 559 (21 Apr. 1980).
Fourth Report. *Race Relations and the 'Sus' Law No., 2*, HC 744 (5 Aug. 1980).

*Session 1980–81*

Second Report. *Numbers and Legal Status of Future British Overseas Citizens without other Citizenship*, HC 158 (16 Mar. 1981).
Fifth Report. *Racial Disadvantage*, HC 424-i (20 July 1981).

*Session 1981–82*

First Report. *The Commission for Racial Equality*, HC 46 (23 Nov. 1981).
Second Report. *Racial Attacks*, HC 106 (27 Jan. 1982).
Third Report. *NHS Charges for Overseas Visitors*, HC 121 (18 May 1982).
Fifth Report. *Immigration from the Indian Subcontinent*, HC 90 (23 July 1982).
Seventh Report. *Revised Immigration Rules*; Evidence from Timothy Raison, Minister of State, HC 526 (25 Oct. 1982).

*Session 1982-83*

Second Report. *Ethnic and Racial Questions in the Census*, HC 33 (5 May 1983).
Third Report. *British Nationality Fees*, HC 248 (4 May 1983).

*Published minutes of evidence of scrutiny sessions with the Secretary/ Minister of State:*

*Session 1980-81*

HC 89, Home Office (18 Dec. 1980).
HC 15-vi, Home Office (26 Feb. 1981).

*Session 1981–82*

HC 405-i, Home Office (14 June 1982).
HC 405-ii, DHSS (5 July 1982).
HC 405-iii, DES (12 July 1982).
HC 405-iv, Home Office (26 July 1982).

## NOTES

1. N. Glazer and K. Young, *Ethnic Pluralism and Public Policy* (Heinemann, 1983).
2. J. Bulpitt, *Territory and Power in the United Kingdom* (Manchester University Press, 1983).
3. E. Guba and H. Lincoln, *Effective Evaluation* (Jossey-Bass, 1983).
4. HC 588 1, *Session 1977–78. First Report from the Select Committee on Procedure* (HMSO, 1979) recommendation 31.
5. HC 588 1, recommendation 40. The Foreign Affairs Committee and the Treasury and Civil Service Committee were also granted the power to appoint a Sub-Committee.
6. D. Englefield, *Commons Select Committees, Catalysts for Progress?* (Longman, 1984) appendix 5, p.122.
7. All HASC draft reports are submitted to the main Home Affairs Committee and are published as HAC reports. In order to distinguish the Sub-Committee reports from those of the main Committee, however, the author has taken the liberty of referring to the former as HASC reports.
8. See, for example. D. Donnison in M. Bulmer (ed.) *Social Research and Royal Commissions* (Allen & Unwin, 1980).
9. HC 434, *Session 1979–80. First Report. Proposed Immigration Rules and the European Convention on Human Rights*, 11 Feb. 1980. Proceedings, 10 Dec. 1979. One Conservative member was absent at this meeting, thereby enabling Labour members to win the vote (5 : 4). The Conservative chairman may cast his vote only in the event of an even vote.
10. For further details of these procedures see, for example, J. Nixon and N. Nixon, 'The Social Services Committee: a Forum for Policy Review and Policy Reform', *Journal of Social Policy*, vol. 12, part 3 (July 1983) pp.346–7.
11. HC 121, *Session 1981–82, Third Report. NHS Charges for Overseas Visitors*. On this occasion Alex Lyon tabled an amendment which took the form of a short minority report.
12. *Parliamentary Debates*, House of Commons, vol. 969, 1978–79, col. 44.
13. HC 92, para 7.
14. Ibid., para 2.
15. All HASC members present for the Debate voted with the Opposition. Jill Knight, Conservative, was absent.
16. This is a reference to a comment made in HC 744, Session 1979–80, p.iv, clause 8: '. . . if there is no measure to repeal 'Sus' . . . members of the Committee will themselves place such a bill before the House.'
17. Zig Layton-Henry, Race and the Thatcher Government, supra, ch.3, pp.80–2.

18. *Guardian*, 7 Aug. 1980.
19. Layton-Henry, op cit., p.22; *The Times*, 27 Jan. 1982.
20. See, for example, 'Minority Minister gets down to business', *Guardian*, 13 Feb. 1982.
21. N. Glazer and K. Young, *Ethnic Pluralism and Public Policy* (Heinemann, 1983) p.292.
22. The Government's Reply to the Fifth Report from the Home Affairs Committee, Session 1980/81, *Racial Disadvantage*, Cmnd 8476 (HMSO, 1981).
23. N. Glazer and K. Young, op. cit., p.292.
24. HC 405 i–iv, Session 1981–82.
25. In Nov. 1984, DHSS published a report entitled *Services for Under Fives from Ethnic Minority Communities*. This was produced by the Inter-departmental sub-group on under fives for ethnic minorities, set up as a direct response to recommendation 39 of HASC's *Racial Disadvantage* report.
26. HC 405ii, para.89.
27. HC 405-iv. In 1981 there were 140 Urban Programme projects, account for £2 millions, which provided for ethnic minority interests. In 1982 there were 206 projects, costing about £7 millions.
28. HC 405iv, para.200.
29. See, for example, *The Times*, 27 Jan. 1982.
30. HC 405iii, para.156.
31. *The Times*, 27 Jan. 1982.
32. HC 663, *Session 1979–80. Second Report from the Social Services Committee, Perinatal and Neonatal Mortality, 1980.*
33. HC 308, para.2.
34. H. Booth, 'Ethnic and Racial Questions in the Census: the Home Affairs Committee report', *New Community*, vol. XI, nos (1/2 Autumn/Winter, 1983).
35. Ibid.
36. Government's Reply to the Second Report from the Home Affairs Committee, Session 1982/83, *Ethnic and Racial Questions in the Census*, Cmnd 9238 (HMSO, 1984).
37. Government's Reply to the Third Report from the Home Affairs Committee Session 1982/83, *British Nationality Fees*, Cmnd 9183 (HMSO, 1984).
38. Ibid.
39. *Annual Report*, Joint Council for the Welfare of Immigrants, 1982–83 (London, 1983).
40. HC 434, 1980, para.20.
41. Proposals for the Revision of the Immigration Rules, Cmnd 7750 (HMSO, 1979).
42. HC 526. *Session 1981–82. Seventh Report. Revised Immigration Rules, 1982.*
43. HC 989, *Session 1979–80*, col. 1717–18.
44. B. Jones and R. Wilford, *A Preliminary Research Report on the Welsh Affairs Select Committee*, paper presented to Political Studies Association, UK, Politics Workshop, Cardiff (Sept. 1980) p.7.
45. *The Times*, 20 May 1981.
46. HC 46, para.6.
47. See, for example, Nixon and Nixon, op.cit., p.342.
48. HC 46–1, *Session 1981–82, First Report. The Commission for Racial Equality*, November, 1981. Proceedings, at which Lyon sought an amendment to the chairman's draft report.

49. HC 92, para.6.
50. See Nixon and Nixon, op.cit., p.346. The previous Select Committee on Race Relations and Immigration was also noted for its choice of controversial subjects for enquiry. See S. Himelfarb, 'Consensus in Committee: the Case of the Select Committee on Race Relations and Immigration', *Parliamentary Affairs*, vol. XXXIII, no. 7 (Winter 1980) pp.54–66.
51. The Education, Science and Arts Committee and the Foreign Affairs Committee jointly undertook this enquiry following publication of the White Paper in which the government indicated its intention to introduce full cost fees for overseas students. Cmnd 7746, *The Government's Expenditure Plans 1980–81*, p.6, para. 33.
52. C. Morris, 'The Opposition's View' in D. Englefield (ed.) *Commons Select Committees: Catalysts for Progress?*, op.cit., p.43.
53. P. Kemp, 'A Civil Servant's View' in D. Englefield, op.cit., p.55.
54. *Parliamentary Debates*, House of Commons, vol. 985, col. 1763 (5 June 1980).
55. J. Craigen, 'The Backbencher's View' in D. Englefield, op.cit., p.21.
56. N. Johnson, 'An Academic's View' in D. Englefield, op.cit., p.61.
57. G. Dewry in D.M. Hill (ed.), *Parliamentary Select Committees in Action: a Symposium*, Strathclyde Papers on Government and Politics, no.24 (1984).
58. HC 92, op.cit.
59. In practice, however, other Committees have operated informal sub-committees in order to deal with their wide remits. HC 92, op.cit., para. 35.
60. Problems of work load and a resultant conflict of interests in Parliamentary duties are not, of course, experienced by HASC members only. See, for example, Nixon and Nixon, op.cit., p.341.
61. HC 588–1, rec. 53.
62. Nixon and Nixon, op. cit., p.342.
63. David Smith, Policy Studies Institute, was appointed as specialist adviser for the Sub-Committee's *Racial Disadvantage* enquiry.
64. Parliamentary Debates, vol.963, cols. 356–7 (20 Feb. 1979).
65. H.C. 92, para.63.
66. Parliamentary Debates, vol. 985, col. 1763 (5 June 1980).
67. HC 92, para.65.
68. I have suggested, elsewhere, that the Home Office retains responsibility for race relations by default: 'It is an area in "policy space" which is occupied by many bureaucracies and where none seeks sovereignty', 'The Home Office and Race Relations Policy: Coordination and Initiation?', *Journal of Public Policy*, vol. 2 part 4 (Oct. 1982) p.369.
69. Bulpitt argues, for example, that, in respect of race relations policy, the Thatcher Government has continued the tradition of non-centralist responsibility or intervention. See Ch.1.

# 6 Non-White Policy Preferences, Political Participation and the Political Agenda in Britain*

## DONLEY T. STUDLAR

Early studies of the politics of race in Britain, including those of the author of this chapter, were criticised for focusing on the attitudes and behaviour of the white electorate and white politicians rather than exploring the views of non-white immigrants and leaders. From an empirical viewpoint, the major problem in analysing mass non-white attitudes was that the numbers of non-whites in any mass survey were too small for extensive analysis.[1] Census data did not enumerate ethnic groups, and small area surveys were likely to be unrepresentative of broader populations.[2] On the elite level, non-white leaders were often self-selected, with minimal followings and little political impact. Although these problems have not disappeared, there now exists a sufficient base of data, at least on the mass level, to draw conclusions about countrywide non-white political behaviour with greater confidence. This paper will use these data in order to examine non-white political participation and policy preferences over approximately the last decade in British politics. Of course, one cannot discuss the politics of race without making some references to the views of the overwhelmingly dominant white majority population (95%) and the even more overwhelmingly dominant white politicians (100% in the House of Commons). The major theoretical focus of this chapter will be on what influences the setting of the political agenda in the area of race.

## THE SETTING OF POLITICAL AGENDAS:
## RACE AND POLITICS IN BRITAIN

Agenda setting is not a topic which has been widely studied in British politics although it has received more attention in recent years.[3] This neglect of agenda setting as an area of study is probably due to two factors: firstly, the assumption that the agenda was determined by the leaders and the manifesto of the victorious party in a general election; and secondly, the adoption of the sociological assumption that the social class background of social and political leaders determined their views on issues.[4] In the United States, where there was less reason to assume either of these conditions, there has been more research into agenda setting, some of which has spilled over into comparative politics.[5] Even in US politics, however, there are only limited studies on the subject because of the inherent difficulties of conceptualising the key term 'agenda' and the problem of assessing patterns of influence such as that of the media.

The study of the politics of race in Britain, however, is exceptional in the amount of attention researchers have paid to the problem of agenda setting, beginning with studies of the initial legislation of the 1960s.[6] Ira Katznelson's provocative study explored why race had lain dormant as a political issue until the early 1960s and how British parties and leaders had acted to minimise the impact of the issue thereafter.[7] Subsequent studies were similarly concerned with the problematic status of race and immigration as parts of the political agenda.[8] Unlike many political problems in Britain, race did not become part of the political agenda because of the leading role of central political figures.[9] Since the issue was forced on central leaders, race obviously did not fit the usual assumptions about the British political agenda. Recently there has been a renewal of interest in the agenda status of race, stemming from the racial dimension in the urban riots of 1980, 1981 and 1985. Recognising that race has previously had only intermittent agenda status in British politics, commentators have debated whether the riots will place race more permanently on the issue agenda.[10]

'Race' as an agenda item, over the last 25 years, has comprised at least three distinguishable dimensions – civil rights (race relations) legislation, immigration policy, and urban aid programmes. Race may also increasingly affect other policy areas, most particularly police (law and order) and education.[11] Of these five areas, the immigration aspects of race have received the most attention from both the public and politicians. Since the 1981 Nationality Act, however, immigration has received only marginal attention. Race relations legislation of progressively broader scope has been passed in 1965, 1968, and 1976, but enforcement is still weak. Urban aid is least often recognised as a race-related programme because of its ambiguous provisions regarding ethnic minorities.[12] Although there is increasing recognition that relations between police and blacks, especially in London, constitute an important problem, there is less appreciation of the desire of Asians to be protected from racist attacks or of the education-related dimensions of race.[13]

Cobb *et al.*, have developed three broad models of agenda-setting. *The outside-initiative model* involves groups outside the formal decision-making apparatus generating sufficient public support to pressure office-holders to put the issue (not necessarily a specific solution) on the formal governmental agenda. The issue originates in the public agenda, then moves to the formal agenda. *The mobilisation model* involves an opposite movement, from formal agenda to public agenda. Governmental leaders initiate the policy but need mass support for its implementation. In contrast to the first two models, *the inside-access model* is a completely elitist model which attempts to exclude the mass public as much as possible. Getting an issue on the formal agenda is sufficient for its initiators.[14]

Race-related issues have achieved sporadic agenda status in Britain mainly through the outside-initiative and mobilisation models. Outside initiative was clearly the applicable model in the case of the first immigration-control legislation, which set the tone for what was to follow. The mobilisation model was of some importance in the cases of the Kenyan Asians crisis of 1968, the Ugandan Asians crisis in 1972, and the 1981 Nationality Act, but this mobilisation was made much easier by the latent concern already existing about immigration questions.[15] Specific questions thus led to an activation of public involvement on immigration questions. The interesting question of why immigration did not become a more permanent part of both public and formal agendas has been explored already,[16] but it is worth further consideration later.

Race relations legislation appears more to be a case of the mobilisation model rather than the outside-initiative model. The three Race Relations Acts were basically the result of Labour governments indicating a desire to consider the issue, sometimes under pressure from other government agencies. The 1958 Nottingham and Notting Hill race riots contributed to persuading several Labour Party politicians that race relations legislation was necessary, while later in the 1960s non-governmental studies such as the survey by Political and Economic Planning on the extent of racial discrimination in Britain were important arguments to the case.[17] In each instance, there was extensive consultation with affected interest groups both inside and outside the government.[18] The general public, however, was less interested in race relations issues than in immigration control ones. Nevertheless the appeal to fair and equal treatment for British subjects already resident in the United Kingdom provoked a more favourable response from the public towards non-whites than did immigration control against nonresident subjects.[19]

A more problematic dimension of race politics has been the urban aid question. Although Harold Wilson announced the financially modest urban aid programme with some fanfare in 1968, more direct assistance to areas affected by immigration is available under the Local Government Assistance Act of 1966. In both instances, one can argue that the mobilisation model applied to the general policy. These were acts designed to help remedy urban decay and deprivation and were part of the general economic modernisation programme of British governments in the 1960s. The racial dimension of both pieces of legislation was ambiguous, and in neither instance did it occasion substantial controversy. Nevertheless these Acts were aimed at dealing, among other things, with problems connected with large urban concentrations of non-whites. What happens when the racial dimension of urban aid becomes explicit was revealed in the furore over the Ethnic Groups (Local Grants) Bill, which the Labour Government put forward in 1978. Opposition to a race-based distribution of funds rather than an area-based one was voiced from several quarters. The Bill fell with the Labour Government in May 1979 and has never been revived.[20]

The issue of urban aid as a policy to tackle racial disadvantage reappeared in the wake of the 1981 urban uprisings. Not the least interesting aspect of this episode was the fact that, for the first time, non-whites played a major part in putting an issue on the agenda. Previous disturbances such as those in 1958 had been initiated by whites.[21] Violence and threats of violence are, after all, one of the few methods that small, weak groups have of influencing the agenda. The urban aid allocated in response to the riots soon became concentrated on the Liverpool area, and even here large amounts of money were not forthcoming. The actual effects of the much-publicised Merseyside Task Force and Environment Minister Michael Heseltine as 'Minister for Merseyside' may be more cosmetic than substantive.[22] The general question of urban aid, then, has been more firmly connected to race through the outside initiative of the riots. Under the political conditions of economic stringency, the Thatcher Government, and general cultural resistance to explicitly ethnic-related financial aid, this does not necessarily mean permanent agenda status or policy outcomes favourable to non-white interests.

Police–black relations have been a festering issue since at least the late 1970s, especially in London. The Brixton uprising which led to Lord Scarman's report emphasised the flashpoint of this problem, and considerable attention has subsequently been devoted to it. As with post-1981 urban aid considerations, this is an outside-initiative issue that non-whites, aided by innovative and deviant thinkers within police ranks, have stimulated. The larger questions of responsiveness of local police forces to the needs of non-white residents have not yet, however, been addressed politically.[23]

Similarly, in education the race issue is only beginning to surface in a more explicit manner. The mobilisation and inside access models have predominated. Hitherto inexplicit and ambiguous policies have been the norm, and the few outside initiatives arising from nonwhite groups have been diluted in this process.[24] As the permanency of their settlement in the United Kingdom becomes evident to more non-white groups, especially Asians, their demands concerning local school arrangements are likely to increase. The connections between education and race and the concomitant problems of policies, resources, and responsibilities may thus become more evident.

Despite these manifold dimensions of race as an issue and the various events and legislation unfolding since the late 1950s, race has never achieved permanent agenda status in Britain. The explanations that have been offered for this are more complementary than competitive. Benyon has adapted Anthony Downs' work on the issue-attention cycle to help explain what has happened since the 1981 riots. He suggests that interest in the problems raised by the riots is declining and that race issues are slipping into a familiar category known as the 'post-problem stage', in which interest recurs only spasmodically.[25]

Whatever the applicability of the issue-attention cycle to race issues, there are other underlying reasons for the sporadic appearance of race on the issue agenda. Most obviously, but often overlooked, is the fact that race as an issue directly affects relatively few Britons. Not only are non-whites relatively small in number, but they are concentrated, firstly in England, secondly in urban areas, and thirdly in residential enclaves within urban areas.[26] Furthermore British political culture is not receptive to ethnically-based demands and policies, as the foregoing analysis of urban policy indicates.[27] The general nature of the race issue, involving status demands that are difficult to bargain over, also has been cited as a factor contributing to lack of permanent status.[28] The most widely accepted view, however, is that the nature of British political institutions is the key influence on the way race as an issue has been handled. Specifically, Katznelson argues that separate institutions were set up to handle race problems outside the normal political channels; in this way, racial 'buffering' took place to keep race-related problems off the political agenda. While Katznelson's argument has never been universally accepted, it is the most well developed and influential explanation of the agenda status of race.[29]

Recently, a new light has been shed on the political buffering argument. Without specifically citing Katznelson's work, Bulpitt[30] suggests that what Katznelson calls political buffering is not a special case at all, but the normal operating procedure for British governments in dealing with a vast array of political problems. Bulpitt calls this model of the polity 'central autonomy', by which he means that central authorities in the Cabinet and Whitehall want to keep many issues of concern to regions and local areas in Britain off the central political agenda as far as possible. In order to do this, central authorities are willing to grant considerable autonomy over policy to local authorities in the periphery. Perhaps the best example of this was the authority granted to the Stormont Government to keep the problems of Northern Ireland away from the centre after the formation of Ulster, an arrangement that worked for almost fifty years. What issues does the centre want for its own decisions? According to Bulpitt, 'high politics' includes foreign policy, defence, macro-economic policy, and law and order. 'Low politics', the politics of the periphery, includes other domestic issues with which individual citizens are concerned, such as education, housing and the police. Race also qualifies as a peripheral, low politics issue. Like

Katznelson, Bulpitt's argument really incorporates political culture and the nature of issues as well as political institutions, but the emphasis clearly lies on the latter. Unlike Katznelson, however, Bulpitt is arguing that the treatment of race issues is characteristic of the British political process rather than a special case. Buffering through whatever procedures are available at the time is the rule, not the exception.

Bulpitt's challenging interpretation of British politics raises anew the question of the agenda status of race, not least because he sees the demands of non-white groups concerning control over the police and education as an incipient challenge to established methods of operation in British politics – an impingement of the periphery on the centre. His view converges with that expressed elsewhere in recent years about the dynamics of the race issue. There is thus a need to reassess this important question, with particular focus on the views and demands of non-whites in their recent roles as subjects as well as objects of the polity. What are the attitudes of non-whites on political issues? Are their priorities different from those of whites? What strategies are they likely to pursue in inserting their demands into the political process? How do their participation rates compare with those of whites? What do their views and their participation mean for the British political agenda?

## NON-WHITE POLICY ATTITUDES

The views of non-whites on policy issues have been only rarely analysed, and no comparisons have been done over time. Although the data are patchy, one can use an extensive 1978 NOP survey, the pooled 1979 Gallup pre-election surveys, and two surveys done in 1983, the Harris poll of non-whites for 'Black on Black – Eastern Eye', and the BBC-Gallup election survey of 8–9 June, to provide information on political opinions over time. The number of non-white respondents in these surveys ranges from 99 in BBC–Gallup to 996 in the Harris. All except the latter are countrywide surveys which have white respondents with whom the non-whites can be compared. While the Harris survey is limited to non-whites and is subject to the environmental effect which has bedevilled CRC and CRE surveys, it has the asset of asking not only about important issues, but also about preferred alternatives on these issues, as well as having a much larger number of non-whites than any other survey.[31]

The 1978 NOP survey provides a useful benchmark with which to start. Nevertheless it may be unwise to generalise on the basis of this survey, since it was prompted by Mrs Thatcher's February 'swamping' comment, which immediately made race and immigration more of an issue in the minds of both white and non-white voters. The non-whites were chosen from constituencies with 2% or more non-white residents, thus making the results susceptible to environmental influences. Comparing a survey in a non-campaign situation with one taken during the election campaigns of 1979 and 1983 must also be done carefully since the stimuli of the situation are different. Nevertheless this was one of the first surveys not only to have a large non-white sample, but also to compare blacks, Asians, and whites on non-racial as well as racial questions.

TABLE 6.1  *Problems perceived as important*

|  | Overall % | Black % | Asian % |
|---|---|---|---|
| Prices/Cost of living | 72 | 68 | 62 |
| Unemployment | 71 | 69 | 65 |
| Strikes/industrial relations | 64 | 44 | 38 |
| Immigration/race relations | 50 | 54 | 40 |
| Education | 29 | 31 | 16 |
| Northern Ireland | 27 | 10 | 12 |
| Housing | 26 | 43 | 27 |
| Devolution | 8 | 3 | 2 |
| All other | 21 | 13 | 7 |
| Don't know | 2 | 3 | 11 |
| N | (1651) | (300) | (304) |

SOURCE   National Opinion Polls, 1978.

What Table 6.1 shows is that while Mrs Thatcher's comments made immigration/race the fourth highest overall issue (third among both blacks and Asians), economic matters of prices/cost of living, unemployment, and strikes/industrial relations (among whites) remained more important issues. Education and housing stand out as issues on which blacks were much more concerned than Asians.

When asked about problems in their local area (Table 6.2), blacks cited more problems on average than Asians, including considerable disparities on such questions as unemployment, violence, racial

TABLE 6.2  *Main problems in local area*

|  | Overall % | Black % | Asian % |
|---|---|---|---|
| Violence/vandalism | 37 | 36 | 20 |
| Noise | 8 | 7 | 11 |
| Colour/racial prejudice | 6 | 22 | 13 |
| Unemployment | 36 | 34 | 23 |
| Overcrowding (housing) | 12 | 25 | 15 |
| Increasing prices (housing) | 23 | 19 | 18 |
| Lack of space for parks/walks | 13 | 18 | 9 |
| Drug addiction | 3 | 3 | 4 |
| Alcoholism/drunkenness | 6 | 4 | 12 |
| Traffic | 29 | 16 | 12 |
| None of these | 16 | 17 | 35 |

SOURCE   National Opinion Polls, 1978.

prejudice, and housing. Asians were more prone to cite the moral problem of alcoholism. Blacks were in most instances closer to the norms for white people in citing issues than were Asians. Furthermore, Asians' level of knowledge on issues appeared to be much less than that of blacks or whites. Blacks mentioned more issues, both countrywide and local, and Asians were substantially more inclined either to answer 'don't know' or to cite no problems on the prompt list. There was also a problem in obtaining interviews with Asian women.[32] Despite the fact that the blacks interviewed tended to have resided in Britain longer than the Asians, they were more disenchanted with British life and more willing to say they wished to leave the country. This may be related to their reasons for coming (Table 6.3), which tended to be more economic and less social (family, living conditions, education) and political than Asians.

The tentative conclusion can be drawn that the longer length of residence, individualism, and materialism of blacks led to their expressing more opinions about British life but less satisfaction with it than Asians, who were more recent arrivals, more communal, less individualistic, and less opinionated, but more satisfied. However, both groups were integrated to the extent that their views of important issues did not vary widely from the opinions of whites.

TABLE 6.3    *Reasons for immigration, (first generation immigrants only)*

|  | | Black % | Asian % |
|---|---|---|---|
| To get a good education for self | | 9 | 14 |
| To get a good education for children | | 8 | 9 |
| To get a better job/to get a job | | 45 | 25 |
| To earn more money | | 11 | 8 |
| To get better housing conditions | | 3 | 4 |
| To get better living conditions | | 6 | 13 |
| To join family | | 19 | 25 |
| To be given welfare state benefits | | – | 1 |
| For political reasons | | 3 | 10 |
| Other | | 18 | 9 |
| Don't Know | | 6 | 5 |
| | N | (269) | (296) |

SOURCE    National Opinion Polls, 1978.

The questions asked in Gallup's 1979 pre-election surveys were somewhat different. Rather than inquiring about a whole range of problems, Gallup simply asked which problems the respondent considered most urgent and second most urgent (Table 6.4). The answers varied even less by ethnic identity of the respondent than those of 1978.

All three groups saw unemployment and the cost of living as the most serious, with immigrants and housing rating low for both groups. Non-white opinions were noteworthy, however, in that very few of them were concerned about specifically international problems. When one combines answers to the two questions, that is, whether a certain problem was mentioned as one of the two most important or not, non-whites were found to be statistically different from whites in their greater tendency to mention immigrants as a problem and the lesser likelihood of their mentioning labour relations, pensions, or law and order. Nevertheless these differences were modest. Both blacks and Asians were more likely than whites not to mention any problems at all, with Asians again manifesting the fewest opinions about political issues. Overall, then, the differences observed in the 1978 data appear to have narrowed under the pressure of an election campaign. Immigration was no longer rated an important issue, economic questions remained primary for all groups, and black-Asian distinctions were fewer. Nevertheless, Asian lack of opinion about political problems facing Britain remained persistent.

TABLE 6.4 *Two most important issues, 1979*

|  | White % | Black % | Asian % |
|---|---|---|---|
| Cost of living/prices/inflation | 48 | 54 | 55 |
| Employment/unemployment | 39 | 42 | 41 |
| Labour relations | 22 | 16 | 13 |
| Other economic affairs | 13 | 7 | 14 |
| Law and order | 11 | 4 | 5 |
| Taxation | 8 | 13 | 4 |
| Housing | 5 | 10 | 6 |
| Immigrants | 5 | 9 | 6 |
| Social security benefits | 5 | 2 | 5 |
| Education | 4 | 6 | 5 |
| Pensions, elderly | 4 | 1 | 1 |
| Health, hospitals | 3 | 0 | 5 |
| Common market | 3 | 1 | 2 |
| National unity | 2 | 2 | 0 |
| Ireland | 2 | 3 | 0 |
| Roads and transport | 1 | 2 | 0 |
| Defence and nuclear weapons | 1 | 1 | 0 |
| International affairs, peace | 1 | 0 | 0 |
| Other problems | 6 | 6 | 3 |
| None/don't know | 12 | 17 | 26 |
| N | (10,411) | (109) | (112) |

SOURCE   Gallup Poll, Pre-Election Surveys, 1979.

Data on non-white political views at the time of the 1983 General Election are richer in questions asked, but poorer in representativeness. Gallup dropped the ethnic question for its pre-election survey. However, the BBC-Gallup survey of 8 and 9 June (polling day) did have 99 non-white respondents in its sample of 4143, and an imposing array of information was solicited. It is risky, however, to assess black and Asian opinion separately with such a small number of respondents (60 Asians, 39 blacks), and little analysis of this sort will be done. The Harris survey for 'Black on Black–Eastern Eye', however, serves as a useful supplement of non-white attitudes. Once again the differences between whites and non-whites on issues were minimal during an election period. The BBC-Gallup survey (Table 6.5) reveals the priorities of both groups to be similar.

The two most important issues to whites were unemployment and defence; for non-whites the important issues were similar, but unemployment was ranked highly by an even larger proportion (83% v. 70%) and defence was rated a major issue by only one half as many in the group (20% v. 38%). Prices and health were considered the third and fourth issues by both whites and non-whites. Law and order and immigrants were not of major concern to either group. When asked about specific policy alternatives and party positions, non-whites were more likely to respond 'don't know', but generally favoured government-based solutions over private enterprise ones and Labour alternatives over Conservative

TABLE 6.5   *Two most important issues, 1983 (Gallup)*

|  | Whites % | Non-whites % |
|---|---|---|
| Unemployment/jobs | 70 | 83 |
| Defence/nuclear weapons/arms | 38 | 20 |
| Prices/cost of living/inflation | 20 | 19 |
| Health/hospitals/NHS | 11 | 16 |
| Education/schools | 6 | 4 |
| Law and order/crime/vandalism | 4 | 9 |
| Taxation/income tax/VAT | 3 | 5 |
| Pensions/service for the old | 8 | 3 |
| Strikes/trade unions/industrial relations | 3 | 3 |
| Common market/Europe | 5 | 2 |
| Immigrants/race relations | 1 | 1 |
| Falklands war | 1 | 3 |
| Nationalisation/public ownership | 1 | 1 |
| Welfare benefits | 1 | 0 |
| Incomes policy | 1 | 0 |
| Northern Ireland/Ulster | 0 | 0 |
| International peace | 1 | 0 |
| Other economic issues | 3 | 3 |
| Other problems | 11 | 8 |
| None/don't know | 4 | 7 |
| N | (4,044) | (99) |

SOURCE   BBC–Gallup Election Survey, 1983.

ones (data not shown). Despite favouring Labour on most issues, non-whites, like the rest of the population, had reservations abut Labour leadership and policies.

The economic downturn of recent years in Britain appears to have hit non-whites especially hard. A larger percentage of non-whites than whites are unemployed, and more of them both reported a worsening personal financial situation over the last year and foresaw poor personal prospects for the year ahead.[33] In short, the 1983 BBC-Gallup survey showed non-whites continuing to focus on domestic issues, and even more concerned about economic matters than whites, because of their own strained material circumstances. Despite some misgivings about Labour leadership and policies, tradition and socio-economic circumstances kept them firmly in the Labour camp.

The Harris survey, taken two weeks before the BBC–Gallup survey, helps fill out the picture of the non-white electorate in 1983 (Table 6). Unlike other surveys,[34] this one showed Asians being as willing to offer issue opinions as blacks. The ranking of issues is somewhat different. Again unemployment led the list for both blacks and Asians, but it was followed by immigration/nationality, cost of

TABLE 6.6   *Two most important issues, 1983 (Harris)*

|  | Blacks<br>%   (rank) | Asians<br>%   (rank) |
| --- | --- | --- |
| Unemployment | 67% ( 1) | 71% ( 1) |
| Cost of living | 27% ( 2) | 19% ( 3) |
| Education | 23% ( 3) | 17% ( 4) |
| Immigration/nationality | 17% ( 4) | 36% ( 2) |
| Police/law and order | 16% ( 5) | 8% ( 8) |
| Housing | 16% ( 5) | 9% ( 6) |
| Health service | 13% ( 7) | 13% ( 5) |
| Nuclear weapons/defence | 8% ( 8) | 9% ( 6) |
| Taxation | 3% ( 9) | 5% ( 9) |
| Trade unions | 2% (10) | 4% (10) |
| None/don't know | 4% | 5% |
| N | (469) | (527) |

SOURCE   Harris Survey for 'Black on Black–Eastern Eye', 1983 living, education, health, housing, and police/law and order above nuclear weapons/defence, taxation, and trade unions. Fitzgerald tentatively suggests that there may be an age or generational phenomenon among Afro-Caribbeans and Asians concerning immigration and education, with the young losing interest in the former issue and gaining interest in the latter.[35] Even though these data revealed more concern among non-whites about non-economic matters (immigration, police), than does the BBC–Gallup survey, the principal issues were again economic, especially unemployment. This survey further confirms the low priority non-whites have consistently given to international matters and labour relations, even though their union membership level approaches that of whites.

When their opinions are solicited about various solutions to problems, there are some interesting comparisons between the views of blacks and Asians.[36] On unemployment and the cost of living, both groups prefer government spending to stricter enforcement of non-discrimination provisions. Their perceptions of the law and order problem, however, are very different. Asians are more concerned to stop racial attacks while blacks see a need for more local control over the police. In education, both groups advocate more attention to the needs of non-whites. On the housing issue, substantial differences between the two groups reflect their respective situations, blacks and council house tenants preferring a freeze on rents, while Asians as private mortgage-holders want reduced cost mortgages. Differences between black and Asian perspectives on immigration are perplexing, with almost one quarter of the Asian respondents saying 'Don't know' to a set of four alternatives. In general, then, non-whites are more in agreement with each other on broad economic questions than on most other matters. Their priorities on alternative policies are similar on education, but considerably different on police/law and order, housing, and possibly immigration/nationality. The chances of a unified stance on policy alternatives, much less policy priorities, seems remote on the basis of these data.

## NON-WHITE POLITICAL PARTICIPATION

How have non-whites expressed their views in terms of political participation? Non-whites have been notable in their staunch support for the Labour Party while other social groups have been reducing theirs.[37] While this is a familiar point (Table 6.7), some supporting data from the 1983 BBC-Gallup survey reveal interesting facets of this process.

TABLE 6.7  *Party preference and political participation, 1979 Gallup Surveys**

|  | White | Black | Asian |
|---|---|---|---|
| *Party preference* |  |  |  |
| Mean pro-Labour | 1.9 | 3.0 | 2.7* |
| Voted Labour 1974 | 46 | 83 | 82 * |
| Voted Labour 1979 | 40 | 68 | 67 * |
| Mean pro-Conservative | 1.8 | .7 | 1.0* |
| *Participation* |  |  |  |
| Mean Participation Score | 1.2 | 1.2 | .9 |
| Non voter 1974 | 20 | 42 | 32 |
| Non voter 1979 | 20 | 33 | 26† |
| Never discusses political matters | 34 | 32 | 40 |
| Never persuades others to share views |  |  |  |
| No stickers on car | 75 | 84 | 87† |
| Never wears badge or button | 79 | 86 | 90† |
| Never hangs up poster | 74 | 81 | 78 |
| Would not join street demonstration | 86 | 86 | 90 |
| Would not go to own party meeting | 85 | 84 | 86 |
| Would not go to other's party meeting | 94 | 95 | 96 |
| Would not canvass | 92 | 89 | 95 |
| Would not give money | 86 | 86 | 93 |
| Would do none of these things | 53 | 51 | 44 |

* All figures except means expressed as percentages.
† p≤ .01
SOURCE  Welch and Studlar (1985).

In 1983, while there was some transfer of support from consistent black voters and even more among consistent Asians towards other parties, especially the Alliance, from Labour, newly eligible non-white voters cast their ballots overwhelmingly for Labour.[38] In the immediate future, the major problems for Labour would seem to be getting its non-white supporters, especially blacks, to the polls rather than generating party loyalty. Reinforced by their largely working-class social standing, non-whites will probably continue to be overwhelmingly Labour supporters.

What is much more questionable, however, is the contention that nonwhite voters are so concentrated in crucial urban areas that these seats constitute 'ethnic marginals' in which a deterioration of ethnic support for Labour would be fatal.[39] A recent ecological analysis of the 1983 election results shows heavily non-white immigrant constituencies to be largely working class as well; hence most of these areas constitute part of the traditional urban Labour core which survived even the Conservative landslide in 1983. True ethnic marginals are few and far between.[40]

Less explored than non-white voting behaviour are other aspects of non-white political participation. Some limited countrywide data do exist on this topic, however, and they illuminate the political situation of British non-whites. Data from the 1979 pre-election Gallup surveys (Table 6.7) showed whites, blacks, and Asians to be virtually indistinguishable in how often they participated in ten different political activities: political discussion, persuasion, displaying car stickers, wearing badges, hanging posters, joining a street discussion, visiting a party meeting, going to an opposition party meeting, canvassing and contributing financially.[41] Blacks and whites had equivalent rates of participation in most instances, with Asians usually trailing slightly. When it came to voting, however, blacks were significantly less likely to participate than whites or Asians, confirming what has usually been found elsewhere.[42] The paradox of participation is that while blacks are apparently better integrated than Asians into most forms of British political participation, they are less well integrated when it comes to voting. What is more, the voting gap appears to be increasing. Does this finding suggest a fundamental alienation on the part of the black electorate? If so, why do they otherwise participate at normal rates?

Classic alienation, or even apathy, would not appear to be the answer. Instead, in the more voluntary activities in which few people generally participate, blacks are as numerous, proportionately, as whites, and more so than Asians. West Indian cultures have often been characterised as highly individualistic, especially in comparison with more communal Asian ones,[43] and accordingly, in voluntary activities, individualism results in appreciable West Indian participation, especially in comparison with Asians. Voting, however, is less voluntary, more of a 'citizen duty', and more subject to mobilisation behaviour. As the more hierarchical and communal group, Asians are more readily mobilised to turn out at the polls than are the more individualistic West Indians. This seems a plausible explanation for the paradox of participation.

## IMPLICATIONS: POLICY PREFERENCES

Despite the limitations of the data, one can make some generalisations about the policy views of non-whites. It is also possible to assess the significance of these views for the British policy agenda, based on consideration of non-white electoral participation and other aspects of the political process. This section will deal with the first point, the concluding section will consider the second.

What can we conclude about non-white political attitudes? First, they are very similar to white political attitudes in most respects. In recent years economic problems have been in the forefront of problems mentioned by both groups, especially during election campaigns. If anything, the economic downturn of the last several years has made the harder-hit non-whites even more concerned about economic problems.

Since non-whites prefer governmental approaches to solving economic problems to private ones, economic issues are one of the key links between them and the Labour Party. The class and trade union status of non-whites reinforces both their economic outlook and Labour inclination. Since non-whites are not disproportionately employed in state services and industries, however, they are not especially heavily represented in the 'old' working class.[44] The different housing situations of blacks and Asians also does not lead to variations of general economic outlook although it does affect preferred policy alternatives. In general, the minimal differences between non-whites and whites in ranking important issues indicates that non-whites have become well integrated into mainstream British politics. There are some caveats, however, to this generalisation.

Non-white attitudes are relatively stable. Their priorities have not greatly changed over the decade, but there is some evidence of gradual shifts taking place. Non-whites remain uninterested in specifically international qustions and, somewhat surprisingly, in industrial relations. Immigration as an issue has declined, although it remains more important for Asians than blacks. In both instances, however, the second generation, often native-born, has less concern. Education and relations with the police are becoming more important issues for non-whites, but are still not challenging economic issues as the major priorities. The riots of the early1980s do not seem to represent a watershed in the thinking of the non-white public. Nevertheless they do appear to have had some effect in making relations between the police and non-whites a more widely recognised problem.

When one examines alternative proposals on issues, the pluralism of the non-white community becomes more evident. Asians and blacks do not view such issues as immigration, housing and law and order in the same light. Being a mortgage holder or a council house tenant, a recent or longer-term immigrant, a subject of racial attacks or police inquiries, makes a significant difference in these instances. This indicates that non-whites are not ideologically unified, either within their own groups or with the Labour Party. Most non-whites who vote Labour are not strong party identifiers and choose Labour out of perceived general group interest rather than because of specific issue positions.[45] Blacks are also more likely to view themselves as members of the working class, which makes them more closely tied to Labour than Asians.[46] Nevertheless the ethnic consciousness and mobilisation capacities of Asians makes them more dependable Labour voters when they decide that Labour supports their interests. When it comes to specific issues, however, blacks and Asians have difficulty in forming coalitions.[47] For that matter, Asians are well known to be riven with divisions within their own group as well, divisions which do not show up in more general survey data.[48]

In short, there is no such thing as a distinctive nonwhite political agenda, at least as can be ascertained from survey data. The major priorities are shared with white voters, and divisions within the non-white community over other issues and alternatives preclude effective coalition-building. The prospects for getting particular non-white problems on the central political agenda through conventional political processes are poor although the chances may be better in local areas where non-whites, especially of one culture and outlook, form a substantial share of the population. There is always the possibility that a broad, effective umbrella group of non-whites may be formed with a leadership that can command mass support, but it is highly unlikely.

## CONCLUSION: ELECTORAL POLITICS, BUREAUCRATIC POLITICS, OR STREET POLITICS?

It is ironic that pluralism and lack of organisational cohesiveness among non-whites should be hindering their political advance because white attitudes, long considered by some analysts to be the major hurdle for non-whites to overcome, are showing signs of becoming more favourable to non-whites. As immigration has declined as an issue, as more non-white British are native-born, and as non-whites have moved into more areas, greater acceptance, if not tolerance, of non-whites has manifested itself. There has always existed a set of attitudes within the British public favourable to equal treatment for non-whites. Most Britons would prefer that large numbers of non-whites immigrants had never arrived on their shores, but, once here, they basically accept them as British subjects and are willing to have laws which guarantee their rights. One might term this situation 'antagonistic acceptance'.[49] Thus the Race Relations Acts, weak though they may be, have never occasioned an outcry from the public. Enoch Powell, in his famous speech of April 1968, was ostensibly attacking the 1968 legislation, but what the public embraced was his jeremiad against immigration, not against equal treatment for those non-whites already established as British citizens. Repatriation has rarely commanded majority public support. In the 1983 General Election immigration 'dropped off the bottom of the political agenda'.[50] Surveys have documented that Britons are more sympathetic to native-born non-whites than they are to non-white immigrants, that most Britons think non-whites *are* treated the same as whites in most circumstances, and that most whites think non-whites *should* be treated the same.[51] This does not mean that whites are necessarily tolerant or that they welcome contact with non-whites. It does mean that they have had time to adjust to the idea of a multi-racial and multicultural society and that traditional British notions of fair play do operate once a group has shown itself to be established in the country on a permanent basis. In short, today non-whites are more accepted as legitimate members of the British political community. If non-white demands can be formulated in such a way that they appear to be aiming for equality rather than special treament, the white climate of opinion could be receptive, or at least non-hostile.

Electoral politics, however, has hitherto not been an effective vehicle for non-white demands. One indication of this is that the first two Race Relations Acts of 1965 and 1968 were passed before non-whites were sufficiently numerous and politically alert to be considered a group worth wooing by political appeals. Only one piece of specifically ethnic legislation (the Race Relations Act of 1976) has been passed subsequently. Despite overwhelming non-white support for Labour, the promised repeal of the 1971 Immigration Act was never even proposed by the 1974–79 Labour Government.[52] Immigration control has been made even more restrictive by the 1981 Nationality Act of the Conservative Government.

Electoral politics has been more beneficial to the political system than to non-whites. It has instilled participatory values and Labour Party loyalty into a group which might otherwise pose persistent difficulties for the British polity. Labour has been able to replace its declining white working class support with another group, one that has few electoral alternatives. As has recently been made more evident, nonwhites have not substantially cast 'ethnic' votes in Parliamentary elections.[53] Their votes have basically been the result of their social class circumstances and Labour loyalty; deviation from Labour on ethnic grounds, which would be the ultimate test of ethnic voting, has been rare. Even Asians, who seem more capable of this behaviour, have not really used such political leverage. Until evidence to the contrary comes to the fore, Labour can afford to take non-white votes for granted, promising them something but delivering little. Not only has Labour not been able to put a non-white candidate into the House of Commons, it has not even tried very hard, to judge by how few non-whites it has put forward.[54] For their part, the Conservatives have also aided non-white integration into the polity by extending at least a reluctant electoral welcome.[55]

The first-past-the-post electoral system is not favourable to ethnic minority representation,[56] and the supposed ethnic marginals are extraordinarily few in number. The non-white population is simply too small, too scattered, and too politically divided to have much impact. However discomfiting it may be to theorists of democracy, electoral politics on the Parliamentary level offers few benefits for non-whites, at least in their current situation.

Participation in parties and elections, then, will not necessarily lead to race-related issues reaching the formal agenda, much less resulting in outcomes preferred by non-whites. At best, such participation may help legitimise non-whites' position as full citizens in British society and thereby improve their potential access to central decision-makers. But what would be the consequences of less electoral participation? It is difficult to conceive of nonvoting stimulating serious repatriation moves when the 1981 riots did not. As for the support electoral politics gives to interest group spokesmen, ethnic minority leaders always repesent small, weak groups because of the lack of a unified non-white front. Their success with white politicians depends much more on finding sympathetic whites, in and out of political office, than it does on any threat, explicit or implicit, of swinging non-white votes. Again, the Race Relations Acts are good examples.

In short, non-white political success in conventional politics depends much more on the politics of the bureaucracy rather than on electoral politics. Jordan and Richardson argue that the characteristic British policy style is 'the logic of negotiation'.[57] Such a policy style is not especially favourable to nonwhite interests, on several grounds. Non-whites are weak in conventional political resources such as numbers, cohesion, finances, skilled leaders and the recognised legitimacy of their grievances. Even the non-white interest groups that do exist have had difficulty in establishing normal consultative relations with government agencies. Jordan and Richardson have argued that the sectorisation of policy in the government bureaucracy aids interest group influence on policy. Yet in the race relations field, there is no government department continuously exercising (or seeking) 'sovereignty'. Instead, race occupies a policy space in several different departments. If anything, fragmentation of bureaucratic responsibility for race-related matters has increased in the last few years. Even the most serious attempt at coordination, the Standing Advisory Council under the chairmanship of the Home Secretary, met infrequently. Furthermore, it invited minority ethnic group members to sit only as individuals, not as representatives of groups. Such arrangements hardly facilitate successful bargaining by non-white groups.[58]

Not only are ethnic minority groups disadvantaged by the institutions and processes involved, but their influence is also hampered by the nature of the issue they are forced to pursue. Zero-sum demands and status (equal rights) demands are generally more difficult to grant than are more materialist petitions.[59] Even when material rewards are at stake, as for instance in the urban aid programme, the very fact that non-white groups are involved can make the issue one of status. Normal procedure is for the British government to avoid tackling such issues head on, that is, by putting them on the formal agenda. Private members bills are the preferred alternative.[60] In the United States many race-related problems have reached the formal agenda through the political intervention of the courts, but this method of dealing with status disputes is less readily available in Britain.[61] Indeed, Rose has argued that the ability to make political problems justiciable is a crucial difference in resolving civil rights problems in the American South compared to Northern Ireland.[62]

Increasingly comparisons have been made between the experience of Jews in the United Kingdom and that of non-whites. With smaller numbers but better organisation than non-whites, Jews have found electoral participation to be less beneficial for their purposes than bureaucratic bargaining. Like non-whites, Jews discovered the Labour Party to be an unreliable ally in office despite great shows of support in opposition which attracted Jewish votes.[63] Unlike non-whites, Jews have made few claims of being capable of delivering a block vote or of swinging elections, and even the existence of a Jewish vote was officially long denied.[64] Even though they are a distinctive ethnic group, Jews have been able to adapt to British politics without emphasising ethnic issues. For the most part their behaviour has been privatistic and pluralistic. The fact that their main ethnic concern, British policy toward Israel, is a foreign policy matter more suitable to bureaucratic bargaining than to electoral politics has facilitated their adaptation to British political norms.

The situation of non-whites is obviously not the same as that of Jews in several respects. Their major ethnic concerns are status issues that are internal, not external, to the polity, and they exhibit less political cohesion. Accordingly, they will have more difficulty in adjusting to British political norms in pursuit of their goals. Nevertheless, there is already some evidence that at least some Asian groups may be able to follow the Jewish pattern of integration into British politics. For other Asian groups and for almost all blacks, however, that path will be harder to follow.

Asians have been more successful at bureaucratic politics because, as has been noted in the electoral context, they can generally mobilise more political resources. The paradox of participation is understandable because voting is just one manifestation, and by no means the most important, of Asian organisational skills. While the blacks are more integrated into British politics on information, class and general participatory criteria, they are less politically influential than the comparatively less informed, more isolated and less participatory Asian communities. This can be explained through the fact that bureaucratic politics is an arena in which a small but reasonably well organised group can perform with some success, especially with sympathetic allies in office. Electoral politics, on the other hand, has comparatively little to offer such groups, and even less to small, poorly organised groups.

That still leaves the politics of the street, the explosion into violent confrontations that have been a sporadic feature of British life in recent years, especially concerning race and notably in 1981 and 1985. Violence itself is not the only aspect of street politics; the threat of violence is equally important.[65] As Gamson has astutely noted, such activity is one of the most effective mechanisms of influence for small groups lacking in conventional organisational resources.[66] Subsequent to Gamson's analysis, terrorist groups in Britain and elsewhere, notably the various versions of the Irish Republican Army, have demonstrated his point. Relatively powerless groups tend to exhibit amorphous, sporadic and unorganised violence which will be crushed, intimidated, or wither away from fatigue and lack of results. The latter fate seems to be the case for the 1981 riots. After a flurry of government activity in the immediate aftermath, efforts subsequently subsided. Even a recurrence of violence would not necessarily lead to different results, and Norton has argued that politically relevant violence is a recurrent phenomenon in Britain and should not be seen as an indicator of instability.[67] Indeed, given the problems of the last twenty years, he finds it remarkable that there has not been more violence. To paraphrase Rap Brown, political violence is as British as plum pudding, and small amounts of it can safely be ignored.

But organised, systematic violence for political ends has to be handled differently. Why have British governments, even Conservative ones, found it desirable from time to time to negotiate with the IRA? It is precisely because the IRA creates such horrendous social control problems that attempts to co-opt it must be made.

The sort of politics of the street represented by the IRA is unlikely among British non-whites. Asians, who are by several indicators the most isolated group,[68] are peaceful, fearful of violent repercussions, and wedded to leaders who are reasonably adept at the politics of bureaucracy. Blacks, on the other hand, are individualistic, lack organisation, and are probably too sceptical to mount an effective concerted attempt at political violence. Instead, what will probably occur at infrequent intervals among British non-whites is precisely the sort of undisciplined, anomic violence experienced during 1981 and 1985. This form of street politics is not likely to yield substantial political benefit unless it can be utilised by non-white leaders as a threat to elicit political concessions.

If electoral politics is ineffective, bureaucratic politics is only effective to a limited extent, and this is mainly advantageous to Asians. Street politics alternatively provides an immediate catharsis for activist participants. But where does this leave the problem of agenda setting on race-related issues? In general the setting of the political agenda in these matters will remain in the hands of the (white) political elite, where most issues reside anyway. As with previous race relations legislation, the key actors are not the public, but interest groups, politicians and civil servants. Important elements of these groups must agree to pursue race-related policies if they are to be placed on the agenda. With the eclipse of immigration control as the principal race issue, the most applicable agenda-setting model is no longer the outside-initiative one, but the mobilisation model. The circumstances most conducive for race to become a formal agenda issue would be a public 'permissive consensus' on the need to improve race relations, which would allow a government seriously committed to dealing with this problem to pursue its preferred policies.

Is race finally going to be a permanent part of the British political agenda? Although being more susceptible to elite influence would seem to augur well for its prospects, there are some other features which indicate difficulties in doing so. For one thing, the British elite is masterly at keeping controversial issues off the agenda, or at least in structuring the alternatives so that minimal change will occur. The institutions that facilitate this process remain in place, the political unpalatability of dealing with race as an issue continues, and the operational code of leaving 'low' politics and peripheral issues to lesser authorities shows no signs of abating. These influences in keeping race off the central political agenda have, if anything, been reinforced by the experience of the last 25 years. Politicians are not keen to make their reputations on championing the interests of non-whites.[69] Politicians will prefer to deal with economic and related social problems, hoping to have sufficient success that racial problems, linked as they are to economic difficulties at present, will diminish. The chances of a major initiative on the police, education, or urban aid by even a Labour Government are thus generally slim.

There is profound irony in this situation. It was frequently argued in the 1960s and early 1970s that what was needed to improve race relations was for politicians to take a positive lead rather than follow the public pressures for immigration control. For reasons already enumerated, that was difficult for them to do. With the decline of the immigration dimension of the question, however, there is more freedom for politicians to follow their principles rather than their constituents. Chastened by the experience of the last quarter century, however, they may be reluctant to do so. If politicians do not take the initiative, race may remain dormant as a political issue until the next explosion of violence.

Doing good by doing little is still an attractive option. But is it what is really needed?

## NOTES

* Support for research resulting in this paper was provided by a sabbatical leave grant from Centre College, Danville, Kentucky, and the hospitality of the Department of Politics, University of Warwick. Special thanks to Jim Bulpitt, Zig Layton-Henry, and Stan Taylor of Warwick. Professor Ivor Crewe of the University of Essex gave helpful criticism. Bob Wybrow of Gallup, John Hanvey of Harris Polls, and Nick Moon of National Opinion Polls authorised use of data from their organisations. Professor Richard Rose of the University of Strathclyde made his 1979 Gallup data available. The author bears sole responsibility for interpretation.

1. D. Butler and D. Stokes, *Political Change in Britain*, 2nd edn (St. Martin's Press, 1974); I. Crewe and B. Sarlvik, 'Popular Attitudes and Electoral Strategy' in Z. Layton-Henry (ed.), Conservative Party Politics (Macmillan, 1980). Throughout the chapter, the following terminology will be employed: blacks = Afro-Caribbeans; browns = Asians; non-whites = blacks & browns.

2. D. T. Studlar, 'The Ethnic Vote, 1983: Problems of Analysis and Interpretation', *New Community*, II (1983) pp.92–100. In delineating these various dimensions of race-related problems, I do not mean to suggest that the connections among them are necessarily manifest to politicians or the public. Factor analysis of public opinion during election campaigns show immigration and race relations issues to be highly associated with foreign aid questions in the public mind (Crewe and Sarlvik, op. cit. 1980). Such analyses are dependent, however, on what questions are asked, as well as how they are asked. The other three dimensions of race presented here have rarely been utilised in public opinion surveys, but they do appear to be important analytically.

3. J. J. Richardson and A. G. Jordan, *Governing Under Pressure* (Martin Robertson, 1979); J. K. Stringer and J. J. Richardson, 'Managing the Political Agenda: Problem Definition and Policy Making in Britain', *Parliamentary Affairs*, 33 (1980) pp.23–39; I. Budge and D. Farlie, *Explaining and Predicting Elections* (Allen & Unwin, 1983); R. Flickinger, 'The Comparative Politics of Agenda Setting: the Emergence of Consumer Protection as a Public Policy Issue in Britain and the United States', *Policy Studies Review*, 2 (1983) pp.429–43;

R. Goodin, 'Banana Time in British Politics', *Political Studies*, 30 (1982) pp.42–58.

4. P. Stanworth and A. Giddens (eds), *Elites and Power in British Society* (Cambridge University Press, 1974).

5. E. E. Schattschneider, *The Semisovereign People* (Holt, Rinehart & Winston, 1960); R. W. Cobb and C. D. Elder, *Participation in American Politics: the Dynamics of Agenda Setting* (Johns Hopkins University Press, 1972); J. L. Walker, 'Setting the Agenda in the U.S. Senate: a Theory of Problem Selection', *British Journal of Political Science*, 7 (1977) pp.424–45; J.W. Kingdon, *Agendas, Alternatives and Public Policies* (Little Brown, 1984); R. W. Cobb, J. Keith Ross and M. H. Ross, 'Agenda Building as a Comparative Political Process', *American Political Science Review*, 70, pp.126–38.

6. P. Foot, *Immigration and Race in British Politics*, (Penguin Books, 1965); K. Hindell, 'The Genesis of the Race Relations Bill', *Political Quarterly*, 36 (1965) pp.390–405; E. J. B. Rose *et al.*, *Colour and Citizenship* (Oxford University Press, 1969).

7. I. Katznelson, *Black Men, White Cities* (Oxford University Press, 1973).

8. D. T. Studlar, 'Political Culture and Racial Policy in Britain', *Patterns of Prejudice*, 8 (1974) pp.7–12; 'Immigration and Racial Change' in W. B. Gwyn and R. Rose (eds), *Britain: Progress and Decline*, Tulane Studies in Political Science (New Orleans 1980); D. Kirp, *Doing Good by Doing Little* (University of California Press, 1979).

9. Foot, op. cit.; D. T. Studlar, 'British Public Opinion, Colour Issues and Enoch Powell: a Longitudinal Analysis', *British Journal of Political Sciences*, 4 (1974) pp.371–81; 'Elite Responsiveness or Elite Autonomy: British Immigration Policy Reconsidered', *Ethnic and Racial Studies*, 3 (1980) pp.207–23.

10. K. Young, 'Ethnic Pluralism and the Policy Agenda in Britain' in N. Glazer and K. Young (eds), *Ethnic Pluralism and Public Policy* (Heinemann, 1983); J. Benyon, 'The Riots, Lord Scarman and the Political Agenda' in J. Benyon (ed.), *Scarman and After* (Pergamon Press, 1984); D. T. Studlar, ' "Waiting for the Catastrophe": Race and the Political Agenda in Britain', *Patterns of Prejudice*, 19 (1985) pp.3–15.

11. J. Bulpitt, *Territory and Power in the United Kingdom* (Manchester University Press, 1983); L. Lustgarten, 'Beyond Scarman: Police Accountability' in Glazer and Young, op. cit.; Benyon, op. cit.

12. J. Edwards and R. Batley, *The Politics of Positive Discrimination* (Tavistock, 1978); Young op. cit.

13. Z. Layton-Henry, *The Politics of Race in Britain* (Allen & Unwin, 1984).

14. Cobb *et al.*, op. cit.

15. Butler and Stokes, op. cit.; Studlar, 'British Public Opinion, Colour Issues', op. cit.

16. Katznelson op. cit.; Studlar, 'Political Culture and Racial Policy in Britain'; 'Elite Responsiveness or Elite Autonomy'; Kirp, op. cit.; Layton-Henry, *The Politics of Race in Britain*.

17. W. W. Daniel, *Racial Discrimination in England* (Penguin Books, 1968).

18. Hindell, op. cit.; Rose *et al.*, op. cit.; Layton-Henry, *The Politics of Race in Britain*, op. cit.

19. Community Relations Commission, *Some of My Best Friends . . .* (CRC, 1976).

20. T. Burgess, 'A Racialist Bill?', *New Society*, 22 Mar. 1978; *The Economist*, editorial, 17 Mar. 1978.

21. M. Fitzgerald, *Political Parties and Black People* (Runnymede Trust, 1984).

22. M. Parkinson and J. Duffy, 'Government's Response to Inner-City Riots: the Minister for Merseyside and the Task Force', *Parliamentary Affairs*, 37 (1984) pp.76–96.
23. M. Kettle, 'The Police' in H. Drucker *et al.*, *Developments in British Politics* (St. Martin's, 1983); Lustgarten, op. cit.; Bulpitt, op. cit.
24. Kirp, op. cit.; B. Jacobs, 'Black Minority Participation in the USA and Britain', *Journal of Public Policy*, 2 (1982) pp.237–62.
25. A. Downs, 'Up and Down with Ecology – the "Issue–Attention Cycle" ', *The Public Interest*, 28 (1972) pp.38–50.
26. I. McAllister and D. T. Studlar, 'The Electoral Geography of Immigrant Groups in Britain', *Electoral Studies*, 3 (1984) pp.139–50.
27. Studlar, 'Political Culture and Racial Policy in Britain', op. cit.; Kirp, op. cit.
28. Katznelson, op. cit.; Studlar, 'Elite Responsiveness or Elite Autonomy', op. cit.
29. Layton-Henry, *The Politics of Race in Britain*, op. cit.
30. Bulpitt, op. cit., pp.29–30.
31. Studlar, 'The Ethnic Vote, 1983'. All these data should be considered suggestive rather than definitive. Methodological reservations include the number of nonwhites in surveys, the tendency of survey respondents to over-report voting, and the capacity of parties to create concern over issues, at least in the short term.
32. National Opinion Polls, *Political Social and Economic Review*, 14 (1978), p.3.
33. *B.B.C. Election Survey* (Gallup, 1983), pp.159, 166.
34. M. Anwar, 'Public Reaction to the Scarman Report', *New Community*, 10 (1982) pp.371–3.
35. M. Fitzgerald, 'Preliminary Notes on Data from Harris Survey for Black on Black/Eastern Eye Election Special 1983', unpublished ms.
36. Ibid.
37. Studlar, 'The Ethnic Vote, 1983', op. cit.; I. Crewe, 'How Labour Was Trounced All Round', *Guardian*, 14 June 1983.
38. *BBC Election Survey*, pp.330, 332.
39. Community Relations Commission, *Participation of Ethnic Minorities in the 1974 General Election* (London: CRC, 1975); M. Anwar, *Votes and Policies* (CRE, 1980); M. Fitzgerald, 'Ethnic Minorities and the 1983 General Election', *Runnymede Trust Briefing Paper*, December 1983.
40. McAllister and Studlar, op. cit. I. Crew, 'the Black, Brown and Green Votes', *New Society* (12 April 1979) pp. 76–8.
41. See also Z. Layton-Henry and D. T. Studlar, 'The Electoral Participation of Black and Asian Britons: Integration or Alienation?', *Parliamentary Affairs*, 38 (1985) pp.307–18.
42. Community Relations Commission *Participation of Ethnic Minorities in the 1974 General Election*; Anwar, *Votes and Policies*; Fitzgerald, 'Ethnic Minorities and the 1983 General Election'.
43. D. G. Pearson, *Race, Class and Political Activism* (Brookfield, Vt: Renouf, 1981).
44. I. Crewe, 'The Electorate: Partisan Dealignment Ten Years On', *West European Politics*, 6 (1983), pp.183–215.
45. B.B.C. Election Survey, pp.96, 369.
46. Fitzgerald, 'Preliminary Notes', op. cit.
47. M. Fitzgerald, 'The Parties and the "Black Vote" ' in M. Harrop and I. Crewe

(eds), *Political Communications in the 1983 General Election* (Cambridge University Press, 1985).

48. McAllister and Studlar, op. cit.
49. Studlar, 'Immigration and Racial Change', op. cit.
50. Crewe, 'How Labour Was Trounced', op. cit.
51. Community Relations Commission, *Some of My Best Friends . . .*, National Opinion Polls, *Political Social and Economic Review* (1978); C. Airey, 'Social and Moral Values' in R. Jowell and C. Airey (eds), *British Social Attitudes: The 1984 Report* (Gower Press, 1984).
52. C. T. Husbands, 'Race and Immigration' in J. Griffith (ed.), *Socialism in a Cold Climtae* (Allen & Unwin, 1983) p.176.
53. I. Crewe, 'Representation and the Ethnic Minorities in Britain' in Glazer and Young, op. cit.; Fitzgerald, 'Preliminary Notes'; McAllister and Studlar, op. cit.; S. Welch and D. T. Studlar, 'The Impact of Race on Political Behaviour in Britain', *British Journal of Political Science*, 15 (1985) pp.528–40.
54. M. Fitzgerald, 'Ethnic Minorities and the 1983 General Election', op. cit.
55. Layton-Henry, *The Politics of Race in Britain*, op. cit.
56. Crewe, 'Representation and the Ethnic Minorities in Britain', op. cit.
57. G. Jordan and J. Richardson, 'The British Policy Style or the Logic of Negotiation', in J. Richardson (ed.), *Policy Styles in Western Europe* (Allen & Unwin, 1982).
58. J. Nixon, 'The Home Office and Race Relations Policy: Co-ordinator or Initiator?', *Journal of Public Policy*, 2 (1982) pp.365–78.
59. P. D. Schumaker, 'Policy Responsiveness to Protest Group Demands', *Journal of Politics*, 37 (1975) pp.488–521.
60. Studlar, 'Political Culture and Racial Policy in Britain', op. cit.
61. J. L. Waltman, 'Change and Rumours of Change: Courts and the Rule of Law', in D. T. Studlar and J. L. Waltman (eds), *Dilemmas of Change in British Politics* (Macmillan, 1984).
62. R. Rose, 'On the Priorities of Citizenship in the Deep South and Northern Ireland', *Journal of Politics*, 38 (1976) pp.247–91.
63. G. Alderman, *The Jewish Community in British Politics* (Oxford University Press, 1983) pp.128–9.
64. Ibid., p.viii.
65. Cobb and Elder, op. cit., pp.152–4.
66. W. A. Gamson, *Power and Discontent* (Homewood, Ill.: Dorsey Press, 1968); 'Stable Unrepresentation in American Society', *American Behavioural Scientist*, 12 (1968) pp.15–21.
67. P. Norton, *The British Polity* (New York, Longman, 1984).
68. Welch and Studlar, op. cit.
69. D. Judge, *Backbench Specialisation in the House of Commons* (Heinemann, 1981).

# 7 Political Dilemmas in Multi-Racial Education

SALLY TOMLINSON

For a period of some twenty years after children of ethnic minorities from overseas had entered British schools in significant numbers, central and local education authorities managed to diminish the political significance of their presence. Supported by prevailing liberal educational pedagogies and the doctrine that Kirp has described as 'doing good by stealth'[1] successive Labour and Conservative secretaries of state for education, and their officials avoided formulating direct, centralised policies to deal with a system which was moving from a mono- to a multi-cultural composition. Those local education authorities which found themselves incorporating large numbers of minority pupils defined the problem on a short-term remedial basis of 'the needs of immigrant children', dealt with matters largely on an ad hoc basis, and looked in vain for central guidance.

Over the past five years however, there has been considerable policy development towards what had broadened into education for a multi-racial, multi-cultural society. 'Education for All' was the concept adopted by the Swann Committee of enquiry into the education of ethnic minority pupils as a phrase which 'describes more accurately the approach to education which we wish to put forward, since it reflects the responsibility which we feel all those concerned with education share in laying the foundations for the kind of pluralist society we envisage.'[2]

Pressure for new developments and approaches has come from both inside and outside the British education system. European legislation on minority rights, action by minority groups within Britain, and pressures from schools and teachers have influenced educational policy-makers towards more explicit pluralist and anti-racist policy-making.[3]

Central government has made some revision of its funding policies for minorities, and has encouraged the more careful preparation of teachers for a plural society. Local Education Authorities (LEAs) have begun to commit themselves to written policy statements on multi-cultural education. These new developments, while welcomed by many educationalists and minority parents, have highlighted the political dilemmas which are becoming familiar world-wide, as education systems designed for white majorities struggle to incorporate ethnic minorities on terms acceptable to the minorities. In particular there is a dilemma inherent in the provision of culturally pluralist education which takes account of minority desires and values, but still allows for equality of opportunity for the minority pupils; there is the dilemma of actually implementing multi-cultural policies at school level; and there is the dilemma of 'educating for all' in a society which provides evidence of remaining incorrigibly racist. Also, given the decentralised nature of power and responsibility in the English education system, it is debatable how far developments at central level will affect Local Authorities, and how far local policies will actually affect schools.

This chapter summarises multi-cultural education policies developed over the past twenty-five years, examines recent policy developments and discusses the dilemmas noted above. It concludes that while the growing 'racialisation'[4] of contemporary educational policies is to be welcomed, there is no guarantee that these political dilemmas will be resolved, or that multi-cultural education will actually assist the creation of a more tolerant multi-racial society.

## POLICIES FOR ASSIMILATION

Educational responses to ethnic minority pupils from the early 1960s were closely linked to political views of the relationship of immigrant minority groups to the rest of society. The pragmatic approach of all parties to race matters – encapsulated in the Wilson government's view that explicit support for ethnic minorities loses votes[5] – was reflected in educational policy during these years. In 1965 a Labour Government spokesman articulated 'the melancholy view that only immigrants most likely to be assimilated into our national life' should be permitted to stay in Britain'[6] and education was expected to play a crucial role in the process of assimilation. The Commonwealth Immigrants Advisory Committee recommended in their second report that education policies should centre round the cultural assimilation of immigrant children into the British way of life, and suggested that some form of dispersal of these children was preferable to *de facto* segregation in 'immigrant schools'.[7] The drafting of this report coincided with a political crisis in two West London schools, in which white parents protested about the presence of large numbers of immigrant children. The then Conservative Minister for Education visited the schools and subsequently suggested that a limit of 30% of such children should be permitted in any one school. A Department of Education and Science publication (DES 7/65) suggested 'spreading the children' and dispersal became the one major central policy recommendation to LEAs. In the event, only a few LEAs ever operated dispersal, and the policy attracted criticism from diverse sources until it was ruled illegal in 1975.

The second policy actively promoted by central government to assimilate minority children was the teaching of English as a Second Language (ESL). The DES produced a pamphlet on *English for Immigrants* in 1963 and the only large research grant for minority education in the 1960s was given for the production of ESL material.[8] Teaching ESL has been the only policy to which central and local governments have consistently committed themselves. Little and Wiley reported from their 1979 survey of LEAs that the majority of local authorities with minority children equated the special needs of these children largely with ESL, but that even this activity was underdeveloped and underfunded.[9]

Funding policies to assist the education of minority pupils have always been distinctly inexplicit. It is highly questionable whether funding educational activities from the Home Office, which has been the major cash source for 'immigrants from the Commonwealth' via the 1966 Local Government Act has, again in Kirp's phraseology 'done good by stealth'. Section 11 of the Act empowered the Home Office to pay grants to those local authorities who employed staff 'in consequence of the presence within their areas of large numbers of immigrants from the Commonwealth whose language or customs differ from those of the rest of the community', This peculiar method of funding has been consistently criticised, not least by local authority Chief Education Officers (CEOs) who would have preferred a national funding strategy. Indeed in 1976 a group of CEOs were of the opinion that the method of funding had hindered the emergence of national policies for the education of ethnic minority children.[10]

In common with an inexplicit funding policy, central education authorities attempted to diminish the political significance of the presence of racially and ethnically different pupils by insisting that they were merely a segment of that wider intractable group, the 'disadvantaged'. Taking a cue from the prevailing 1960s liberal belief in compensatory education, and from political pressures to keep a low profile on minority pupils, the DES attempted to subsume the problem of minority pupils under those of urban deprivation and disadvantage. The 1974 circular on *Educational Disadvantage and the Needs of Immigrants* 'saw a need to provide for all those suffering from educational disadvantage'.[11] A Centre for Disadvantage was established at Manchester which did press quietly for more coherent policies on minority education, but this centre was closed down in 1980. While minority pupils were considered to share many characteristics with 'disadvantaged' white pupils, particularly their lower school achievement, it has always been ironic that indices which have purported to measure social deprivation have included the actual presence of immigrant minorities as a disadvantaging factor (see, for example, the 1967 Plowden Report). The commitment of central government to a 'disadvantaged' view of minorities ignored this irony and the view has persisted. A Home Office circular in 1978 claimed that 'the government's basic analysis is that a good deal of the disadvantage that minorities suffer is shared with the less well-off members of the indiginous population'.[12] Social disadvantage, rather than factors of race and ethnicity, were held to be a prime determinant of the school performance of ethnic minorities. This resulted in a political atmosphere in which, despite growing verbal dissatisfaction from minority parents and communities, issues of race and culture were played down until the 1970s.

## CHANGES IN POLICY DIRECTION

Policies concerned with ESL, dispersal and disadvantage were both assimilative and inexplicit and successfully diminished, for a time, the political significance of racial and cultural differences among pupils. Of equal importance were the non-policy decisions made by central government. As Stephen Lukes has argued 'non-decision making' can be seen as a form of 'decision making' because it 'allows for consideration of the ways in which decisions are prevented from being taken on potential issues over which there is a observable conflict of interest'.[13] Central government has enormous power *not* to make policy decisions and non-decisions are in fact part of policy-making. Even during the 1970s, at a time when there was a greater shift towards the centralisation of educational policy making in general, proposals for more central direction on the education of minority pupils were met with constant reference back to LEAs and schools.

Between 1973–81 some 228 policy proposals to improve the education of minority pupils and prepare all pupils for life in a multi-racial society had been put forward by a series of committees and commissions. The committee set up by government in 1979 to enquire into the education of ethnic minority children made eighty-one of these recommendations and regretted that 'we have received some evidence about the lack of leadership given by the DES in the field of multi-cultural education'.[14]

By the end of the 1970s pressures both inside and outside the education system made low-profile inexplicit policies untenable, and the development of both cultural pluralist and 'racialised' policies more likely. A major external pressure came from minority communities and parents. Immigrant parents had come to Britain with expectations that their children would acquire, through educational qualifications, social and occupational mobility. They did not wish to see their children as part of a permanently disadvantaged minority. Although, in crude socio-economic terms, the majority of the parents were working class, their expectations of education were distinctly middle-class. By the 1970s many parents were disappointed and disillusioned with the education their children were receiving and were developing their own forms of supplementary or even segregated education. Caribbean parents and educationalists had created, by a variety of initiatives, a black education movement whose central belief was that schools designed for white majority pupils could not offer equal opportunities to black children.[15]

The decade of the 1970s also produced a world-wide debate about the merits of assimilation versus pluralistic existence in almost all societies in which immigrant minorities had come to settle.[16] In Britain, demands from minority communities – particularly Sikh,

Muslim and Hindu communities – to retain their own linguistic, religious and cultural traditions, constituted a strong pressure to change practices and produce policies which would take account of cultural pluralism. In the late 1970s a resurgence of fundamentalist Islamic values worldwide also began affecting Muslim views of education in Britain. The Muslim Education Council set out a case for separate state-subsidised education in 1978[17] and by 1983 a Muslim Parents Association in Bradford requested that five schools be re-classified as voluntary-aided Muslim schools. Under these kinds of pressure it was likely that both central and local government policies for minority eduction would become more explicit.

## PRESSURE FOR POLICY CHANGE

The external pressure which probably exerted the most immediate influence on educational policy-makers were the civil disturbances of 1981. Troyna has argued forcibly that the higher profile taken by central and local policy-makers since 1981 are less a result of benevolent concern, than of a fear that further disturbances may result if the education system is not seen to make some attempts to improve the education of black pupils.[18] Certainly, the Scarman Report linked minority school failures, unemployment, and a propensity to riot, in a way calculated to galvanise policy-makers into action, even if it was based on tenuous evidence.[19]

Within the education system itself major pressures to develop pluralist policies came from the schools, particularly in terms of curriculum reform. By the late 1960s movement had begun to counter negative Eurocentric images of former colonial countries as 'places only inhabited by savages' and also to counter any racism exhibited by white pupils to their black colleagues. Over the following years teachers also began to establish that there were tenuous links between the negative presentation of non-whites in the school curriculum and lower academic school performances.[20] By the end of the 1970s there was considerable agreement that curriculum reform was needed in all schools and not just those with minority pupils.[21] The DES gave tentative support to curriculum reform in the 1977 consultative green paper on *Education*, which was produced by a Labour secretary of state, and asserted that 'the curriculum appropriate to our Imperial past cannot meet the requirements of modern Britain'. In 1981 the Department's advice to LEAs included the liberal maxim that education in a multi-racial society should 'instil tolerance of other races, religions and ways of life'.[22]

Other pressures for change have come from groups within education whose political allegiance has moved from early identification with liberalism in education to the more radical left. *The National Association for Multi-Racial Education* initially developed in the early 1970s as a left-liberal teachers' pressure group but has since moved towards a neo-Marxist political standpoint. In 1985 it changed its name to the *National Anti-Racist Movement in Education* and was drawn to the Marxist writings of Sivanandan and Mullard as a theoretical base for its political activities. The organisation has developed a radical programme which links 'anti-racist education' to 'anti-sexist and anti-classist education . . . in order to help produce and reproduce the socio-educational relations of liberation'.[23]

## EVIDENCE OF CHANGE

At the level of local education policy, detailed evidence has only recently begun to emerge. Mullard *et al* reported in 1983 that 36 LEAs out of 105 claimed to have formulated written policy statements on multi-cultural education.[24] Cashmore and Bagley on the other hand have written that, of the 72 LEAs they surveyed, only 12 had made no move at all in a multi-cultural direction, even though most authorities had not got as far as a written policy.[25] An examination of written policies does indicate that there is a division between pluralist approaches and those which stress anti-racist equal opportunity policy, although the division is not as clear cut as some critics would suggest. For example, the northern authority of Kirklees set out in 1981 to produce a set of recommendations to guide all local authority services in their relations with minority communities. The authority held discussions with 'those members of the minority communities who have particular interests in the education service' and decided that policies should foster home-school links and minority involvement in the educational decisions made about their children. While these activities may not be explicitly anti-racist, they do seek to minimise a potentially racist situation developing out of a paternalist LEA imposing its decisions on minority communities.[26]

The authorities which have claimed explicitly anti-racist directions in their policy statements are Berkshire and the Inner London Education Authority (ILEA). In both these areas discussion with parents has centred on how the education system as a whole contributes to racism in society and perpetuates inequality of opportunity for minority pupils. Berkshire set up a committee for multi-cultural education in 1981, which produced a discussion paper *Education for Equality*.[27] The paper urged that schools and teachers should emphasize equality rather than assimilation or cultural diversity but in practice many of the Berkshire recommendations to develop links with minority communities and involve parents in educational decision making appear identical to the Kirklees recommendations.

ILEA was the first authority to produce a policy statement, in 1977, setting out its commitment to education for a multi-racial society and proposing initiatives which should be undertaken to bring this about. These included the development of multi-cultural curriculum materials, the provision of aid to voluntary agencies (particularly for mother-tongue teaching and supplementary schools), the setting up of resource centres and an increase in multi-cultural specialist personnel, the creation of a unified language service, and in-service teacher courses. The expanded inspectorate published an *aide-mémoire* on education for a multi-ethnic society in 1981[28] and by this time the elected leaders of the authority had moved to an overt commitment to anti-racist education. 'Anti-racism is critical to the work of the authority . . . the creation of new policies which fail to grapple with racism is likely to prove worthless.'[29] Under the guidance of Frances Morrell, the Labour ILEA leader, the authority has made a specific commitment to improve the educational achievements of working class pupils, minority pupils, and girls, and to 'anti-racist, anti-sexist' education. ILEA also specifically repudiated the policy of subsuming minorities under the label 'disadvantaged'. A 1983 publication noted that 'there is a school of thought, supported by the present government, that the educationally disadvantaged (working class children, girls and black children are included in this group) are a minority of the school population . . . for whom separate and different educational provision should be made. We wish explicitly to disassociate ourselves from that school of thought'.[30]

Overall, the changes in policy direction at LEA level have been more apparent and explicit since 1981, though the work of Rex,

Troyna and Naguib has indicated that these initiatives may have resulted in only a limited and partial impact on most schools.[31] There is a rhetoric that in order to offer equality of opportunity in education, minority parents and communities will have to be more closely involved in education decisions made about their children through consultation, home–school links and parent–governorship representatives. There is also a growing commitment to the belief that cultural diversity should be respected and that cultural traditions, symbols and values of minority communities be respected. In particular, more schools now accept that linguistic traditions via mother-tongue teaching, religious education by the communities, different cultural symbols (particularly food and dress) and the gender arrangements of minorities, should be respected by schools. There is also a growing adherence to curriculum reform, to reduce the ethnocentric content of the curriculum and make it more appropriate for both minority and majority pupils. There is a greater commitment to the notion that all teachers should have some initial training for education in a multi-racial society and that in-service courses be developed, this latter commitment being shared by central government. The new Council for the Accreditation for Teacher Education, established by the Secretary of State for Education in 1983, does include in its brief the encouragement of a multi-cultural dimension in all future teacher training, and the Council for National Academic Awards has produced a policy statement on multi-cultural, anti-racist education for all public sector teacher training institutions.[32]

The major form of providing extra funding for the education of minority pupils is still Section 11 of the 1966 Local Government Act, although the Home Office reviewed these grants and in 1982 issued a circular to all LEAs setting out new conditions for the grant. In particular, LEAs applying in future must have consulted what the circular rather quaintly describes as 'the local Commonwealth immigrant community' or the Local Community Relations Council. The authority must also demonstrate that the grant received is actually being spent on the 'needs of Commonwealth immigrants'.[33]

Adequate funding and resources are crucial if changes are actually to be implemented. The Swann Committee of enquiry considered that new policy developments would be limited by the terms of the 1966 Act and recommended new legislation to make funding more appropriate for schools and LEAs.[34]

## POLITICAL DILEMMAS

New policy development in multi-racial education is a response to political developments between ethnic minority groups and the white majority society in Britain. The background to these developments is not simply 'racism' on the part of white individuals or institutions, it is the politically open question as to how far the descendants of immigrant minorities of the 1960s will be afforded full citizenship rights, and allowed equal opportunies within a plural society. Education is now moving to a more central position in this debate. Questions concerning the responsibility of schools to transmit a common core of beliefs and values while respecting cultural diversity, and the ability of all schools to change white perceptions of ethnic minorities are being raised across the political spectrum. One catalyst in the increasing polarisation of 'left' and 'right' perspectives on multi-racial education has recently been Ray Honeyford, the Bradford headteacher of a predominantly Asian school. He published an article in the right-wing journal *The Salisbury Review* which argued that schools which were committed to multi-cultural education might neglect indigenous pupils and give preferential treatment to minorities.[35] While this might have been an acceptable case politically in the 1960s, this had become more controversial in the 1980s. He was subsequently suspended by his Conservative-controlled LEA and his case raised in Parliament. A Conservative MP for a neighbouring LEA claimed that Honeyford was the victim of a 'campaign' waged by Marxists,[36] and the non-political National Association of Headteachers supported legal action on behalf of Mr Honeyford. The case received national media coverage (especially on Thames Television's programme *TV Eye* on 2 May 1985) and has assisted in further polarising political positions.

However, the education system in Britain still generally inclines to a liberalism which other institutions have abandoned and the provision of equal opportunities for minority pupils and a recognition of cultural diversity do still appear to be major policy goals. The pursuit of these goals, however, entails a series of political dilemmas.

## THE DILEMMA OF 'EQUAL OPPORTUNITY'

Firstly, a major dilemma centres around the possibility of providing equal opportunities for minority pupils within educational structures which do not guarantee such opportunities. The ILEA policy statements have pointed to the unequal opportunities which working class, female and black pupils are offered[37] and the notion of pursuing equality of opportunity within an education system geared to an 'incorrigibly competitive and hierarchical society'[38] is in any case highly problematical. The development of comprehensive education was initially regarded by its supporters as a move towards a more egalitarian society, but the ending of the tri-partite system did not increase the opportunities for large numbers of children. The chances of pupils of working class parents being selected and prepared for academically-oriented education which allows access to higher education have not improved and inner city comprehensive schools, which are the schools attended by most minority pupils, do not generally offer a high-status academic curriculum.[39] The arrival of minorities did, of course, enhance the opportunities of white parents and their children, who were able to move to more desirable jobs, schools and areas in the 1960s. The schools attended by minority children are now more likely to contain the residual white 'disadvantaged' children, and to be geared to lower level academic work and increasingly to the new ideology of 'children with special needs'.[40] Many inner city schools are beginning to realise that they incorporate all levels of ability as far as minority children are concerned, but they do not necessarily have the skills or resources to develop these abilities. Thus the present structures of education make it unlikely that promises of 'equality of opportunity' for minority pupils to acquire social and economic mobility via educational qualifications can ever be realised.

## THE DILEMMA OF CULTURAL DIVERSITY

Secondly there is a political dilemma in deciding how far minority cultures, languages, religions and values can be recognised, respected and incorporated into schools, without disadvantaging minority pupils, or undermining the cohesion produced by a 'national' system of education. This dilemma is occurring worldwide and is by no means exclusively British. The problem of reconciling the competition that occurs between pluralist groups in a society, with the need to preserve cohesion in the nation-state as a whole is highlighted in education systems that are moving from mono-cultural to multi-cultural perspectives.[41] In Britain, however, there is as yet little serious suggestion that minority cultures should 'compete' equally with majority culture, and a Eurocentric perspective still dominates the curriculum. But the belief that minority groups should have a right to determine what sort of education their children receive is growing and leading to conflict. The issue of Muslim education in Bradford has already been noted, and certainly the clash between Western and Islamic views about how girls should be educated seems to be an example of an apparently insoluble dilemma.

## THE IMPLEMENTATION OF POLICIES

The actual implementation of multi-cultural policies in schools also poses a series of policy dilemmas. Although some pressures towards multi-cultural education came from schools, notably the curriculum reform movement, and from teachers' pressure groups, there is no guarantee that even written policy statements by LEAs will change school practice or even be accepted by some schools. Jeffcoate has taken the view that 'local authority policy statements on anti-racist and multi-cultural education seem destined to end up in the waste-paper basket . . . and rightly so'.[42] Troyna and Ball, on the other hand, after surveying a group of headteachers' reactions to their authority's multi-cultural policy, have concluded that 'as change-agents' these policies were 'not worth the paper they were written on'. They argue that if multi-cultural, anti-racist education is to be taken seriously in schools, it is important for the authority to inform schools why the policy has been developed, what the policy goals are, and what guidelines and evaluation criteria for implementing the policy are available.[43]

The reluctance of many schools to implement such policies reflects a more general conservatism in Britain, especially among its political leaders, to affirm that the society *is* multi-racial, and that equal opportunities, particularly in education and employment, will be offered to minority groups. White parents have consistently remained hostile to the idea of their children attending schools with ethnic minority pupils – from the protests in 1963 by Southall parents alluded to earlier in this chapter, to the Nottinghamshire parents who in 1983 objected to a temporary exchange of children between an inner city and a suburban primary school because it meant mixing with 'those immigrants from the city centre'.[44] As long as there is no central political affirmation and action which will demonstrate that non-white minorities are indeed equal citizens, there is no reason to suppose that white parents' views will change, or that they will not continue to feel aggrieved if their children are educated among minority children. The evidence presented in Annex C of the Swann Report, detailing visits to schools in 'all-white' areas, suggests that the fundamental problem for the majority of LEAs is that of producing and implementing multi-racial policies in white areas.[45]

## THE SWANN REPORT

The final report of the committee of enquiry on the education of minority pupils made a brave attempt to grapple with the political dilemmas inherent in the re-education of a hostile majority society so that 'the foundations for a genuinely pluralist society' could be laid.[46] In chapter six the committee began by reaffirming their belief that the ad hoc measures taken around the country to implement some version of 'multi-cultural education' were based on political expediency and had resulted in large areas of the country remaining 'oblivious to the changed and changing nature of British society'.[47] They rejected the view that in a decentralised education system central government should not dictate policies to LEAs and schools, particularly if the alternative was the perpetuation of different 'brands' of multi-culturalism. They observed that 'the term multi-cultural education appears to have encouraged schools and LEAs in all-white areas to believe that the issues involved are of no concern to them since they see themselves as mono-cultural'.[48] The committee also adopted the phrase 'Education for All' to reflect the responsibility that all those concerned with education should share in developing a pluralist society which allows for the equality of opportunity for *all* pupils. They concluded the chapter with a summary of seven steps in the argument for 'Education for All' and seventeen strategies for implementation. Overall, the committee's concept of 'Education for All' can be considered a radical–liberal commitment to reform within the existing education system, rather than a neo-Marxist commitment to an unspecified alternative education system:

'  –   The fundamental change that is necessary is the recognition that the problem facing the education system is not how to educate children of ethnic minorities but how to educate *all* children.

–   Britain is a multi-racial and multi-cultural society and all pupils must be enabled to understand what this means.

–   This challenge cannot be left to the separate and independent initiatives of LEAs and schools. Only those with experience of substantial numbers of ethnic minority pupils have attempted to tackle it, though the issues affect all schools and pupils.

–   Education has to be about something more than the reinforcement of the beliefs, values and identity which each child brings to school.

–   It is necessary to combat racism, to attack inherited myths and stereotypes and the ways they are embodied in institutional practice.

–   Multi-cultural understanding has to permeate all aspects of a school's work. It is not a separate topic that can be welded on to existing practices.

–   Only in this way can schools begin to offer anything approaching *equality of opportunity* for all pupils which it must be the aspirations of the education system to provide.'[49]

CONCLUSION

This chapter has reviewed changing policies towards multi-cultural education over the past twenty-five years and concluded that there have been moves from the low-profile assimilative policies of the 1960s and 1970s, to the beginnings of more overt 'racialised' policies in the 1980s. One striking feature about the debate on multi-racial education is that it has now moved to a central position in the British race relations debate, and there is an increased polarisation of political views between the left, the centre and the right. Liberal ideologies still generally underpin the education system and the professional preparation of teachers, and have encouraged many educationalists to begin to take serious account of minority views on pluralism, racism and educational change. Both central and local authorities have responded to minority pressure groups, talk of 'consultation', and are willing to incorporate minority views about how their children should be educated. However, it is likely that the strongest pressures to produce more overt policies stemmed from fears of a repeat of the 1981 street conflicts. Changed educational policies incorporate a series of political dilemmas, especially relating to the degree that central government should dictate to local government, how far 'education for all' should actually become a dominant rather than a marginal concern to schools, and how far education in all-white areas should challenge the entrenched beliefs of the majority of white Britons. It is not surprising that policies have not yet seriously addressed the problem of persuading those who live in all-white areas that they do not live in a mono-cultural society, and the real challenge of the late 1980s will be to those LEAs who do not incorporate minority communities or pupils. While the education system is now being recognised as a crucial mechanism to help prevent political conflict between minorities and the majority society in the future, there is still little rational discussion of the dilemmas involved or the policies required. Until this happens, assertions that any variety of multi-cultural education can assist in the creation of a tolerant, plural society will remain on the level of platitude.

## NOTES

1. D. Kirp, *Doing Good By Doing Little: Race and Schooling in Britain* (University of California Press, 1979).
2. Department of Education and Science, *Education For All* (HMSO, 1985), p.317.
3. T. Corner, *Education in Multi-Cultural Societies* (Croom Helm, 1984).
4. J. Williams, *From Institutional Racism to Anti-Racism* MSc Dissertation, University of Aston, 1984.
5. R. H. S. Crossman, *Diaries of a Cabinet Minister* (Magnum Books, 1979) p.73.
6. Quoted in S. Patterson, *Immigration and Race Relations in Britain* (Oxford University Press, 169) p.109.

7. Commonwealth Immigrants Advisory Committee, Second Report, Cmnd 2266 (HMSO, 1976).
8. J. Derrick, Teaching English to Immigrants (Longman, 1966).
9. A. Little and R. Willey, *Multi-Ethnic Education – the Way Forward*, Schools Council Working Paper, No.18 (London, 1981).
10. Community Relations Commission, *Funding Multi-Racial Education – a National Strategy* (CRC, 1976).
11. Department of Education and Science, *Educational Disadvantage and the Needs of Immigrants* (HMSO, 1974) p.5.
12. Home Office, *Proposals for Replacing Section II of the Local Government Act*, Circular 97/82 (HMSO, 1978).
13. S. Lukes, *Power: a Radical View* (Macmillan, 1974).
14. Department of Education and Science, *The School Curriculum* (HMSO, 1981) p.73.
15. S. Tomlinson, *Home and School in Multi-Cultural Britain* (Batsford, 1984).
16. J. Bhatnager, *Educating Immigrants* (Croom Helm, 1981).
17. Union of Muslim Organisations, *Education Council – Background Papers* (UMO, 1978).
18. B. Troyna, 'Policy Entrepreneurs and the Development of Multi-Ethnic Education Policies – a Reconstruction', *Education Management and Administration*, 12 (1984).
19. Lord Scarman, *The Brixton Disorders 10–12th April 1981* (Penguin Books, 1982).
20. D. Milner, *Children and Race – Ten Years On* (Ward Lock, 1979).
21. Little and Willey, op. cit.
22. DES, *The School Curriculum*, op. cit., p.3.
23. C. Mullard, *Anti-Racist Education – The Three 'O's* (National Association for Multi-Racial Education, 1984) p.56; A. Sivanandan, *A Different Hunger: Writings on Black Resistance* (Pluto Press, 1982).
24. C. Mullard, L. Bonnick and B. King, *Racial Policy and Practice – A Letter Survey*, Race Relations Policy Unit (University of London, 1983).
25. E. Cashmore and R. Bagley, 'Colour Blind', *The Times Educational Supplement*, 28 Dec., 1984.
26. Kirklees Metropolitan Council, Report of the Inter-Directorate Working Party on Multi-Ethnic Kirklees, Kirklees 1981.
27. Berkshire Education Committee, *Education for Equality: Report of an Advisory Committee on Multi-Cultural Education* (Berkshire, 1981).
28. Inner London Education Authority, *An Aide Memoire to the Inspectorate* (ILEA, 1981).
29. Inner London Education Authority, *Race, Sex and Class I: Achievement in Schools* (ILEA, 1983).
30. Ibid.
31. J. Rex, B. Troyna and M. Naguib, *Development of Multi-Cultural Education Policies in Four LEAs*, unpublished report to the Swann Committee (London, 1983).
32. Council for National Academic Awards, Discussion paper on Multi-Cultural Education and the Professional Preparation and In-Service Development of Teachers (CNNA, 1984).
33. Home Office, *Section 11 of the Local Government Act*, Circular 97/82 Home Office (London, 1982) p.3.

34. DES, *Education for All*, op. cit., p.359.
35. R. Honeyford, 'Multi-Ethnic Intolerance', *The Salisbury Review*, no.4 (1983).
36. B. Lodge, 'MP Rebukes Education Chiefs Over Actions in Race Row', *The Times Educational Supplement*, 19 Apr. 1985.
37. ILEA, *Race, Sex and Class*, op. cit.
38. B. Shaw, *Comprehensive Schooling – the Impossible Dream* (Basil Blackwell, 1983) p.37.
39. A. H. Halsey, A. F. Heath and J. M. Ridge, *Origins and Destinations* (Clarendon Press, 1980).
40. S. Tomlinson, 'The Expansion fo Special Education', *Oxford Review of Education*, vol.11, no.2 (1985) pp.156–62.
41. B. Bullivant, *Pluralism, Cultural Maintenance and Evolution* (Multi-Lingual Matters Press, 1984) p.106.
42. R. Jeffcoate, *Ethnic Minorities and Education* (Harper & Row, 1984) p.171.
43. B. Troyna and W. Ball, 'Styles of LEA Intervention in Multi-Cultural Anti-Racist Education', *Educational Review*, 37, 2 (1985) pp.165–73.
44. K. J. Richards, 'A Contribution to the multi-cultural education debate', *New Community*, 10, 2 (1983) p.232.
45. DES, *Education for All*, op. cit., pp.244–69.
46. Ibid., p.316.
47. Ibid., p.315.
48. Ibid., p.317.
49. Ibid., pp.769–71.

# 8 Training for What?: Government Policies and the Politicisation of Black Youth Unemployment

JOHN SOLOMOS

## INTRODUCTION

In the last decade or more the question of unemployment among young black workers, particularly in relation to the 16–25 age group, has become one of the central concerns of race relations policies. Every incoming government has declared itself in favour of the pursuit of equal opportunity in the youth labour market, and equal access to jobs for all young people, regardless of racial background, ethnic origin or colour. In addition, state agencies of various kinds, ranging from the Commission for Racial Equality, the Manpower Services Commission and the police, have become preoccupied with the implications of relatively high levels of unemployment among young blacks for social order and stability.[1] What is equally clear, however, is that the increasing politicisation of this issue has done little to break down the entrenched processes of discrimination against young blacks in the labour market.

Why has this situation arisen and what reasons can be given for the apparent gap between policy intentions and practices? This paper will approach this question in two steps. Firstly, and in a highly abbreviated manner, it will analyse the reasons for the increasing politicisation of 'black youth' as a specific social category. Here we shall focus on the underlying assumptions and political ideologies that have guided state intervention in this field, and the policy responses that have taken shape over the last decade:

Secondly, it will analyse critically the various meanings which have been attached to the notion of 'equal opportunity' and assess the actual outcomes of current policies for young blacks. This involves specifying the alternative courses of action open in the 1980s, especially in the light of the measures announced by the government in the wake of the 1981 Scarman Report.

A few preliminary points however need to be made on the more general context of race policies and their relationship to the black youth question. Firstly, it is important to emphasise that policies in relation to young blacks cannot be analysed apart from the broader setting of policy initiatives on race relations, for there are surprisingly few attempts to link initiatives concerned with youth to racism in education, employment, and social welfare. Secondly, policies for the young black unemployed need to be set within the context of employment policy generally. Furthermore in the light of the experience of the 1980–81 'riots', youth unemployment cannot be separated from the role of the police and those social control agencies that tend to define law and order as a problem related to high levels of unemployment among minority groups.[2]

While this paper will not go into these relationships in detail, an attempt will be made to show that the political meaning of 'black youth unemployment' has been constructed partly in relation to this wider set of issues which have preoccupied governments over the last decade.

## AN OVERVIEW OF GOVERNMENTAL RESPONSES TO BLACK YOUTH AND UNEMPLOYMENT

Murray Edelman has argued that the study of government responses to social problems must begin with an analysis of how the 'problem' is defined, proceed through an account of the policy options which are developed for coping with it, and conclude with a critical analysis of the objectives specific policy initiatives have been designed to meet.[3] He has also pointed out, in the context of a study of political language and social reform, that public policies rest on the beliefs and perceptions of those who help to make them, whether or not these are accurate. Guided by the experience of various programmes aimed at helping the unemployed in the United States, he argues that:

A reference in an authoritative public statement or in a Social Security law to 'training programs' for the unemployed is a metonymic evocation of a larger structure of beliefs: that job training is efficacious in solving the unemployment problem, that workers are unemployed because they lack necessary skills, that jobs are available for those trained to take them. Because each component of this interrelated set of beliefs is dubious, job training has been largely ineffective as a strategy for decreasing unemployment. But people who are anxious to fight unemployment and eager to believe the problem can be solved without drastic social change are ready to accept this kind of reassuring cue.[4]

In analysing the formulation, development, and implementation of policy initiatives it is therefore important to know not only the formal premises on which they are based, but also the underlying assumptions and prejudices which help define what the problems are and how they can be resolved. These assumptions in turn cannot be separated from the actions and rhetoric of governments, since these also help shape beliefs about the nature of public problems and their causes. As examples of this dialectical process of 'problem' definition and policy response Edelman cites the American 'War on Poverty', the 1960s urban riots, and the growth of social welfare institutions.[5]

In this section we want to develop this point in relation to the recent history of how the state and its associated agencies have responded or not responded to the question of relatively high levels of unemployment among the younger generation of black workers. The argument will proceed in two stages. Firstly, the underlying assumptions on which successive governments have relied in their definition of the youth unemployment problem will be critically analysed. Secondly, the policy prescriptions and forms of state intervention which derive from these assumptions will be outlined and analysed against the context of the actual changes which they have brought about.

**Underlying Assumptions**

From the late 1960s onwards there have been two dominant themes in official thinking about the 'second generation' question or the 'black youth question': firstly the image of the second generation as a 'social time bomb' and secondly the social construction of young blacks as suffering from a 'complex of disabilities' deriving from their own background and their lack of integration into the wider society.

The first image has been a recurrent theme since the late sixties, and has gained a sharper focus since the 1980–81 riots.[6] Writing in the aftermath of the 1960s riots in America, A. H. Halsey captured the meaning of this image when he argued that the central question about the second generation was 'will they revolt?'.[7] More substantially a number of official and semi-official documents took up the 'social time-bomb' theme and used it to emphasise the need for state intervention in order to defuse the danger of an explosion.[8] This theme was given more emphasis by the 1974 report by the Community Relations Commission on *Unemployment and Homelessness*, which warned that black youngsters in many urban areas were a 'social time-bomb' waiting to be detonated by the onset of widespread unemployment.[9]

The 'social deprivation' or 'complex of disabilities' theme has probably been most central to official thinking on this question. Beginning with the 1969 Select Committee report on *The Problems of Coloured School Leavers*, which emphasised the 'complex of disabilities' suffered by young blacks, subsequent reports have linked the experience of living in deprived inner city areas to that of being a member of a disadvantaged community.[10] In a number of reports produced by government departments, parliamentary committees, and official race relations agencies it is precisely this notion of disadvantage that has gained widest acceptance, although it is linked implicitly to other notions of 'unrealistic aspirations', 'psychological maladjustment', 'cultural conflict', 'language disabilities', 'weak family units', and a 'cycle of deprivation'.[11] In essence various sections of the black communities are seen as suffering from two types of disadvantage. Firstly, there are the problems associated with a deprived physical environment, bad housing, unemployment, and educational underachievement. All of these are made relatively worse for minorities because of racial discrimination.[12] Secondly, blacks are perceived as suffering from forms of social disadvantage related to newness and problems of adjustment, language and literacy problems, cultural difference and lack of 'integration'. It is the combination of these two forms of disadvantage which are in varying degrees seen as producing the 'complex of disabilities' characteristic of black communities.

Both of these dominant images have been translated into different, and sometimes contradictory, policy initiatives. These range from remedial programmes aimed at compensating for social disadvantages to remedial programmes for 'helping' the black communities. As a number of writers have pointed out, both of these approaches have exhibited a tendency to focus on the weaknesses of the black communities as the source of all problems, and have implicitly assumed various inadequacies and handicaps on the part of either whole communities or specific groups within them. This approach, which has been variously called 'social pathology' or 'blaming the victim',[13] is one of the recurrent themes in institutional responses to young blacks in British society over the last two decades. As Gus John has perceptively noted:

> The state, the police, the media and race relations experts ascribe to young blacks certain collective qualities, e.g. alienated, vicious little criminals, muggers, disenchanted, unemployed, unmarried mothers, truants, class-room wreckers, etc. The youth workers, community workers, counsellors and the rest, start with these objective qualities as given, and intervene on the basis that through their operations they could render young blacks subjectively different, and make them people to whom these objective qualifications could no longer be applied. When this is done in collaboration with control agents themselves, as in police–community liaison schemes, or instances in which professional blacks collaborate with schools in blaming black kids for their 'failure', it is interpreted as progress towards 'good community relations'.[14]

Although it could be argued that other images of young blacks have been used by various agencies, apart from those identified by John and others,[15] there are two important elements of his account which help explain how the various responses to 'problems' faced by young blacks can become part of the process of discrimination against them, however well-intentioned they may be.

The first, and perhaps most important, mechanism is the ascription to young blacks of certain immutable collective qualities, which are then transformed into more conventional notions by policy-makers and officials working in control agencies. A good example of this type of ascription is represented by the way in which the 'second generation' theme developed during the 1960s and 1970s out of rather imprecise notions about 'disadvantage', 'social handicap', and the 'threat of violence'.

The second mechanism, which in a sense grows out of the first, is the tendency on the part of government to intervene on the assumption that through their operations they could render young blacks more 'normal'. Since individual deviance from the norm is defined as the 'problem', an inbuilt tendency exists to seek causal explanations of the problems faced by young blacks through reference to cultural and personal inadequacies rather than in relation to more general inadequacies in British society. A pathology of individuals tends to predominate over a pathology of institutions.[16]

It is on the basis of these twin assumptions that socio-political ideologies about black youth have been constructed, although recently there have been some modifications. It is important to note that the entire intervention model of programmes for young blacks rests on assumptions about inadequacies which have to be remedied, albeit in combination with some measures to deal with 'discrimination'. These assumptions have in turn been buttressed by research and reports which make a number of interlocking claims about the nature of black culture, community structures, networks and family relations.[17] At the same time, the emphasis on these characteristics has tended to structure debate in such a way that racism as a structural phenomenon becomes only one small part of the overall race relations landscape, and by no means the central one.

More fundamentally, perhaps, the tendency to combine images of environmental disadvantage with images of personal handicap has helped produce rather stereotyped views of young blacks caught in a cycle of deprivation which leads to forms of alienation, criminality, and disaffection from the values of society – in other words, views of them as a 'problem'.

Nevertheless, it would perhaps be a mistake to see all government interventions in this field as guided by implicit or explicit assumptions about cultural handicap and deviance. There is at least some recognition within agencies such as the Commission for Racial Equality that there is a danger of blaming young blacks themselves for being unemployed, while ignoring the racist practices which make them more likely to be unemployed, or the economic and political mechanisms which result in a lack of jobs. As one widely publicised report from the Commission states:

> It is sometimes easy for those in authority to regard young people as 'the problem'. To do so is to confuse cause and effect. The real 'problem' lies in the inadequacies of society and the inability to respond to the needs and challenges of new generations of young people – especially those with different ethnic backgrounds, colour and/or culture.[18]

Similar opinions can be found in the report of the Home Affairs Select Committee on Racial Disadvantage and a Home Office study of ethnic minority attitudes, as well as other reports.[19]

The dominant perception of young blacks as a 'problem', particularly in relation to social order, has, however, not been shifted by such critical reports. Along with popular media images, official images of young blacks still seem to be preoccupied with the 'threat' posed by these young people rather than by the institutionalised processes of discrimination and racism that doubly oppress them. This has led to policy being biased towards solutions at the individual level while ameliorative measures are diverted at groups particularly hard hit by the recession. Although such measures have been helpful to individual young blacks in some form, they have done little to change common sense perceptions of young blacks as a 'social problem' or to challenge racist stereotypes.

During the post-1981 period 'the threat' perceived as emanating from young blacks has, if anything, become more widespread in public opinion. The role of the young unemployed in areas such as Brixton and Toxteth in the 1981 confrontations with the police, and subsequent low-level confrontations, has helped popularise the commonplace notion that unemployment can be linked with social disorder. As the MSC London Regional Office noted in its report for 1982:

> One effect of the civil disturbances that took place in early summer 1981 in various parts of London and elsewhere in the country was to increase interest in ethnic minority employment, as some commentators sought to link rising unemployment, especially among young blacks, with increasing social tensions in areas of ethnic minority concentration.[20]

This has in turn led to a politicisation of the black young unemployment issue in ways which had not been experienced hitherto. In addition to the parliamentary debate, government agencies such as the MSC and CRE and mainstream government departments began to look more closely at their role in dealing with the issue. Perhaps the clearest way in which the events of 1981 helped sharpen the political nature of the black youth unemployment debate can be gauged from the way in which, as one commentator put it, the riots made the social control of the black unemployed part of the national political agenda as well as the agenda of institutions such as the police and the MSC.[21]

## Policies and Programmes

As has been pointed out, a number of initiatives have been taken in the past decade to 'help' young blacks, particularly from the late 1970s onwards. These have mainly consisted of two types of intervention, each with its own institutional base in a government agency. The first type, closely associated with the work of the Commission for Racial Equality, has involved measures which are seen as helping the second and third generation of young blacks to integrate more fully into British society.[22] The second type, which is more recent in origin, is associated with the Manpower Services Commission, and involves the provision of training for unemployed young blacks within the context of schemes such as the Youth Training Scheme (previously the Youth Opportunities Programme).

### Integrative Measures

From the time of the 1969 Select Committee report onwards there has been a fear in official thinking that if young blacks were denied equal treatment they might become alienated from society and so become less likely to be integrated into it. This has been a particularly influential theme in the work of race relations bodies, which have seen their role as one of helping to integrate minorities and minimising social disturbances arising from immigration. A number of reports through the seventies were produced by the Select Committee on Race Relations and Immigration, the Community Relations Commission, and the Commission for Racial Equality which reflected this ideology of integration.[23] These resulted in initiatives directed at schools, the Careers Service, the youth service, and the police – which were intended to help the integration of young blacks into the wider society by either 'increasing understanding' or by giving them special help to meet their 'problems'.[24]

This integrative ideology, however, had only a partial impact by the time of the 1980–81 riots. The reason for this lay partly in the fact that bodies such as the CRE had limited resources with which to implement their policies, and partly because warnings about future problems were not heeded by the main government departments. The 1974 report by the CRC on *Unemployment and Homelessness* is a case in point. Although it achieved a wide circulation and influenced the perceptions of professionals about young blacks, e.g. in relation to the link between unemployment and relations with the police, the CRC and later the CRE could do little to put into practice its generalised calls for concerted action to achieve greater equality for young blacks. Six years later, however, a similar report, called *Youth in Multi-Racial Society*, had a wider impact on actual policies pursued. This was not because it produced new evidence, since its analysis was quite similar to the 1974 report. It warned that young blacks were becoming 'alienated', 'disillusioned' and 'disaffected' from society, and stated that 'unless society is able to tackle their needs, there is a danger that we will create a whole generation of alienated black adults'.[25] The reason the report did have more impact was that it was published at the same time as the Bristol 'riot' of April 1980, and its warnings about racial conflict could therefore be related to actual events on the streets.

Seen in these terms, it is clear that the role of race relations bodies, with their limited power and resources, can best be understood as channels for symbolic action such as the issuing of reports, attempts to influence government departments and limited programmes of 'special help'. In the aftermath of the 1981 riots this role became even more clear through the attempts by the CRE to influence the provisions made for young blacks by the MSC, and numerous conferences and seminars were organised by the Commission over the 1981–84 period, for educationalists, social workers, youth workers and employers about the problems faced by the young black unemployed.[26]

*Training Initiatives*

The second type of initiative dates from the late 1970s, although the 'riots' of 1980 and 1981 played a crucial role in forcing the black youth unemployment issue on to the general political agenda. It is also related to the first type of intervention, since increasingly the placement of young blacks on training schemes has come to be seen as a way of helping them integrate into the labour market and society more generally.

As regards training, the period until 1981 was characterised largely by *ad hoc* measures of a fairly limited nature. This included a joint working party set up by the Manpower Services Commission and the Commission for Racial Equality on the special needs of the black unemployed. The party's report concluded that young blacks were one of the groups most vulnerable to unemployment, particularly in the context of the recession in the post-1976 period. It also warned that a minority of disaffected young people from the ethnic minority communities were losing touch with statutory agencies and required 'special help' in order to ensure that they did not drift into crime and lawlessness.[27]

As a result of this and other reports, the role of the MSC in relation to young unemployed blacks began to expand, though it concentrated its attention on specific groups of young blacks it deemed 'at risk' rather than young unemployed blacks as a whole. This approach was related to the approach which emphasised the importance of 'special needs' outlined above, though it was also partly the result of a general lack of political interest on the question of the black unemployed. In the aftermath of the riots of 1981 however, there was a notable increase in the attention given by the MSC to ethnic issues, which as one report argued represented 'one of the most difficult challenges in the field of social, economic, environmental and employment policy'.[28] Partly as a result of pressure from the CRE during the two years after the 1981 riots, the MSC has integrated an equal opportunities policy into the Youth Training Scheme, funded research on the adequacy of its provisions for young unemployed blacks, and adopted a more high profile role in debates about inner city problems.

The response after 1981 is thus of interest in that, far from abandoning the earlier emphasis on the 'special needs' of the black unemployed, the MSC has re-worked this notion to suit its more interventionist stance. It is significant, for example, that in the MSC's definition of 'particular labour market problems' the issue of racism is hardly mentioned, and the emphasis is put on ameliorative and remedial measures to help black workers (particularly the young) adjust to labour market realities. This bias is reflected in the MSC's own definition of its role in this field:

> Many people from ethnic minority groups – particularly those in inner cities – suffer a significant labour market disadvantage. This problem cannot be solved by the Commission alone but the Commission will give priority to ensuring that all such groups have equal access to its services through provision of adequate information and publicity . . . and by encouraging staff to respond flexibly to the needs that are identified. Particular efforts will be made to ensure that all young people, regardless of race or sex, have equal access to the new Youth Training Scheme, and that the Scheme makes adequate provision for young people with special needs.[29]

According to the MSC's perception, therefore, the fundamental issue of labour market disadvantage is beyond its control. While it does not clearly specify what is within its control, it comes down to making sure that its training services cater for the 'special needs' of disadvantaged groups. The conditions which produce discrimination in the labour market are thus removed from debate, or at least minimised.

At a more practical level the impetus produced by the 1981 events did push the MSC to adopt not only an 'equal opportunity statement' but to publicise, albeit in a limited fashion, the CRE's *Code of Practice* for employers to its managing agents and to sponsors of YTS schemes. It has publicly stated the need for all schemes run under the rubric of YTS to comply with legislation forbidding discrimination and to provide positive opportunities for disadvantaged groups. A paper to the Youth Training Board in April 1983 clarified this approach by pointing out that, although equal opportunity for ethnic minorities all too often may not be a reality in working life, '. . . YTS should not replicate inequality'.[30]

Such statements have now become common in MSC documents, and are in turn given as proof that the Commission and the government are fully aware of the 'special needs' of the young black unemployed. Recent research on YTS would seem to show, however, that there is in fact an emerging gap between the promise of equal opportunity and the implementation of this promise.[31] A research project funded by the MSC itself concluded that within YTS the notion of 'special needs' was too often associated with ideas about social deprivation and personal inadequacy which combined with racist stereotypes to allocate a majority of young blacks to Mode B schemes, which are commonly regarded as second class.[32] This has in turn led to an under-representation of young blacks on Mode A schemes, especially those which also seem to offer the greatest likelihood of future permanent employment.

While such preliminary findings are not conclusive, they do raise important questions about the limits of existing initiatives as a means to improving the employment prospects of young blacks. The channelling of young blacks into dead end schemes, or at least ones which are less likely to result in permanent jobs, raises the problem of whether schemes which are supposed to challenge existing stereotypes and discrimination may not in fact be reinforcing existing inequalities. With levels of unemployment among young blacks in the 16–25 age group being between two or three times higher than unemployment among young whites in the same age group, the assumption that the placement of young blacks on training schemes represents a move towards equality of opportunity seems to be a tenuous argument.

## 'EQUALITY OF OPPORTUNITY' AND THE LIMITS OF REFORM

Perhaps the clearest conclusion to emerge from the above discussion is that successive governments, particularly through agencies such as the CRE and MSC, have publicly committed themselves to ensuring 'equality of opportunity' for young blacks, while doing little to challenge the structural basis of racism in the labour market. Governments have concentrated their energies on the public espousal of 'equality of opportunity', and politicians from both major political parties have warned about the dire consequences of allowing young blacks to drift into a subculture of 'alienation' and 'resistance' to the forces of law and order.[33] Even the present government, with its espousal of a capitalist free market ideology, has acknowledged that there is a need for measures to help disadvantaged groups within the black communities and that the 'government will play its part in preparing young people from the ethnic minorities for work'.[34]

Given this public commitment, however, it is equally clear that there is no firm evidence in support of the argument that government measures have actually helped young blacks achieve greater equality in the period of transition from school to work or more generally in society or in the labour market. Whether in terms of actual levels of unemployment or differential access to training courses for the young unemployed there is considerable evidence that indicates a pattern of continuing inequality and lack of progress over the last few years. A similarly disturbing conclusion has been suggested by a number of European studies of the children of migrant workers, which tend to support the argument that the structural inequalities suffered by the first generation are being reproduced for the second and third generations.[35]

Part of the problem is that the strategies pursued by successive governments to promote 'equality of opportunity' have been singularly unsuccessful in challenging the deeply entrenched patterns of racism and discrimination in employment, let alone developing more 'positive' avenues for black workers.[36] This has been recognised in a number of recent documents by the CRE, which has called for a strengthening of its powers through reform of the 1976 Race Relations Act.[37] In addition, however, another fundamental problem is that any measures taken by the CRE or the MSC can have little impact on the future of employment as such, which is determined more by the measures taken by the major departments of government, and particularly by the Department of Employment and the Treasury. Against this background, there are severe limits on the actual possibilities of achieving real equality of opportunity as opposed to symbolic gestures. As we have seen, report after report throughout the seventies and early eighties has talked rather loosely about equal opportunity as the basic objective of government initiatives for young blacks, as well as for race relations more generally. But even after this long period of debate, little clarity has been achieved in relation to this central notion.

The MSC's stance on equal opportunity reflects this confusion. The Commission upholds two principles in relation to ethnic minority groups. Firstly, it argues that its services are open to all groups regardless of colour or ethnic background. Secondly, it recognises that ethnic minorities may have particular labour market needs for which there needs to be special provision. These principles are significant in the sense that the Commission can use them to claim on the one hand that according to its own definition, it allows for equality of access to all, while on the other hand it explains the inequalities in practice according to the particular problems intrinsic to ethnic minorities. Young blacks, and older black workers, the Commission thus concludes, have to be helped to adjust to the realities of the labour market by special measures, which resemble the kind of provisions which are supposed to help the educationally disadvantaged black children in schools.[38]

A number of observations can be made about these conceptions of 'equality of access' and 'special provisions', but the most important relate to the systematic confusion surrounding the notion of 'equality of opportunity'. Terms like 'equal opportunity' or 'equal access' have become ideological charter words over the last decade, but their practical meaning tends to lack clarity. Do they mean the implementation of measures to ensure equality in the labour market for young blacks? Do they refer to measures for the recruitment of young blacks to training schemes? Or are promises of 'equal opportunity' symbolic gestures to alleviate a sensitive political problem, which will not achieve much in terms of equality in practice?

These questions have become more complicated when one looks at the broader political context of state interventions. Benyon has pointed out that the massive expansion of provisions for young blacks in the aftermath of the 1980–81 'riots' took the form of *ad hoc* panic measures aimed at preventing a recurrence of these events or, at the least, ensuring that the employment issue was depoliticised.[39] In practice, the main objective has been not to use 'training' to solve the unemployment problem, or increase 'equality of opportunity', but to move young blacks (and whites) off the streets and into an institutional context where they could more easily be controlled. Ideologically the provision of 'training' is seen as a way of ensuring 'equality of access', which is defined by the MSC as (a) the avoidance of discrimination on its training programmes and (b) the provision of help to black youth to overcome their 'special problems'. This is a limited definition, though, since both the MSC and the CRE have never made clear what the outcome of equal access to youth training schemes will be. In this context 'training' has become little more than what Edelman has called a symbolic political goal[40] and one which is shaped by, rather than itself transforming, the inequalities which produce high levels of black youth unemployment.

## SOCIAL POLICY, RACISM AND BLACK YOUTH IN THE 1980s

The previous discussion may seem a somewhat over-pessimistic assessment, though there are a number of reasons why such a dismal course of development can be predicted. Apart from the notable failure of the existing training programmes to have any major impact on levels of youth unemployment generally, there are several reasons for doubting the actual effects of initiatives aimed at providing young blacks with 'equality of opportunity'. The most important of these relate to the weakness of enforcement measures, the ambiguous nature of the concept of 'equality of opportunity', and the contradictory links between this concept and measures aimed essentially at preserving social stability and order.[41] The last factor has gained particular importance in the aftermath of the 1980–81 riots, and has effectively pushed government responses since then further along the road of seeing the black youth question as essentially one of social control.

This climate of opinion represents an important blockage in the way of effective action against institutionalised racialism as it affects young blacks. Although a whole array of measures are being undertaken or proposed in relation to issues such as 'equal opportunity', 'community policing' and 'urban renewal', the objectives underlying them usually remain vague or contain conflicting elements. In the aftermath of the Scarman Report there was some hope that the content of policies on race relations would become more explicit and that more effective mechanisms for bringing about greater quality in access to basic services and employment would be established. Hope was aroused among a large section of the black communities that more fundamental changes in their conditions were on the way. The available evidence on the implementation of policies is inconclusive, but the levels of black unemployment have remained high and there is little evidence to show that the youth training schemes are helping young blacks overcome the racism which prevails in the labour market. Moreover, there is at least some plausibility to the argument that the success of programmes such as YOP and YTS in helping black youngsters has been seen largely in quantitative rather than qualitative terms.[42]

In sum, the weakness of existing definitions and assumptions which have helped shape policy intervention in this area is that they have taken for granted a number of images of black youth which have tended to ignore the issue of racism and emphasised instead personal or communal handicaps. Far from being based on 'objective' analysis, the various stages of response discussed in this paper would seem to indicate the importance of common sense fears about 'race' in the construction of race policies. The symbolic evocation of the danger represented by young blacks has at best produced a series of contradictory responses and counter-responses, and at worst helped popularise images of young blacks which are negative. It shows though little sign of bringing about the kind of social reform necessary to improve the material conditions of young blacks.

This is partly because, as a number of authors have pointed out, there are severe limits on the impact of political intervention on structurally based patterns of inequality.[43] Furthermore, these limits result from the previous inability of successive governments to mount a concerted offensive against institutional discrimination given their underlying assumptions concerning the 'problems' faced by young blacks. At most, agencies such as the MSC have been able to promise to take account of the 'special needs' of the black unemployed, but they have been able to do little to mount a concerted challenge against the causes of racial inequality in employment. The promise held out by the setting up of the Scarman Enquiry of a national effort to bring about more 'equality of opportunity' for young blacks has thus fizzled out to such an extent that the CRE has now warned of a recurrence of the events of 1980–81.[44]

At the local level there have been some improvements in provision. The role of the Greater London Council and its coordinated reorganisation of training provisions through the Greater London Training Board is one example of initiatives at this level, though few authorities have either the resources or the political will to match the GLC in this respect. Although the GLC has been critical of the role of the MSC in relation to young blacks, as well as young women, it has attempted to develop existing provisions in directions which would enhance the equal participation of white and black trainees on the various MSC backed schemes, particularly YTS. In addition it has made racism the central issue, rather than the supposed cultural handicaps faced by young blacks.[45]

Such local initiatives notwithstanding, the national picture since 1981 gives little support to the idea that substantial changes have taken place. According to the CRE's assessment:

So far the response (to the Scarman report) by the Government and others has been disappointingly inadequate. It lacks the sense of urgency that runs through Lord Scarman's report in particular. Of course, it is more difficult in a time of recession, when unemployment is high and resources are scarce, for a massively expensive effort to be made. But it is precisely at such a time that the vulnerable sections of society suffer most, and even steps that require only a comparatively modest outlay are not being taken by the Government.[46]

This pattern of low level response has been criticised repeatedly by bodies such as the CRE and at a more political level by the Labour Party. Yet, as Layton-Henry argues in this volume, 'positive initiatives to assist racial minorities have been minimal and *ad hoc*, even after the most serious violence that any post-war British government has had to face outside Ulster'.[47] Moreover there seems little recognition of the complex ways in which more general policies pursued by the present government, e.g. on industry, urban redevelopment, employment and trade may be acting to the disadvantage of groups which are already in a weak position.

From the standpoint of the mid-eighties, it appears that promises concerning equal opportunity and 'special needs' have done very little to alter the social standing of young blacks. In the labour market the idea of 'training for jobs' has little real meaning in inner city areas where over half of young blacks are unemployed, with little or no likelihood of finding future employment. The failure to achieve reform and the emergence of political conflicts around the issue of racism reveal policy options that are severely limited and inherently contradictory.

Part of this contradiction is exemplified by the former Home Secretary, William Whitelaw, who argued that 'it is a deplorable reflection on our society that in all too many instances young people from the ethnic minorities find it harder to get work than their white colleagues with the same background and experience'. He nevertheless still felt inclined to emphasise the importance of a 'strong economy' in holding out hope for the future:

. . . people in the ethnic minorities stand to benefit particularly greatly from a strong economy. I believe that the best single thing we as a government can do for ethnic minorities in this country is to control inflation and create a climate where real jobs flourish and unemployment falls.[48]

Looked at in this way, any measures to provide 'special help' are likely to be subordinated to the overall objective of creating the conditions for a 'strong economy' and 'real jobs'. The chances too that the government will pursue what Lord Scarman has called 'an effective co-ordinated approach to tackling inner city problems' remains slim. This will not necessarily mean a recurrence of the events of 1980–81 during the late eighties, but the pursuit of a policy on training which means training for unemployment, and a strengthening of the police as a mechanism of social control which will not solve the problems faced by young blacks in employment or other areas. At best such measure may 'keep the streets clear and the young people quiet'.[49] The tensions and the political dilemmas will remain.

## CONCLUDING REMARKS

It is certainly difficult to predict the future course of development in an area which has proved to be rather difficult for successive governments to manage. The central assumptions which underlie current policies are based on the rather loose concepts of *equal opportunity* and *special needs*. As this paper has sought to show, however, these are concepts which have been interpreted in such a way as to suggest that access to jobs and training is unequal because of the cultural and personal characteristics of those who lose out in the competition for jobs. At a broader level this standpoint has been criticised for blaming those without work for being unable to find jobs, and so acting as a variation of social programmes that 'blame the victim':

> Governments who are reluctant to change the way in which the economy is run, and who lack policies for economic growth, naturally welcome the idea that what is at fault is not the socio-economic system but the individuals who are its victims. If we can tackle youth unemployment by retraining youth, and giving them illusive work experience, then why tamper with the existing mechanisms for distributing wealth and opportunities?[50]

This description relates to the general function of youth training programmes since the late 1970s. But it could be applied equally to the ways in which the issue of black youth unemployment has been managed. Though there is no shortage of expressions of concern for the plight of young blacks in the labour market, this has not been reflected in measures that tackle the economic, social and political processes that reproduce racial inequality. Rather measures have been limited to providing help in overcoming 'special problems' that are defined largely in cultural terms and general statements about 'equality of opportunity'. Such measures are unlikely to have much impact on patterns of discrimination against young blacks in the labour market, particularly when set against the background of government policies which do not aim to reduce overall levels of unemployment but aim rather to create 'real jobs'.[51].

Because black youth unemployment highlights social inequalities that are a profound source of anxiety for both the state and the black communities, it is likely to remain a central issue on the race relations agenda and to attract attention from both the media and political actors. Given the history of recent measures aimed at providing young blacks with greater equality of opportunity, there is little reason to hope for drastic changes in the current situation. Rhetorical promises and symbolic actions can do little to overcome entrenched patterns of racial inequality, without accompanying measures which change the structural bases of racism at work and in society as a whole. In this sense the best hope for any radical change in the position of young blacks may lie in the development of political initiatives that challenge the roots of racism rather than policies which ameliorate the situation without actual change in the conditions which give rise to the underlying problems.[52]

Whether such measures are likely to be undertaken in the context of the current political–ideological climate remains to be seen, and the experience of the last decade does not give much room for optimism. On the contrary, the publication of the recent White Paper on *Employment – the Challenge to the Nation* seems to signal a firm commitment by the present government to the principles of the 'free market' which takes little or no account of the impact of racial discrimination in the labour market. The underlying philosophy of the White Paper is that the role of political intervention in the labour market must be to remove any obstacles to its efficient functioning. Within this philosophy there seems to be little room for any concerted action against racism and discrimination in the labour market.[53]

Against this background, the prospects of decisive political intervention to produce more equality in the field of employment, or other areas, remains only a distant possibility. In this context it is more plausible to see initiatives for young unemployed blacks as 'training for unemployment'. If this is the case, however, they are likely to produce their own political reactions, and on a scale perhaps greater than that experienced during the riots of 1980 and 1981. This is the main reason why the question of youth will remain a central aspect of the race relations agenda for some time to come.

## NOTES

1. This issue is discussed from various angles in B. Troyna and D. Smith (eds), *Racism, School and the Labour Market* (National Youth Bureau, 1983).
2. A fuller discussion of the relationship between youth unemployment and law and order issues is to be found in J. Benyon (ed.), *Scarman and After* (Pergamon, 1984) pp.163ff.
3. M. Edelman, *Politics as Symbolic Action: Mass Arousal and Quiescence* (Chicago University Press, 1972) ch. 1.
4. M. Edelman, *Political Language: Words that Succeed and Policies that Fail* (Academic Press, 1977) p.16.
5. M. Edelman, *Politics as Symbolic Action*, op. cit., pp.23ff.
6. For a fuller discussion of the 'social time bomb' image over time see: G. Fisher and H. Joshua, 'Black Youth and Social Policy', in E. Cashmore and B. Troyna (eds), *Black Youth in Crisis* (Allen & Unwin, 1982) pp.129–42.
7. A. H. Halsey, 'Race Relations: The Lines to Think On', *New Society* (19 Mar. 1970) pp.472–4.
8. Department of Education and Science, *Immigrants and the Youth Service* (DES, 1967); Select Committee on Race Relations and Immigration, *The Problems of Coloured School Leavers* (HMSO, 1969).
9. Community Relations Commission, *Unemployment and Homelessness* (CRC, 1974).
10. An elaboration of this point can be found in my paper on 'Black Youth Unemployment and Equal Opportunities Policies', in B. Troyna and D. Smith (eds), *Racism, School and the Labour Market*, op. cit., pp.46–60.
11. The recurrence of these images in debates throughout the sixties and seventies is analysed in some detail, and from rather different perspectives, in: G. John, *In the Service of Black Youth* (National Association of Youth Clubs, 1981); G. Gaskell and P. Smith, *Race and 'Alienated' Youth: a Conceptual and Empirical Enquiry* (London School of Economics and Political Science: Department of Psychology, 1981); S. Field, *The Attitudes of Ethnic Minorities* (HMSO, 1984).
12. Home Affairs Committee, Sub-Committee on Race Relations and Immigration, *Racial Disadvantage* (HMSO, 1981).

13. A comparative and conceptual discussion of these notions can be found in R. P. Lowry, *Social Problems* (D.C. Heath, 1974); W. Ryan, *Blaming the Victim* (Vintage Books, 1978).

14. G. John, *In the Service of Black Youth*, op. cit., p.155.

15. A full discussion of the development of official ideologies about young blacks can be found in my paper 'Problems, But Whose Problems?: the Social Construction of Black Youth Unemployment and State Policies', *Journal of Social Policy* (forthcoming).

16. The distinction between a 'pathology of individuals' and a 'pathology of institutions' is derived from Edelman, *Political Language*, op. cit., pp.9–10.

17. A discussion of some of these assumptions, drawing largely on evidence from the late 1970s, can be found in E. Lawrence, 'Just plain common sense: the "roots" of racism' in CCCS Race and Politics Group, *The Empire Strikes Back: Race and Racism in 70s Britain* (Hutchinson, 1982) pp.47–94.

18. Commission for Racial Equality, *Youth in Multi-Racial Society* (CRE, 1980) p.10.

19. Solomos, 'Black Youth Unemployment and Equal Opportunities Policies', op. cit., pp.56–8.

20. Manpower Services Commission, London Regional Office, *London Employment Review 1982* (MSC, 1982) pp.25–6.

21. An overview of these shifts can be found in J. Benyon (ed.), *Scarman and After*, op. cit., pp.3ff.

22. Clear statements of this position can be found in: 'Community Relations Commission, *Unemployment and Homelessness* (1974) and Commission for Racial Equality, *Youth in Multi-Racial Society* (1980). A critique of the basic arguments can be found in G. Fisher and H. Joshua, 'Black Youth and Social Policy', in E. Cashmore and B. Troyna (eds), *Black Youth in Crisis*, op. cit., pp.136–42.

23. A fuller discussion of this ideology can be found in J. Solomos, 'Problems, But Whose Problems?: the Social Construction of Black Youth Unemployment and State Policies', op. cit., *passim*.

24. A discussion of the influence of this approach in relation to education can be found in B. Troyna, 'Multicultural Education: emancipation or containment?' in L. Barton and S. Walker (eds), *Social Crisis and Educational Research* (Croom Helm, 1984) pp.75–97.

25. Commission for Racial Equality, *Youth in Multi-Racial Society*, op. cit., pp.58–9.

26. A description of these activities is beyond the scope of this paper, but the CRE's *Employment Report* provides a regular list of the Commission's initiatives in this field, which have shown a marked increase in the post-1981 period.

27. Manpower Services Commission and Commission for Racial Equality, *Ethnic Minorities and the Special Programmes for the Unemployed* (Manpower Services Commission, 1979) pp.5–7.

28. Manpower Services Commission, *Corporate Plan 1982–86* (Manpower Services Commission, 1982) p.16.

29. Manpower Services Commission, *Corporate Plan 1983–87* (Manpower Services Commission, 1983) p.30.

30. Manpower Services Commission, 'Equal Opportunities for Ethnic Minorities, Unpublished Document from Special Groups Branch, Training Division, p.1.

31. S. Fenton *et al.*, *Ethnic Minorities and the Youth Training Scheme*, Research and Development Paper No.20 (Manpower Services Commission, 1984). R. Means *et al.*, 'Implementation of Social Goals in Labour Market Policy: the Case of Black Youth, Equal Opportunities and the Youth Training Scheme', *Policy and Politics*, 13, 1 (1985) pp.72–83.
32. S. Fenton *et al.*, *Ethnic Minorities and the Youth Training Scheme*, op. cit., pp.10–12.
33. A discussion of this point can be found in R. Jenkins and J. Solomos (eds), *Race and Equal Opportunities in the 1980s* (Cambridge University Press, forthcoming).
34. W. Whitelaw, 'Speech to the Birmingham Community Relations Council', 11 July 1980, p.3.
35. See S. Castles, *Here for Good: Western Europe's New Ethnic Minorities* (Pluto Press, 1984).
36. R. Jenkins and J. Solomos (eds), *Race and Equal Opportunities in the 1980s*, op. cit., concluding chapter.
37. Commission for Racial Equality, *The Race Relations Act 1976 – Time for a Change?* (CRE, 1983).
38. See J. Williams, *From Institutional Racism to Anti-Racism: the Relationships between Theories, Policies and Practices*, unpublished MSc Thesis, University of Aston, 1984.
39. J. Benyon, 'Unemployment, racial disadvantage and the cities', in J. Benyon (ed.), *Scarman and After*, op. cit., pp.163–83.
40. M. Edelman, op. cit., *Political Language*, pp.10–11.
41. D. Dunn, 'Black Youth, the Youth Training Scheme and the Choice at 16', *Multiracial Education*, 11, 3 (1983) pp.7–22.
42. R. Means *et al.*, 'Implementation of Social Goals in Labour Market Policy', op. cit., pp.80–3.
43. C. Offe, *Contradictions of the Welfare State* (Hutchinson, 1984), provides a balanced overview of some of the most important debates on this question.
44. Commission for Racial Equality, *Annual Report for 1983* (CRE, 1984) pp.3–4.
45. Greater London Training Board, *GLC – Training for Jobs* (GLC, 1984). The full implications of the GLC's initiatives in this field have still to be studied, so it is quite difficult to assess the actual changes which they have helped to bring about. An assessment from the GLC itself can be found in a report called *On the Road to Equality* (GLC, 1984).
46. Commission for Racial Equality, *Annual Report for 1982* (CRE, 1983) p.3.
47. See Chapter 3 in this volume.
48. W. Whitelaw, 'Speech to the Birmingham Community Relations Council', op. cit., p.3.
49. K. Roberts, 'Youth Unemployment and Urban Unrest', in J. Benyon (ed.), *Scarman and After*, op. cit., p.183.
50. M. Loney, 'The Youth Opportunities Programme: Requiem and Rebirth', in R. Fiddy (ed.), *In Place of Work* (Falmer Press, 1983) p.30.
51. An overview and critique of post-1979 employment policies can be found in J. Fairley and J. Grahl, 'Conservative Training Policy and the Alternatives', *Socialist Economic Review 1983* (Merlin Press, 1983) pp.137–53.
52. An early and clear argument along these lines can be found in S. Hall *et al.*, *Policing the Crisis* (Macmillan, 1978) pp.327ff.

53. Department of Employment, *Employment – the Challenge to the Nation*, Cmnd 9474 (HMSO, 1985).

# 9  Spiral of Decline: Race and Policing[1]

## JOHN BENYON

The riots in 1980 and 1981 provoked a variety of explanations. It was claimed that they were the result of criminality, lack of parental guidance or indeed 'seditious, sociological claptrap that is passed on in our schools as education'.[2] Others identified social and economic deprivation as the prime cause, particularly escalating youth unemployment, abysmally inadequate housing, unacceptably low levels of social service provision and decay in central areas.[3] A number of politicians, police officers and news media put forward the conspiracy theory; for example the Commissioner of the Metropolitan Police, Sir David McNee, told journalists

> We have unconfirmed reports that what you have seen tonight was not spontaneous but has been orchestrated and very well planned.[4]

The idea that agitators and subversives are to blame for the thoroughly 'un-British' behaviour of rioting has frequently been used to explain disorders.[5] For example, a story in *The Times* of 6 August 1919, entitled 'Plot Financed from Abroad' stated that 'the authorities' believed the Liverpool riots were 'part of a definite conspiracy, which had its roots abroad, to subvert the present system of government'. This approach was echoed in 1981 under headlines such as those in the *Daily Mail*, 'Search for the Masked Men' (7 July 1981) and 'Extremists' Master Plan for Chaos' (10 July 1981), and the *New Standard* 'Four Behind the Riots' (10 July 1981).

The suggestion that four motorcyclists were going round Britain, like the Riders of the Apocalypse, causing disorder and chaos was clearly absurd, but nevertheless the conspiracy theory was often invoked in the aftermath of the riots. Lord Scarman, though, was in no doubt that the disorders in Brixton 'originated spontaneously. There was no premeditation or plan'.[6] He agreed with those who believed deprivation and disadvantage were factors giving rise to 'a set of social *conditions* which create a predisposition towards violent protest' but he stressed that the riots were precipitated by police action.

## RESENTMENT AGAINST THE POLICE

It was commonly argued that police behaviour was the principle factor which had created the *potential* for disorder and also triggered *actual* rioting, although viewing it as *the* cause of the disorders is too simplistic, for the context of social deprivation and disadvantage, and especially the very high levels of unemployment, seems to have been a key factor.[7] However, policing was perceived as a major grievance, especially by young black people living in the areas where the riots occurred. In Brixton, Lord Scarman seems to have been genuinely shocked at the indignant and resentful attitude of the young towards the police.[8]

In 1976, at the Notting Hill Carnival, another major confrontation had taken place between young people, primarily black, and the police. The district police station was besieged, 95 police officers were injured and other serious disturbances occurred. The police argued that crimes were being committed at the Carnival and according to Sir Robert Mark, the Metropolitan Commissioner, 'crime is not negotiable as far as we are concerned. If there is a crime we will decide how to deal with it'.[9] The Carnival Committee on the other hand suggested that police numbers were provocative, while black youths complained of harassment. According to the Community Relations Council events at the 1976 Notting Hill Carnival showed that relationships between young West Indians and the police

> have broken down to such a degree that mutual distrust, suspicion and antagonism lead to the formation of battle lines so that sometimes trivial incidents quickly escalate into open hostilities.[10]

Similar views were expressed about the St. Paul's district of

Bristol in which a major disorder occurred on 2 April 1980.[11] Here, as in Brixton almost exactly a year later, a confrontation between police officers and local young people led to the riots. In 1981, in Liverpool 8 it was claimed that 'everyone on the streets had a personal grudge against the police'[12] and in Moss Side, Manchester, where serious disorder began on 8 July 1981, a large crowd attacked the district police station. A reporter, Michael Nally, who was present during this riot was in no doubt that the youths were on the streets 'to protest against alleged harassment and ill-treatment by the police'. One youth put forward the views of many:

> I'm here to see the pigs get theirs. They've done this for years. Now they know what it's like to be hit back.[13]

The participants in the 1981 disorders were both black and white, despite media assertions to the contrary. Almost 4000 people were arrested during the disorders in July and of the 3704 for whom data are available, 766 were described as 'West Indian/African', 180 as 'Asian' and 292 as 'other or not recorded'; some 2466 or 67%, were described as 'white'. These figures varied from area to area; while in Toxteth and Moss Side the proportion of those arrested who were 'non-white' was about a third, in Southall and Brixton it was around two-thirds. Nearly seven out of ten of those arrested were under twenty-one years of age.[14]

The poor relations between police and young black people in certain areas has been highlighted in a number of studies.[15] In particular, friction has occurred between police officers and young blacks on the streets, where powers to stop and search people and to arrest individuals 'on suspicion' have been employed. Section 4 of the Vagrancy Act 1824 enabled police officers in London, and in some other large cities such as Manchester and Liverpool, to arrest and charge someone with being a suspected person loitering with intent to commit an arrestable offence. The burden of proof on the police was very low and not only was it *not* necessary to produce the potential victim of the alleged crime or a witness but, indeed, this was rarely done. It was claimed, and widely believed, that police officers abused the legislation and used it to keep young black people off the streets; according to George Greaves, Principal Community Relations Officer in Lambeth:

> So apprehensive had some parents become that their children

might be charged as suspected persons that they either kept them indoors, particularly after dark, or arranged for them to be escorted by an adult if they had to be out.[16]

A detailed study of the 'sus' law found that of the 2112 people arrested in London in 1976 under this legislation, 42% were black – a strikingly high figure.[17] A Home Office Research Study revealed that a black person was *fifteen times* more likely to be arrested for 'sus' than a white person.[18] The growing discontent with this position led the Home Affairs Select Committee in 1980 unanimously to recommend repeal of the legislation[19] and this was put into effect by the Criminal Attempts Act 1981.

## THE SUBSTANTIAL COST OF STOPS AND SEARCHES

General stop and search powers have in the past been provided for certain police forces such as those in London, Merseyside and the West Midlands, and all constables in England and Wales have now been given the power to stop and search a person or a vehicle for stolen or prohibited articles as long as they have 'reasonable grounds for suspicion'. These extended powers are provided in sections 1–3 of the Police and Criminal Evidence Act 1984, which came into effect on 1 January 1986.

There is considerable evidence that stop and search powers are disproportionately applied to young people, men and Afro-Caribbeans. In Liverpool it was reported that the powers were being increasingly used, and were causing friction between young people and the police, and data from Birmingham and Manchester showed high stop rates among young and Afro-Caribbean people.[20] Carole Willis' study in 1982 of four police stations also found that the stop rates for black people were far higher than for the population as a whole, and in Kensington the stop rate for black males aged between 16 and 24 was three times that for all males in this age group. Willis also reported that the recorded statistics underestimate the number of stops by about 50%.[21]

The most detailed data comes from the Policy Studies Institute (PSI) study of the Metropolitan Police.[22] They show clearly that the chances of being stopped by the police vary considerably according to age, sex, ethnic group and use of a vehicle. Young black people are likely to be stopped *repeatedly*, and have a far higher chance of being stopped on foot than young whites: 45% of West Indians aged 15–24 had been stopped during the previous year compared to 18% of white people in the same age group. The data showed that Afro-Caribbean people were 'markedly less happy' than white or Asian people with the behaviour of the police who stopped them, and this was particularly evident amongst young blacks.

The findings suggest that the Metropolitan Police make about one-and-a-half million stops every year, and these result in about 75 000 people being reported for offences (usually traffic violations), and a further 45 000 individuals being arrested and charged. Overall the study found that 8% of stops produce a 'result', and this proportion is the same for each ethnic group. The researchers report that:

> the cost of the present policy, in terms of the relationship between the police and certain sections of the public, is shown to be substantial, and most stops are wasted effort, if they are seen as purely an attempt to detect crime. The findings therefore suggest that the police should look for other more efficient and less damaging methods of crime detection to replace those stops that are currently carried out for no very specific reason: it may be significant, in this connection, that in some other parts of the country the clear-up rate is higher than in London although many fewer stops are carried out.[23]

The validity of these remarks was demonstrated by the infamous operation, known within the police as *Swamp '81*, which was taking place at the time of the Brixton riots. The purpose of this operation was to detect and arrest burglars and robbers on the streets of Lambeth. One hundred and twelve officers were involved and the strategy was to 'flood' particular areas with police who would make extensive use of the stop and search powers. During the course of *Operation Swamp*, from 6 April to 11 April 1981, 943 stops were made. Over two-thirds of the people stopped were aged under 21, and over half were black. The police arrested 118 people and charged 75, but these charges included only 1 for robbery, 1 for attempted burglary and 20 for theft or attempted theft.

As critics have pointed out, judged by its own aims – 'to arrest burglars and robbers' – the operation was not a resounding success and it inconvenienced over 850 innocent people. Lord Scarman reported that *Swamp '81* was a factor which contributed to the great increase in tension' in Brixton and, in short, it was 'a serious mistake'.[24]

## VARIATIONS IN RATES OF ARREST OF ETHNIC GROUPS

Black people, especially those who are male and young, are also *arrested* in disproportionate numbers, according to the available evidence. Stevens and Willis reported that the arrest rate for Afro-Caribbean people, in Metropolitan Police divisions in 1975, was higher than that for whites and Asians for *every* category of offence. The arrest rates for *assault* were found to be 466 per 100 000 population for Afro-Caribbeans, 124 for Asians and 77 for whites; for *robbery* they were 160 per 100 000 for Afro-Caribbeans, 13 for Asians and 18 for whites; and for '*other violent theft*' they were 60 for Afro-Caribbeans, 4 for Asians and 4 for whites.[25]

Stevens and Willis suggested a number of explanations for the variation in arrest rates not accounted for by socioeconomic and demographic variables. *Intrinsic* factors may include forms of social deprivation and disadvantage which were not examined, and different tendencies to take part in crime. *Extrinsic* features entail the differential enforcement of the law or, put another way, a higher likelihood that black people will be picked up (rightly or wrongly) by the police. This may be because they are more likely to frequent places where arrests occur, or because the police concentrate on certain areas, types of offence and on particular sorts of people. Indeed it was found that blacks were the group most likely to be arrested for 'sus' and for 'other violent theft' (mostly snatches of wallets and handbags causing no injury) where, the researchers stated, 'there is considerable scope for selective perception'. The study suggests that police bias is quite plausibly a factor in the disproportionately high arrest rates among black people.

The PSI study of the Metropolitan Police also found that Afro-Caribbean people were far more likely to be arrested than those from other ethnic groups. In the survey of Londoners, 15% of black men reported they had been arrested during the last five years, compared with 10% of white males. Whereas 11% of 15–24 year old whites had been arrested, the corresponding figure for Afro-Caribbeans was 17%.[26] The figures from the survey of police officers matched closely, with officers describing the last person arrested as Afro-Caribbean (Identcode 3) in 17% of cases, although they constitute only about 6% of the London population.[27]

The authors of the PSI study suggest reasons similar to those put forward by Stevens and Willis, and indeed to those advanced by the Metropolitan Police itself in evidence to the 1976–77 inquiry by the Select Committee on Race Relations.[28] Scotland Yard's statistics revealed that in 1975, 12% of those arrested for indictable crime were Afro-Caribbean. The Metropolitan Police considered that this proved a disproportionate involvement in crime, and to reinforce their case they produced statistics based on victims' descriptions of their assailants. The police figures showed that 28% of those arrested for robbery were 'West Indian/African', and 32% of *identified* attackers were described as 'coloured'; similarly, of the total arrests for violent thefts, 37% were 'West Indian/African' and 41% of *identified* thieves were 'coloured'. Nevertheless, the Metropolitan Police were quite content to accept deprivationist and demographic explanations, as long as the Select Committee was made aware of the 'problem' of black crime.

However, the Community Relations Commission subjected Scotland Yard's data, and their interpretation, to considerable criticism, and in this they were powerfully supported by Professor Terence Morris of the University of London. He noted eight points of particular interest:

(1) The arrest rate of 12% for Afro-Caribbeans was entirely consistent with social class variables, so race as a factor could be spurious.
(2) He criticised the equation of arrests with crimes, suggesting that in many respects the number of arrests of black people is likely to be a poor index of the proportion of crimes committed by them.
(3) There was no data produced by Scotland Yard to refute the view that the high arrest rate of Afro-Caribbeans was at least partly a result of discrimination by the police.
(4) He suggested that serious and trivial offences might have been grouped together, and the figures may have been affected by the deployment of police manpower in respect of petty incidents and minor infringements – in short, police discretion was a significant factor.
(5) He expressed surprise at the exclusion of data comparing black and non-black arrest rates for certain offences.
(6) He pointed out that police methods can affect the arrest rates

for some groups in particular areas, if there is a concentrated police presence.

(7) Another criticism concerned the reports of victims describing their assailants: Morris suggested that it would be unwise to rely on these data as the circumstances of the particular offences of robbery and violent theft mean that identification is difficult and there are problems of selective perceptions.

(8) He argued that the presentation and manipulation of the data was 'to say the least perplexing' and in some respects 'seriously defective'.[29]

## POLICING, CRIME AND YOUNG BLACK PEOPLE

The arguments put forward by Morris and the Community Relations Commission persuaded the Select Committee that there was no evidence available to justify any firm conclusions about the relative involvement of West Indians in crime, which was rather less definitive than the Committee's conclusion in 1972 that 'the West Indian crime rate is much the same as that of the indigenous population'.[30] The 1971–72 Select Committee inquiry received the views of many senior police officers in the Metropolitan Police District and elsewhere in England, which were that crime rates among 'immigrant groups' were no higher, and in some cases were lower, than among white people, but by March 1976, in the later Select Committee inquiry, the Metropolitan Police took a rather different stance, as cited earlier. This has prompted authors such as John Lea and Jock Young to ask what happened between 1971 and 1976 to alter the police position.[31] They pointed out that if, as claimed by many, the disproportionately high level of arrests of young blacks shown in the 1975 figures was a result of police discrimination, it seems rather implausible to suggest that this was not also occurring in 1971.

Lea and Young strongly criticise both those who claim that the higher arrest rate for young blacks is a result of police prejudice, and those who consider that it reflects the greater number of crimes committed by them. They emphasise the need to see the interconnection between these two views and to appreciate three related factors. Firstly, the crime rate for black people *is* disproportionately high as a result of deprivation, unemployment and discrimination. An important point, they believe, is the development of cultural conditions which sanction certain kinds of crime, thus accounting for the difference between the levels of crime committed by young Afro-Caribbeans and young Asians. Secondly, at least partly because of racial prejudice, the police respond *readily* to the rise in black crime levels. For the ordinary police officer the deprivationist arguments put forward by senior staff are of no consequence; race is seen as a cause of crime. Thirdly, the two processes reinforce one another leading to 'deviancy amplification'. Rising black crime rates and the increasing police action taken against young blacks therefore become part of a vicious circle.

To some extent it would seem that Lea and Young are over-simplifying the targets of their attack. While it is true that a few writers, such as Bridges and Gilroy,[32] have appeared to argue that the higher black crime figures are *simply* the result of police prejudice, most analysts accept that a significant number of certain types of crime involve Afro-Caribbean young people. As Stuart Hall and his fellow authors stated in 1978 about areas in some British cities:

> Black youth are clearly involved in some petty and street crime in these areas, and the proportion involved may well be higher than it was a decade earlier. Black community and social workers in these areas believe this to be the case, an impression more reliable than the figures.[33]

In these 'crime-prone' areas, unemployment is high, housing is poor, much of the population is young, and there are few opportunities for overcoming the widespread social and economic deprivation. Changes in consciousness, ideology and culture have led to less acquiescence amongst some young black people living in the 'urban colonies', and many of them have chosen separateness rather than incorporation. Inter-generational conflict has resulted in some young people leaving home, but with few if any employment opportunities, and 'colony life' has offered the possibility of alternative means of survival, such as 'hustling'. Hall and his co-authors make it plain that, though understandable and unsurprising, the resort to crime by young people is divisive and, if violence is used, this is disabling and degrading. *Race Today* expressed a similar view:

> We are uncompromisingly against mugging. We see the mugging

activity as a manifestation of powerlessness, a consequence of being without a wage.[34]

## ALIENS AND CRIME: A 'MORAL PANIC'

In law, no such offence as 'mugging' exists, but during the early 1970s, and intermittently since, the news media, spurred on by certain politicians, judges and police officers, devoted considerable attention to crimes which have been popularly described by this term. Different people and groups use it to include various crimes. In 1976, for example, in answer to the question 'how many incidents of mugging have been reported . . .?', a Home Office minister referred to the 4452 cases of robbery in London during 1975.[35] However, robbery includes a number of crimes which would not normally be regarded as 'mugging' – such as robbery from banks and business premises.

Street robbery is not, of course, a new crime and, as the Metropolitan Police Commissioner stated in 1964, 'London has always been the scene of robberies from further back than the days of highwaymen and footpads'.[36] One hundred years earlier, in the winter of 1862–63, 'garotting' was a new name given to an old crime and it 'created something like a reign of terror'. *The Times* commented that it was 'un-British', 'of foreign importation', and no doubt the result of aliens. The garotters' behaviour, said *The Times*, resembled that of the 'Indian "thuggee" '.[37]

The idea that an alien intrusion is causing crime and disorder has commonly been invoked by the media and politicians. As mentioned earlier, 'aliens' and 'agitators' are invariably blamed if 'un-British' behaviour such as rioting occurs, and yet evidence for such 'intruders' is seldom if ever produced. In its issue of 17 August 1972, the *Daily Mirror* introduced the country to a 'new' crime which was alien and un-British: 'As crimes of violence escalate, a word common in the United States enters the British headlines: MUGGING. To our police it's a frightening new strain of crime.' During the next twelve months a 'moral panic'[38] occurred over 'mugging', with frequent media reports, speeches by politicians, police officers and other opinion leaders, and several prominent court cases.

Many of the incidents which were reported involved neither robbery nor violence, but theft such as pickpocketing. Although white youths were involved in a number of the cases, the predominant impression given in the media was that the perpetrators were black. This occurred in three ways: firstly, when the locations of street crime were reported, invariably stress was laid on the inner-city areas where black people lived; secondly, discussions of the American experience related 'mugging' to blacks and ghettos; finally, the association was made explicit either by victims' descriptions of their assailants or by the identification of people arrested and prosecuted. The 'alien' form of this 'un-British' behaviour was thus two-fold: it was an American import and it was perpetrated by 'coloured immigrants'.

The 'mugging' panic reappeared in early 1975 after crime figures were released by Scotland Yard. In a piece entitled 'Danger signals from the streets of Lambeth', Derek Humphry wrote in the *Sunday Times* that 'soaring street crime' was a result of the 'widespread alienation of West Indian youngsters from white society'.[39] The Metropolitan Police figures were based on victims' descriptions of their assailants: 79% of the robberies, and 83% of offences of theft from the person, were alleged to have been committed by black people. However, it was later discovered that the *total* number of offences upon which the robberies statistic was based was only 111, while that for theft from the person offences was 324.[40] The study was based on Brixton but the media largely ignored this context with stories such as those in *The Times*: 'mugging . . . [is] . . . increasing in South London . . . [and] . . . 80 per cent of the attackers are black', in the *Evening News*: '80 per cent of London's muggers are black' and in the *Sunday Express*: 'in a large part of the city 80 per cent of the muggers are black'.[41]

The release of the 'black crime' figures led to an increased focus on race, crime and policing. In May 1975, sentencing five black youths, a judge commented:

> Within memory these areas were peaceful, safe and agreeable to live in. But the immigrant resettlement which has occurred over the past 25 years has radically transformed that environment. Those concerned with the maintenance of law and order are confronted with immense difficulties.[42]

RACE, CRIME AND POLICING 'GO OUT OF COURT'

On 13 October 1976, Peckham police released a press statement prepared by Scotland Yard which detailed street crimes in the area and made reference to a large rise in 'muggings' carried out by black people, usually on white victims. The Home Office had by now attempted to offer a definition of 'mugging' as 'an offence of robbery of personal property which follows a sudden attack in the open where there is no previous association between the victim and the assailant',[43] and on this basis Sir Robert Mark estimated that in 1974, of the 4452 cases of robbery in London, 1977 fell into the 'mugging' category. The Peckham figures, however, seemed to include robberies and theft from the person; they were duly reported sensationally in the press as 'mugging' even though the total arrest figure upon which some of the statistics were based was just 55.

It is clear that the Metropolitan Police statistics provide a dubious basis for relating race and crime. However, if the figures are simply a result of police activity and prejudice, how can the changes in police attitudes between the Select Committee inquiries of 1971–72 and 1976–77 be explained? When one examines the evidence presented to the earlier inquiry three points emerge which may help to answer the question. Firstly, in 1971 statistics on the race of people arrested were generally not kept by police forces and, indeed 1975 was the first year for which 'identcoded' arrest figures were made available. Thus, few meaningful comparisons can be made with the crime data reported to the Select Committee inquiry in 1976–77. Secondly, in those areas where evidence was available *in 1971–72*, arrest and charge figures often *did* tend to show that Afro-Caribbean people were arrested in disproportionately high numbers for certain offences. At Notting Hill police station, over 15% of the people charged with crime were 'coloured persons'. In Wandsworth, 62% of the 135 cases of theft from the person were 'attributable to coloured youths' in 1971, and in Moss Side it was 'estimated' that 75% of crimes of violence, robbery and thefts from the person were committed by 'coloured persons against white persons'. Thirdly, the views of a number of police officers differed from the orthodox opinions of the senior staff. The Committee itself reported:

There seems to be a fairly widespread feeling, shared, as we found in informal discussion, by some police officers, that immigrants commit more crime than the indigenous population.[44]

Maureen Cain found that many policemen considered that 'niggers' were 'in the main . . . pimps and layabouts, living off what we pay in taxes'[45] and some years earlier, in 1966, Joseph Hunte produced a report for the West Indian Standing Conference which alleged racial abuse, harassment and brutality by the police and a general suspicion amongst police officers that black people were criminals. The title of Hunte's report was *Nigger-Hunting in England?*, because, it was said, police officers leaving their stations were heard saying they were going 'nigger-hunting'.[46]

Furthermore, changes had occurred by 1976 which may explain why senior police officers painted a much gloomier picture of race, crime and policing then, than in 1972. For example, by 1975–76 there were more young black people between 13 and 17 years of age – the age group which, according to the Metropolitan Police, was the most prone to commit street crimes.[47] If the same *proportion* of young black people had offended in 1975 as in 1971 there would have been an increase in the *number* of street crimes as the total number of young blacks had increased. In addition, as unemployment rates had increased during this period, particularly in inner urban areas where many young black people lived, it seems plausible to suppose that this may have been related to an increase in the number of young black people who committed offences.

Besides an actual change in the number of offences committed by Afro-Caribbean people, there seem to be four other possible explanations for the change in senior officers' views between 1972 and 1976–77. Firstly, police stereotyping and prejudice may have increased during the period, leading to a greater number of arrests of Afro-Caribbeans in 1975 than in 1971. Secondly, senior police officers may have become persuaded of the extent of black crime by junior officers so that by 1976–77 they were reflecting the views held earlier by constables and sergeants. Thirdly, senior officers, concerned at the amount of criticism about harassment of black people, may have sought to defend their actions, especially their use of stop and search powers and 'sus' charges, by arguing that the involvement of Afro-Caribbeans in crime justified them. Fourthly, there may have been a general change in public and elite opinion.

Perhaps each of these factors played a part in the decision by Scotland Yard to highlight black crime as a 'growing problem'. In

Bulpitt's terms this marked a move away from the liberal language of analysis which characterised the London-oriented Political Establishment. This change in public stance by the police coincides with the period from 1976 onwards when, argues Bulpitt, important aspects of race relations tended to go 'out of Court'.[48] Before this, using an analysis based on the notion of a Centre–Periphery or Court–Country power configuration, the Centre's statecraft had reasonably successfully managed race and politics in Britain. The liberal language of analysis which emanated from the London-based Establishment (the Centre or Court) was predominant amongst politicians, bureaucrats, certain of the quality media and leaders of key institutions such as the police. This liberal approach, generally optimistic about race relations and keen to play down difficulties, was much in evidence in the proceedings of the 1971–72 Select Committee inquiry, and is illustrated by the final words of its report:

> If the best examples of leadership in police and immigrant relations prevailed throughout forces in the United Kingdom, many of the difficulties we have dwelt upon would, within a reasonable space of time, diminish. In some places they could wither away.[49]

The Committee stressed the need for education and patience and the whole tone of their report, and of their investigations, reflected the Establishment's political approach, which was generally a call for tolerance and understanding, a hope that race relations would improve and an aspiration to keep race off the main political agenda.

However, by 1976–77 race was firmly on the agenda under the general headings of crime, law and order and policing, largely placed there by the media and the 'moral panic' over 'mugging', and by the police themselves. The Centre was confronted with a position in which:

> important aspects of the issue tended to go out of Court: increasingly race politics occurred outside the limited confines of Westminster and Whitehall. In other words, the Periphery's traditionally passive role of responding to Centre initiatives declined.[50]

## 'A CRUDE EQUATION BETWEEN CRIME AND BLACK PEOPLE'

Between January 1978 and September 1980 special operations against crime on the streets of Lambeth were organised on four occasions using the Special Patrol Group. Although, according to evidence presented to Lord Scarman by the Metropolitan Police, serious offences in Lambeth and in Brixton increased between 1976 and 1980 by 13%, which was 2% *lower* than the increase for the Metropolitan Police District as a whole. At the same time, the increase in offences of robbery and other violent theft was claimed to be 138% in Brixton compared with 38% for the London area.[51] How could it be that serious offences in general rose at a *lower* rate than elsewhere, but robbery and other violent theft, which includes those crimes called 'mugging', rose at a much *higher* rate than across the whole Metropolitan Police District?

One possible answer is that a vicious circle, similar to that which Lea and Young identified, was at work; some rise in these crimes led to increasing public concern, which focussed police attention on particular areas, offences and stereotypes, namely 'young black criminals'. As Mannheim pointed out:

> Police statistics reflect the activities of the police at any given time and place and are, therefore, greatly dependent on the interest taken by the police in a certain type of crime or certain classes of persons.[52]

This sort of police attention and activity could have led to more crimes being reported. Another possibility is that police in Brixton were categorising offences differently than police elsewhere; for example crimes which in another area would have been classified as 'theft' might in Brixton have been termed 'violent theft'. A careful analysis of the figures convinced Blom-Cooper and Drabble that this was indeed happening. They found that while the rate for robbery and violent theft was *higher*, the rate for 'other theft and handling stolen goods' was *lower* in Brixton than in the Metropolitan Police District as a whole.[53]

As a result of their statistics, the reliability of which can be seen to be suspect, the police in Brixton saturated the area on a number of occasions, and conducted frequent stops and searches, a strategy which culminated in *Operation Swamp '81*. The Policy Studies

Institute study of the Metropolitan Police, which was being carried out during this period, reported that:

> Police officers tend to make a crude equation between crime and black people, to assume that suspects are black and to justify stopping people in these terms.[54]

Afro-Caribbean people, especially teenagers, were far more likely to be stopped than others and the effects of these special operations is 'beyond doubt'. According to Lord Scarman:

> They provoked the hostility of young black people, who felt they were being hunted irrespective of their innocence or guilt. And their hostility infected older members of the community, who, hearing the stories of many innocent young people who had been stopped and searched, began themselves to lose confidence in, and respect for, the police. However well-intentioned, these operations precipitated a crisis of confidence. . .[55]

Lord Scarman's report was published on 25 November 1981, and in it he counselled caution about future 'hard' policing in view of the damage it had caused, and the absence of any tangible benefits. However, just two months later, Deputy Assistant Commissioner Gilbert Kelland was reported as telling his divisional commanders that there should be no let-up.[56] The report in the *Daily Mail* in which this appeared was headed 'More and more muggings but the Yard fights back', and this did indeed mark the beginning of a sustained 'fight back' against Lord Scarman's criticisms, and his recommendations. On 5 March 1982 the *Daily Mail* carried a double page story entitled 'Prisoners Behind Net Curtains' and four days later the *Daily Express* had a similar piece headed 'On Britain's Most Brutal Streets'. Each story was about Brixton and each featured attacks by black youths on elderly white women.

The London crime statistics, released on 10 March 1982, were taken up with apparent gusto by the media, and were grossly distorted by many newspapers. In the statistics released by Scotland Yard, the race of suspects was indicated only in cases of robbery and other violent thefts, and the London total of 18 763 such offences included robberies from banks and other businesses, and non-violent thefts from the person. Indeed, it is reported that in 90% of offences classified as 'other violent theft' no injuries whatsoever are sustained by the victim.[57] Furthermore, this whole category of crime, subject to so much attention, makes up just 3% of all serious crime known to the police and it might be reasonably asked why the other 97% was not rigorously examined by the media.

The *Daily Star*, on 11 March 1982 referred to 'the total of nearly 19,000 muggings', when the number of reported street robberies was 5 889. The *Daily Mail's* front page story was 'Black Crime: the Alarming Figures' and it reported that 55.42% of the assailants were identified as 'coloured' while the 'overwhelming majority' of the victims 'are white and are women. All too often elderly women'. Other newspapers carried similar reports. In short, unscrupulous newspapers published distorted images of crime and race in London, based on figures released by the Metropolitan Police. As one commentator in March 1982 observed:

> Londoners riding home on the proverbial Clapham omnibus – *especially* the Clapham omnibus – last week could have been forgiven for believing that they resided in a city racked by racial hatred, where black muggers loitered threateningly at every street corner waiting to accost them.[58]

In 1983 similar figures were again released 'through the malevolent offices of Mr. Harvey Proctor, the ultra-right-wing Conservative MP', reported the *Guardian* leader, which referred to 'selective manipulation' and 'orchestrated distortion' of the figures.[59] The popular press responded again with headlines such as 'Black Crime Shock' (*Sun*, 23 March 1983), and once more stereotypes and prejudices were reinforced, and the fears and anger of black people strengthened. Since then, these crime figures broken down by race of suspects have not been released in this way, but the damage to relations between the police and many black people had already been done.

## ALLEGATIONS OF POLICE MISCONDUCT

The parlous state of relations between the police and significant sections of the Lambeth public was clearly apparent to Lord Scarman. Aspects of this deterioration were charted in strident terms in the report by the Working Party into Community/Police Relations in Lambeth, which was established by the Borough

Council in March 1979. The position was described as 'extremely grave', and the police were accused of intimidating and harassing working-class people in general and black people in particular. Furthermore, the Working Party had received evidence of 'violence, intimidation and induced confessions', of extensive misconduct, rudeness and incivility.[60] As Francis Wheen reported in the *New Statesman*:

> most of the witnesses quoted in the report do not sound as though they are 'anti-police' by inclination; they are simply people who have been cowed into a mood of brooding resentment.[61]

The Working Party was established in response to a request from the Council for Community Relations in Lambeth, which had resolved early in 1979 to withdraw from a formal liaison committee with the police. This liaison forum had been established only a few months earlier but had begun badly when a special police operation, involving the SPG and extensive use of stop and search powers, took place three days after the inaugural meeting, at which no announcement of the forthcoming operation was made. Matters deteriorated further in February 1979, when three members of the staff of the Council for Community Relations in Lambeth were arrested because they, like the alleged assailants of two plain clothes police officers and a black barman, wore sheepskin coats. The report of the Working Party was published in 1981, three months before the Brixton disorders confirmed its direst warnings. Lord Scarman commented:

> I have no doubt that the style, language and contents of this report succeeded only in worsening community relations with the police. But I am also satisfied that it reflected attitudes, beliefs and feelings widely prevalent in Lambeth since 1979.[62]

There is, however, little doubt that hostility towards the police was widespread in certain areas well before 1979, caused by incidents such as those described by George Greaves in his contribution to *Scarman and After*. In 1976, for example, a black man in his late fifties was walking home along Railton Road in Brixton:

> he was stopped by police and questioned about a parcel of groceries which he was carrying. He was man-handled, and his

groceries scattered in the roadway. A pregnant young woman intervened but she was rebuffed with such force that she fell to the ground . . .[63]

Many specific cases of police misconduct have been documented and one of the worst is that which involved Mr and Mrs White of Stoke Newington in London. During the night of 15 September 1976 seventeen police officers illegally entered the home of the elderly black couple looking for stolen goods, of which none were found. David and Lucille White were arrested and charged with assaulting police officers, for which they were subsequently acquitted. It was pointed out that Mr White was an elderly, frail person and it was over two months before he was sufficiently recovered from his injuries to return to his work. In April 1982, hearing a claim for damages, Mr Justice Mars-Jones adjuged that the police officers were guilty of 'monstrous, wicked and shameful conduct' and a 'brutal, savage and sustained variety of assaults', and they had 'assaulted this defenceless man in his own home with a weapon and beat him up in a brutal, inhuman way . . .'.[64] Mr and Mrs White were awarded damages against Sir David McNee, Commissioner of Police for the Metropolis, of £51 392.

The Whites' case was particularly horrifying but it is only one of a catalogue of cases of alleged police misconduct against black people. Some of these were cited in the evidence presented to the Royal Commission on Criminal Procedure by the Institute of Race Relations, published as *Police Against Black People*, and others have been documented by authors such as Derek Humphry and Paul Gordon.[65] A few cases are well known, such as that which involved the death of the Nigerian David Oluwale and led to the imprisonment of two police officers for assault. At their trial, in 1971 at Leeds, witnesses reported that the officers had repeatedly assaulted the man and one of them had urinated on him.

The majority of alleged incidents of police misbehaviour are, of course, more mundane and seldom reach the headlines. Many examples are contained in the evidence received by the Select Committee inquiries in 1971–72 and 1976–77, and, to take just one example, the memorandum submitted by the West Indian Standing Conference on 27 January 1972 was described by William Deedes MP, Chairman of the Select Committee, as presenting 'a case almost akin to civil war between the West Indians and the police'.[66] In 1976 a member of the Committee, Dudley Smith MP, felt it necessary to inform the President of the Association of Chief Police Officers of the views of the Afro-Caribbean representatives:

> There has been a consistent, continuous allegation on the part of many of the witnesses appearing before us that they are discriminated against by the police. The more reasonable witnesses say that officers, very senior officers like yourself, and other reasonably senior officers, understand the problem and honestly and genuinely to the best of their ability try to operate non-discrimination and the equality of the races. They say that on the other hand, down the line the young policeman and the not so young policeman on the beat or on patrol does not; that he discriminates against blacks; that he does not like blacks; that he regards them as inferior citizens and says in fact, 'What the hell are you doing here? We do not want you' . . . the main discrimination alleged in this country is largely that allegedly committed by the police.[67]

Many of the instances cited in the evidence appeared to be minor, but no doubt irritating, examples of police officers 'pushing their weight around', and some of these had been interpreted as manifestations of racial prejudice when the officers may well have behaved in a similar way with white people. It should be remembered that the police tend to experience the greatest friction with young people in general, and on many occasions it may be the *age* of the person rather than their race which influences the police officer's behaviour towards them.

An example of the sort of treatment by the police which can lead to considerable ill-feeling occurred in 1982. On his sixteenth birthday Mark Bravo, a black youth in north London, bought a motor cycle. During the first week he was stopped by the police on 7 occasions and this began a pattern which continued for several months. His mother kept a record of his encounters during a two-week period in April 1982: *2 April*: stopped 4 times; *4 April*: stopped once; *5 April*: stopped twice; *7 April*: stopped 7 times; *8 April*: stopped twice; *9 April*: stopped twice; *14 April*: stopped 5 times. Mr Bravo eventually received 18 summonses as a result of countless stops between January and the summer; he was acquitted of 10 and those for which he was found guilty included a 'defective registration plate' which contained a crack (£2 fine), careless driving (endorsements), and 'dangerous part' (£10 fine and endorsement).[68]

Of course, every case is distinctive and perhaps there were good reasons for the police to stop this person so often; however in local lore it no doubt goes down as another example of police harassment.

Some police conduct which has led to resentment and anger has been fairly widely reported. For instance, a succession of raids has taken place at the Mangrove Restaurant in Notting Hill. The first occurred in February 1969 and subsequent raids, and resultant charges, such as that against the owner for serving food after 11 p.m., led to considerable unrest in the area.[69]

A particularly notable raid took place in Railton Road, Brixton, shortly after the end of the first phase of the Scarman inquiry, and this too prompted a bitter and angry reaction. On 15 July 1981 at 2 a.m. eleven houses were raided by 176 police officers with a further 391 held in reserve. The police had obtained warrants to look for evidence of unlawful drinking under section 187 of the Licensing Act 1964, and to search five houses for petrol bombs under section 6 of the Criminal Damages Act 1971. No evidence of either was found and, indeed, two of the houses for which warrants were granted as a result of 'police observations' turned out to be derelict and unoccupied. The next day pictures were seen, in the press and on television, of wreckage and destruction in the houses – of smashed windows, sinks, toilets, floorboards, furniture, televisions and possessions. Lord Scarman visited the scene of the havoc surrounded by visibly upset residents, and John Frazer, the local Member of Parliament, stated:

> I could come to no conclusion other than that a large number of policemen had deliberately set out to wreck the houses, to make them uninhabitable, by taking up floorboards, breaking water pipes, removing gas and electric meters, hand rails and bannisters and smashing almost every window.[70]

The resultant outcry led to an internal inquiry by Deputy Assistant Commissioner Dear which exonerated those involved and explained that police officers had been issued with sledgehammers and crowbars 'to effect speedy entry'. Compensation of £8 500 was paid by the Metropolitan Police for structural damage and further sums for damage to personal property, but as Lord Scarman commented, 'compensation is no substitute for destroyed property'.

Not surprisingly, several formal complaints were lodged about the police behaviour. However, the Director of Public Prosecutions decided to take no action. Most people thought that was the end of the story but, for the first time ever, the Police Complaints Board resolved to carry out an investigation under section 8(2) of the Police Act 1976 which empowered them to report to the Home Secretary on matters to which his attention should be drawn 'by reason of their gravity or of any other exceptional circumstances'. The Home Office tried to keep the report's existence secret and it only came to light because of a one-line mention in the Complaint Board's Annual Report. Only after pressure in Parliament was a copy of the special report placed in the House of Commons Library and in it the Board stated that the Railton Road raid had involved 'serious lapses from professional standards' and there had been an 'institutional disregard for the niceties of the law'. The Board also stated that they were 'disappointed' with the response to their criticisms by the Deputy Commissioner and they considered that 'the unprofessional conduct of officers engaged on that operation could be a reflection of their conduct on less sensitive occasions'.[71]

There seems no reason to suppose that the handling of the complaints in the case of the Railton Road raid will have increased public confidence in general, and that of black people in particular, in the way in which complaints are investigated. A common view of the procedure appears to be that there is little point in using it. The British Crime Survey found that less than one person in ten who say they have been annoyed by the police actually make a complaint; 38% consider 'it would be no use', 18% think they might get into trouble and 10% say they are afraid of the consequences.[72] A survey carried out for the Police Federation by MORI in February 1984 revealed a low level of satisfaction with the procedure: 66% said that complaints should be investigated by a body other than the police.

The evidence from the Police Complaints Board shows that the vast majority of complaints are not substantiated. During 1983, for example, the Board completed action on 7199 complaints cases, containing a total of 16 231 matters of complaint; of these 1346 (8.3%) resulted in 'advice' to the officers concerned, and a further 234 (1.4%) entailed disciplinary charges.[73] A study by Stevens and Willis showed that the proportion of complainants who were Afro-Caribbean or Asian increased sharply between 1975 and 1976 and thereafter. Furthermore, the study found that whereas the substantiation rate for Asian complainants, in the Metropolitan Police

District in the first quarter of 1979, was similar to that of whites (Asians: 2 cases substantiated out of 94 lodged; whites: 53 out of 1716), the substantiation rate for Afro-Caribbeans was much lower: 3 out of 283 complaints.[74] The research showed that Afro-Caribbean complainants were more likely to make complaints of assault, but, in general, serious accusations such as assault are very unlikely to be found proven and a complaint of assault by an Afro-Caribbean or Asian which is substantiated is 'rare', and 'very rare' if the complainant is under arrest.

There is little doubt that relations between black people and the police have in general deteriorated, at least in London, and the increased number of complaints from members of the ethnic minorities is testimony to the decline. The Policy Studies Institute report found that whereas 26% of whites felt that some groups 'do not get fair treatment' from the police, 36% of Asians and 62% *of West Indians* agreed with this view. The research also showed that a much higher proportion of West Indians than of whites or Asians are critical of police conduct, but a lower proportion of West Indians (79%) than of other groups (some 90%) said they would make an official complaint if they felt seriously dissatisfied with the police. The report concludes that:

> These findings suggest that between one-third and one-half of West Indians completely lack confidence in the police force, and that two-thirds have at least considerable doubts about standards of police conduct.[75]

## POLICING AND RACIAL ATTACKS

The attitudes of Asian people towards the police appear to be more favourable than those of Afro-Caribbeans, but they are particularly critical of police behaviour in respect of racial attacks. They complain that police refuse to take calls for assistance seriously, and that they do not charge assailants. The appalling extent of racial attacks has been documented in a number of studies, and it is clear that assaults on members of the ethnic minorities are now all too common in some urban areas, particularly in parts of London. The incidence of unprovoked attacks, especially on Asian people, appears to have increased considerably since 1976. During this period Asian shops have been attacked, Asians' houses damaged and burned and a number of Asian people murdered. Peter Fryer reports that 31 black people were murdered by racists between 1976 and 1981, and a report by the Bethnal Green and Stepney Trades Council documented over one hundred racial attacks between 1976 and 1978 in Tower Hamlets alone.[76] The report showed that racial abuse and attacks were common and particularly suffered by Bengalis, who frequently expressed little confidence in the police. Indeed, it was suggested that often the police appeared more concerned with whether the victim was an illegal immigrant than with apprehending and prosecuting the assailants.

It was evident that the National Front was actively encouraging racial hostility in many of the areas where attacks were occurring, even if its *direct* involvement in them was hard to prove. When, during the election campaign in 1979, the National Front provocatively decided to hold a meeting in Southall, it was not surprising that local people and the Anti-Nazi League responded to the challenge. On 23 April 1979, about 3000 people demonstrated against the meeting and 2756 police officers were present to keep public order. However, at the end of the day – 'a day dedicated to peaceful protest against the provocation of an alien racist presence' – hundreds of demonstrators and police were injured, 345 people were arrested and Blair Peach was dead.

> Eye-witness reports, from a wide variety of sources, testified to examples of police behaviour to effect arrest or disperse crowds which ranged from the unreasonable to the downright brutal.[77]

All the accounts of the 'Battle of Southall' seem to agree that the police response was ferocious and included racial abuse. The *Daily Telegraph*, for example, described how the police 'cornered about 50 demonstrators' and then

> several dozen, screaming coloured demonstrators were dragged . . . to the police station and waiting coaches. Nearly every demonstrator we saw had blood flowing from some sort of injury; some were doubled up in pain.[78]

The police claim that they merely responded to attacks by some of the protestors, but other accounts suggest that police conduct was largely to blame, and that the Special Patrol Group in particular meted out violence indiscriminately. There seems little doubt that

the police behaviour, 'left a deep scar on the people of Southall which will take years to heal'.[79] Confrontations also took place at Lewisham, Tameside, Leicester, Coventry and elsewhere.

Racial attacks and harassment have continued to increase during recent years in a number of areas. These have been documented in various reports such as those by the Home Office in 1981, the Runnymede Trust a year later and the Greater London Council in 1984.[80] The GLC Report detailed a number of horrifying incidents and was particularly critical of the police response.

It is clearly nonsense to suggest that the police in general are indifferent to serious crime suffered by members of the ethnic minority population but, as the detailed case studies reveal, a significant number of police officers have failed to deal properly with many incidents. Whether this is out of a misguided belief that good race relations are best fostered by pretending there is no problem, or whether it is caused by racist views, or by lazy officers, is a matter of debate. There is little doubt, though, that a few celebrated cases in which the police have appeared to take tough action against people who are seeking to defend themselves, rather than against their attackers, has led to widespread cynicism about policing policies among many members of the ethnic minorities.

In Bradford twelve Asian youths were charged with very serious offences of conspiracy, but they successfully argued that they had acted in self-defence. The Home Office report on racial violence revealed that there was considerable evidence of such attacks in the city, but police officers involved in the case of the 'Bradford Twelve' in 1982 seemed not even to be aware of the report's existence.

Another significant case came to court on 17 November 1983. Eight young Asian men were accused of various offences including affray, assault and possession of offensive weapons. The prosecution alleged that on 24 September 1982 three plain clothes policemen had been attacked by a gang, including the accused. However, a number of significant inconsistencies were apparent in the police evidence and independent witnesses corroborated the defendants' account that they were peacefully accompanying children on their way home from school. It emerged that the children had been subject to threats and assaults by skinheads, and each of the defendants had been the victim of at least one racial attack. The defence alleged that the three police officers in plain clothes had attacked the group after comments such as 'OK Paki bastard, let's see what you're made of.' Allegations of abuse and assaults during the journey to the police station, and while the defendants were in custody, were denied by the police.

During the five-week trial many accounts were given of racial attacks and harassment in Newham and elsewhere, and of the lack of police interest and help. The *Guardian* reported that the Old Bailey jury heard how

> Asian families in the East End of London lived a nightmarish existence of abuse and attacks from white racialists . . .

Mr Kulwant Singh Mangat, general secretary of the Sikh Temple in Newham stated that his community had little faith in the police, and the court heard of

> Asian homes which were constantly boarded up to protect their occupants from stone-throwing gangs, and of temples and schools where Asian youths had to mount patrols to deter racialist attackers.[81]

It was suggested that not only did the police fail to protect the Asian people, but they often threatened the victims with prosecution, or indeed charged them, when they sought to defend themselves. In court local police said they had never heard of the Home Office report on racial attacks and indeed denied being aware of any racially-motivated attacks in the Newham area. Four of the 'Newham Eight' were acquitted, while the other four were each sentenced to 50 hours community service for the crime of affray, and in the case of one, for common assault. In May 1985 another Old Bailey trial opened, this time of the 'Newham Seven' – again young Asians variously accused of affray, assault, possession of offensive weapons and criminal damage. A catalogue of racial attacks and alleged police indifference was revealed, and the defence case of 'self defence, no offence' was largely upheld by the verdicts on 10 July 1985.

Sir Kenneth Newman, Metropolitan Police Commissioner, announced in his January 1985 report to the Home Secretary, that he was adding racial attacks to his target areas for special attention which also include robbery, burglary, autocrime, drug abuse and vandalism.[82] It remains to be seen how effective the targetting will be, but press and television reports in 1985 suggest that the problem, in parts of London at least, is steadily growing worse.[83]

On 13 July 1985, for example, in Ilford, London, a particularly horrifying arson attack occurred in which Mrs Shamira Kassam, who was eight months pregnant, and her three children, died.

A complaint which a number of Asian people have made is that when they have called for police assistance the officers asked to see their passports and suspected them of being illegal immigrants. Gordon has documented a large number of passport raids carried out since the Immigration Act 1971 and the subsequent establishment of the Illegal Immigration Intelligence Unit at Scotland Yard.[84] The scale of these operations, and the way they have been carried out, has provoked considerable anger amongst ethnic minority communities. Recent cases include police raids on sixty Asian homes in Luton in January 1984, and on Kashmiri homes in Birmingham two months later. Each raid provokes hostility amongst the people who experience it and further alienates members of the ethnic minorities from the police.

## THE ATTITUDES OF ETHNIC MINORITIES

The recent Policy Studies Institute investigation of the British black population, which entailed a survey of 5 001 adult people, confirmed that the ethnic minorities lack confidence in the police. In answer to the question 'are people of Asian/West Indian origin treated the same, better or worse than white people by the police?', 30% of Asians said 'worse' and 26% didn't know. The belief that the police discriminate against them is far more widespread among Asians than the belief that any other institutions do so, such as the courts, schools, trade unions, pubs, building societies, banks, estate agents and even council housing departments, the only exception being employers. Among West Indians the findings are overwhelming: *64% believe that they are treated 'worse' than whites by the police*, with just 16% saying 'the same'; 19% didn't know. Again, far more believe that they are discriminated against by the police than by any other institution.[85]

The survey also revealed that many black people felt that the incidence of racial abuse and attacks had increased during the previous five years and a large number did not believe that they could rely on the police to protect them. 43% of West Indians and 52% of Asian men considered that the problem of racial attacks had worsened (about 20% didn't know), while 42% of Asian men, and

64% of West Indian, men believed that it was 'probably' or 'definitely' *not* true that black people could rely on the police for protection. About half the Asians and West Indians believed that black people should organise self-defence groups if necessary to protect themselves from racialist violence.

It is clear that relations between many black people and the police are poor, and are characterised by hostility, resentment and lack of confidence. The depth of this hostility and distrust among many black people is more considerable than senior police officers and certain politicians may realise, but possibly not as great as some others have argued. The Policy Studies Institute investigation found that black people are just as likely as white people to report crimes to the police, and even young Afro-Caribbean people, who are the most markedly hostile, do not wholly reject the present policing system. The point of view of many black people was expressed with some poignancy by Derek Humphry, at the beginning of his account of police misbehaviour:

> I am critical of the police force in this book because I wish to respect it. . . . the rule of law in Britain should be a rule which is firm and just (and seen to be such) to peoples of all colours, appearances and incomes.[86]

Unfortunately, many black people feel that police treatment of members of the ethnic minority communities is not just and, as this chapter has tried to show, there is considerable evidence to support them.

## THREE CENTRAL PROBLEMS AFFECTING RACE AND POLICING

During a period of rapid change and increased inequalities, disadvantage and unemployment, it is not surprising that the police, as important agents of social control, should experience greater pressures and criticisms. Some of the central problems were examined by the Royal Commission on Criminal Procedure which reported in January 1981[87] and others were highlighted by Lord Scarman in his report ten months later. These inquiries placed a number of issues on the political agenda and after considerable debate the main result was the rather inadequate Police and Criminal Evidence Act 1984, which seems likely to prove irksome, bureaucratic and costly for the police and ineffective in terms of providing an improved service, and safeguards against abuses, for the public.[88]

This legislation does not seem likely to lead to an improvement in

relations between black people and the police although, on Lord Scarman's initiative, Section 101 of the Act does make racially discriminatory behaviour a specific police disciplinary offence. From the evidence reviewed in this chapter and accounts elsewhere, it seems possible to identify three particular problems which may directly affect race and policing: (1) racially prejudiced and discriminatory behaviour, (2) officers' attitudes and conduct in general, and (3) 'institutional racism'.

### Racially Prejudiced and Discriminatory Behaviour by Police Officers

There is now considerable evidence of racial prejudice among police officers. In addition to that which has been cited, Robert Reiner, for example, reported that a large minority of his sample of police officers volunteered racialist, hostile or suspicious views of black people.[89] Research in Chapeltown, Leeds, in early 1981 found common criticism of ethnic minorities by police, and a general stereotyped view of Asians as no great problem, but liars if suspected of wrong-doing, whereas 'West Indians were seen as lazy, easygoing and simple people' and young blacks as troublesome, disrespectful, uncooperative and disorderly. The study also reported that racially offensive language was in common use within the police station.[90] This was dramatically illustrated at the 1984 Police Federation Conference when Peter Johnson, speaking from the platform, referred to 'our coloured brethren or nig nogs'. The Federation Chairman, Leslie Curtis, immediately repudiated the remark and Mr Johnson apologised for his 'slip of the tongue' but, after extensive publicity, he felt obliged to resign from the police service.[91]

The Policy Studies Institute research also found that 'racialist language and racial prejudice were prominent and pervasive'. One view put forward to the researchers was

> I freely admit that I hate, loathe and despise niggers. I can't stand them. I don't let it affect my job though. There are some decent ones, though, like that bloke we've just dealt with.[92]

The study suggested that the remark may accurately reflect experience, in that prejudice does not invariably result in discriminatory behaviour.

The argument has been put many times that police prejudice reflects that in society, but there cannot be many occupational groups, which regard themselves as respectable professionals, in which racialist talk is as pervasive as it is reported to be within the police. Lord Scarman stressed 'we cannot rest on the cynical proposition, which I have heard, that, since the police will necessarily reflect social attitudes, racially prejudiced people are bound to found in their ranks'.[93]

As a result of the Scarman Report, the Police Training Council recommended in 1983 that 'racism awareness training' should be introduced. Initially four pilot schemes were established, and it seems likely that increased emphasis will be placed on training in this area.[94] As well as the inclusion of racially prejudiced behaviour as a specific offence in the Police Discipline Code, Lord Scarman also recommended that concerted attempts should be made to prevent the recruitment of racialists by the police. Research by Colman and Gorman of the University of Leicester did reveal that 'conservative and authoritarian personalities' appeared to be particularly attracted to the police service, and their small sample of recruits showed hostility to black people. Essays by police cadets at the Peel Centre, Hendon, extracts from which were published in newspapers in 1982, revealed some extreme examples of prejudice and racial hatred.[95] Certainly it would seem reasonable to expect that tests could be applied which would prevent people with such violent views becoming police officers, although it would be more difficult to avoid recruiting people who are less openly racialist.

Lord Scarman was also concerned to increase the number of police officers recruited from the ethnic minorities. He found that in the whole of England and Wales in October 1981 there were only 326 black officers, a mere 0.3% of the total; by 1984 this had risen to 0.5%. Evidence from the Policy Studies Institute research, and from a recent article in *Policing*, suggests that black police officers experience prejudice from their colleagues, and in their dealings with white and black members of the public, and have little if any effect on the pervasive racialist talk within the police.[96] There continues to be considerable difficulty in attracting more applicants from the ethnic minorities.

**Police Officers' Relations with the Public**

It seems quite plausible that some police behaviour which is interpreted as racial discrimination or harassment by black people is not that as such but rather 'heavy-handed' or discourteous conduct by police officers, not prompted by racial motives. It should be stressed that studies, surveys and opinion polls consistently tend to show that the public have a reasonably high opinion of the police. The British Crime Survey, for example, revealed that three out of four people considered the police did a 'very good' or 'fairly good' job in their area, and four out of five people who had come into contact with the police in the recent past said they had been helpful and pleasant.[97]

The Policy Studies Institute survey also found that a majority of people who had encountered a police officer commented favourably on his or her attitude, although the figures varied from 79% for white people, to 64% for Asians and 60% for West Indians. The PSI survey asked a number of questions on police success and found that public confidence varied considerably, depending on which aspect of policing was being assessed. For example, 80% thought that the police were 'very successful' or 'fairly successful' at coping with marches and demonstrations but only 31% expressed these opinions about curbing domestic burglaries. Seven out of ten people thought the police were successful at 'getting on with people' but only 43% of black people expressed this view.[98]

The British Crime Survey showed that members of the public who approach the police have markedly varying opinions about them. Older people are more satisfied than younger, women more than men, non-manual workers more than manual, and those living in rural areas more than those in towns. Only one in five young men in inner cities felt that the police had been 'very pleasant', as opposed to four out of five elderly women in rural areas.[99] Of those who had been approached by the police, 52% of young men said that they had received impolite treatment, and over a third aged between 16 and 24, said they had been annoyed.

Contacts between police officers and young people seem to be far from satisfactory. This is particularly evident in the case of young black people, as the PSI study found and as Southgate's research in Chapeltown revealed. Here, police officers complained that young black people would not respond as cooperatively and respectfully as young whites, while young West Indians resented the formality of police officers. Southgate also noted that older officers criticised the ability of younger ones to get on well with the public in general.[100] A high proportion of police constables are young – in England and Wales in 1980 some 36% were aged between 18 and 25 – and it has been argued that they lack the experience and maturity to handle difficult encounters effectively and reasonably amiably.

Lord Scarman drew attention to the importance of proper guidance and supervision for young police officers 'in discharging their difficult, delicate and indispensable function' and he advocated improved monitoring and management of constables on the streets to minimise misconduct. However it is not clear that his recommendations have been vigorously acted upon, and indeed there are considerable difficulties in achieving satisfactory supervision. Police officers are given great discretion in the way they carry out their duties, and much depends upon the attitudes of individual officers and the people they encounter. The expectations and stereotypes of both police officers and members of the public are important in determining how incidents are resolved. This seems to be particularly significant in contacts between young officers and young people, and especially young black people. If their attitudes are hostile, abrasive and disrespectful the result may be an arrest for 'contempt of cop'.[101]

## Institutionalised Discrimination

It has been argued by many people that the prejudice and misconduct of individual officers are not the only reasons for 'racist policing': a prime cause is 'institutional racism'. There is some difficulty about this concept for it seems to be used in the debate about race, crime and policing in at least four different ways. Firstly, it is argued that the policies of the police service are intentionally racially discriminatory, while secondly it is claimed they are unintentionally so. The third usage applies the concept to society in general and to government policies and agencies in particular and argues that some of these are deliberately racist while the fourth way in which it is used is similar but suggests that the racist outcomes may be unintentional.[102]

There is some evidence to support each contention. A number of people have argued that immigration policies are intentionally racially discriminatory and, in fact, they are. The various acts to control immigration, and particularly the concept of 'patriality', have been specifically designed to prevent the entry of Afro-Caribbean and Asian people. 'Immigration law defined the presence of black people – not white racism – as the problem'.[103] Others, while not denying the intentional racism of Home Office policies on immigration and deportation, have pointed out that institutionalised racism is more insidious; Salman Rushdie stated that

> 400 years of conquest and looting, centuries of being told that you are superior to the fuzzy-wuzzies and the wogs, leave their stain on you all; such a stain seeps into every part of your culture, your language and your daily life; and nothing much has been done to wash it out.[104]

As Rex has explained 'racism is something which pertains not simply to the psychology of individuals but to the belief systems which operate in society'.[105] Certain institutions may amplify this racism through sub-cultures, and this seems evident in the police – thus the 'prominent and pervasive' racialism discovered in the Metropolitan Police by the Policy Studies Institute researchers.

Lord Scarman rejected the general allegation that Britain 'is a society which knowingly, as a matter of policy, discriminates against black people' and he 'totally and unequivocally' repudiated the accusation that the direction and policies of the Metropolitan Police are racist. However, evidence cited in this review demonstrates that at the very least, the outcomes of the institution's policies are racially discriminatory – witness the number of black people stopped and searched, and arrested. One must also query why Scotland Yard released racially-based crime statistics, knowing that their comprehensiveness and accuracy was open to question and presumably being aware that they would be construed as linking race and crime, or, put more simply, that they would create a popular image of black people as criminals. Hence remarks such as those of Mr Worsthorne in the *Sunday Telegraph* of 29 November 1981:

> Brixton is the iceberg tip of a crisis of ethnic criminality which is not Britain's fault – except in the sense that her rulers quite unnecessarily imported it.

Targetting of certain crimes or areas by the police can result in institutionalised racism, in the sense of unintentionally discriminating against people on the basis of race, and *Operation Swamp* can be seen as such an example. Research by Landau showed that the police in London appeared to exercise discretion in a biased way in cases involving juveniles. His investigation in five divisions of the Metropolitan Police in 1978–79 entailed the examination of 1708 cases and he found that black juveniles, in comparable cases and circumstances, were more likely to be treated severely and charged by the police than to be referred to the juvenile bureau.[106] Individual cases might be explained by particular officers' prejudice, or by features of the interaction between specific suspects and police officers dealing with them, such as insolence and disrespect, but the cumulative result, whereby young blacks are treated more harshly, may be seen as another manifestation of institutionalised discrimination.

## RACE AND POLICING: THE WIDER CONTEXT

Policing and race cannot be isolated from the wider context within which it takes place. This includes racial discrimination, inner city unemployment, deprivation and crime, and racial disadvantage, which is partly the result of the location of the ethnic minorities but largely a result of past and present discrimination. Another important part of the context is the general change in the style of policing, especially in urban areas, during the last twenty years.

Unlike many countries, Britain does not have a national police force under one unified command, but many fear that there is a trend in this direction. The National Reporting Centre, which was established in 1972 and was prominent during the 1984–85 coal dispute, is claimed by some to be evidence of the trend of centralisation, although perhaps more convincing is the reduction in the number of forces from 126 before 1964 to the present 43. The importance of chief constables has grown apace during this period, accompanied by a decline in the influence of local police committees. Perhaps the most significant change in policing is that it seems to have become *remote* from people. The advent of panda cars, and the consequent removal of many foot patrols, was an important factor in distancing the police, and so too was the establishment of a number of large police forces in the aftermath of the 1964 Act.

Police officers have also seemed to be increasingly prepared to take part in political debate and this may have undermined the previous impression of impartiality. The Police Federation has organised a number of campaigns, notably on the restoration of the death penalty, and Sir Robert Mark, during his period as Metropolitan Police Commissioner, made a series of attacks on politicians and parts of the criminal justice system, such as juries.[107] Other chief officers have had much to say about politics and society; for example, James Anderton, Chief Constable of Greater Manchester, remarked in 1982, 'I firmly believe that there is a long-term political strategy to destroy the proven structures of the police and turn them into an exclusive agency of a one-party state.'[108]

In 1985, Mr Anderton was again warning the Association of Chief Police Officers not to become 'the willing instrument of unscrupulous politicians', and he pointed out too that crime had never been so extensive and he had never known so many demands on the police, and indeed at times he felt 'quite helpless'.[109] He did not point out that there have never been more police officers: the total rose by 12 000 between 1979 and 1985 and expenditure by 154%.

The *image* of policing also seems to have changed considerably during the last twenty five years. Within the service specialisation and 'results', in terms of successful arrests, are seen as means to promotion and this is arguably at the expense of the helpful, service role of officers on the beat. Police officers are frequently seen rushing around in fast cars, or involved in public order operations which are violent. The image of the friendly but firm Dixon, who knew his 'patch' and the people living there, has given way to the 'fire-brigade' policing of *The Sweeney* and *The Bill*. The police 'run the risk of becoming, by reason of their professionalism, a "corps d'elite" set apart from the rest of the community', said Lord Scarman, and he advocated consultation and accountability to prevent 'them from slipping into an enclosed fortress of inward thinking and social isolation which would in the long term result in a siege mentality'.[110] Some have argued that this position has been reached in parts of Britain's inner cities, and that the police feel isolated from hostile and resentful sections of the communities, which in turn view the police as remote and threatening.

The nostalgic view of a 'golden age' of policing in the 1950s and 1960s is clearly an over-simplification. Inner city areas have never been easy to police, for it is here that crime is highest, poverty and poor housing the most widespread, and unemployment a major affliction.

RACE AND POLICING: THE SPIRAL OF DECLINE

Conditions in many of Britain's inner cities are appalling for many of the inhabitants. It is no wonder that the simmering cauldron occasionally boils over in an outburst of anger and bitterness, and it is no surprise that the police should be the targets for this violence. They are the visible symbols of a government which is allowing these areas to decline alarmingly, and they are the daily enforcers of order. When their conduct is considered to be unjust, or abusive, or harassing, then the mixture indeed becomes explosive. Wadding-ton, a regular contributor to the Federation's magazine *Police*, has nicely put the point about policing the inner cities:

> Here, most of all, what is required is impartial, impersonal authority and restrained use of force. In these areas the police may indeed be seen as a visible irritant. It is even more essential, therefore, that they be seen as representatives of the law, above considerations of class and race.[111]

Just so, but as the evidence in this chapter shows, many black people in Britain's cities do not believe the police are impartial or that they are particularly restrained in their use of force. The hostility and resentment of many black people means that in some areas the police receive little co-operation or information and consequently find it difficult to clear up crime. As a result, they adopt heavy-handed methods and sometimes 'bend the rules' to try to catch criminals and this leads to a further deterioration in relations with local people and even greater lack of information. This vicious circle or spiral of decline in police relations with local people, often both black and white, is just one of several trends evident in inner cities.

Racial abuse, harassment and discrimination are common in some areas, as this chapter shows. These are vital causes of 'the crisis of confidence' which Lord Scarman found in Brixton, and which exists elsewhere. He reported that an account of relations between the police and the public in that area was a tale of failure and that must be the judgement in the wider area of race and policing. The spiral of decline in relations between the police and black people could be reversed if appropriate initiatives were firmly implemented, but at present there is little cause for optimism.

## POSTSCRIPT: THE CAULDRON BOILS OVER

Relations between the police and black people were at the centre of the serious disorders which occurred in several English cities during the late summer of 1985. Each riot was precipitated by an incident involving police officers and black people, and each occurred in areas where there was widespread antagonism between some members of the ethnic minorities and the police.

The first eruption took place on Monday 9 September 1985 in the Lozells Road area of Handsworth, Birmingham. The riots resulted in the deaths of two Asian men, Amirali Moledina and his brother Kassamali, who suffered asphyxiation in their burning post office. Thirty other people, mainly police, were reported injured and the value of damaged property was put at £10 million. Further rioting occurred the next day, when Mr Douglas Hurd, the newly-appointed Home Secretary, visited the scene. Other disturbances, widely regarded as 'copycat', were reported elsewhere in the West Midlands, for example in Moseley, Woverhampton and Coventry, and in the St Pauls district of Bristol, which was the scene of serious disorder in April 1980.

The Handsworth/Soho/Lozells area, with a population of 56 300 is regarded by Birmingham Council as 'the most deprived district in the city'. Unemployment is a major affliction, and at the time of the riots 36% of the workforce in Handsworth was out of work, while the figure for people under 24 years was 50%. It is an area which has been noted in recent years for reasonably good relations between young blacks and the police, based on the concept of community policing introduced by Superintendent David Webb in the late 1970s. However, at the end of 1981 he left the police service and although his approach was continued by his successor, he too, moved from the area in April 1985. The new superintendent instituted changes which included moving a number of the area's community police officers to other duties, and clamping down on activities by local youths which had previously been tolerated. In particular police attention turned to the use of cannabis by black youths, and a number of raids took place during the summer. For example, on 10 July 150 officers raided the Acapulco cafe in Villa Road, and seven people were arrested.

These changes in officers and tactics resulted in an increase in tension between youths and the police. In July 1985 two serious disturbances occurred in Handsworth, but both were played down and went unreported by the media. In the first, about seventy youths rioted, attacking police vehicles and officers and looting a shop. It took over two hours to restore order. A few days later, police officers who were questioning a youth were attacked by a large group. The context within which the eruption occurred on 9 September was thus one of deteriorating relations between young people, especially blacks, and the police, as well as one of widespread unemployment and social disadvantage. The tinder merely required a spark, which was provided when a black youth, known as Stepper, became involved in an altercation with an officer over a parking ticket. It is alleged that during the incident, at which more police arrived, a black women was assaulted, but whether or not this occurred what is certain is that two hours later some 45 buildings in Lozells Road were ablaze.

Brixton was the scene of the next outbreak of violent disorder, during the weekend 28–29 September 1985. Police reported 724 major crimes, 43 members of the public and 10 police officers were injured, and 230 arrests were made. As in Handsworth, the trigger event which led to the rioting involved police officers and a black person, on this occasion Mrs Cherry Groce. At 7 a.m. on 28 September, armed police entered her house in Normandy Road, Brixton, looking for her son. Two shots were fired by an officer, and a bullet damaged Mrs Groce's spine causing serious injury. At 6 p.m. the local police station was attacked with petrol bombs, and during the next eight hours large numbers of black and white people took part in burning and looting which caused damage estimated at £3 million. During the riot a freelance photographer, Mr David Hodge, sustained injuries from which he died three weeks later.

Two days after Mrs Groce was shot, rioting occurred in Liverpool 8. In this instance, the disturbances appear to have been precipitated when four black men were refused bail at Liverpool magistrates' court. They had been charged in connection with a fracas in August, but local youths claimed that they were being treated unfairly and picked upon by the police. During the summer there were reports of rising tension in the area, and on 30 August a crowd demonstrated outside Toxteth police station, and then attacked police cars and the station itself. A number of assaults on police officers were also reported. As in Brixton and Handsworth, police relations with young people, and especially black youths, was a significant factor in the explosive mixture, and in Toxteth, too, the disorder was precipitated by an incident involving police officers and black people. Quite why rioting occurred in Peckham in London, on the same night, is not clear. The context appears to be similar to the other instances, that is one of rising tension between young people and the police, and at about 10 p.m. on 30 September the centre of Peckham was effectively sealed off for at least four hours. Police reported 'various sporadic acts of lawlessness', and it was reported that many people, especially blacks, were prevented from returning to their own homes.

The most serious of the disorders occurred at Broadwater Farm Estate, in Tottenham, London. The rioting began at about 6.45 p.m. on Sunday 6 October and during a night of extraordinary violence PC Keith Blakelock was stabbed to death, 20 members of the public and 200 police officers were injured and a large number of cars and some buildings were burned. Guns were fired at the police, causing injuries to several officers and reporters, and the police deployed CS gas and plastic bullets, although these were not used. The next day, the Metropolitan Police Commissioner, Sir Kenneth Newman, stated:

> Yesterday evening the ferocity of the attack on the Metropolitan Police was senseless and beyond belief. . . . To write off such acts as directly attributable to a lack of jobs, or facilities or past unfairness is to indict all those who are unable to work or who are black, white or poor, but do not sink to such depths.
>
> Petrol bombing, arson and looting are alien to our streets. They must not go on. Last night I deployed members of my Tactical Firearms Unit in readiness to use plastic bullets. They were not used, because the containment operation, though grave in its economic and human cost, was successful.
>
> But, I wish to put all people of London on notice that I will not shrink from such a decision should I believe it a practical option for restoring peace and preventing crime and injury. I would have hoped not to have had to express that thought, but yesterday evening's events have made it a regrettable possibility.

The Home Secretary said that he fully supported Newman, and so with the ferocious events at Tottenham the use of plastic bullets on the streets of Britain have become a real possibility.

As in Handsworth, Brixton and Toxteth, the context within which the disturbances occurred in Tottenham was one of deteriorating relations between the police and young people, especially blacks, and the trigger event involved police officers and black people. The chief superintendent for the area, Colin Couch, is a strong believer in community policing, and puts as his first priority the prevention of public disorder. However, it is clear that many of his police constables and sergeants do not agree with his approach. During the summer of 1985 there was evidence of increasing tension, and a prominent member of the Hornsey Police Federation was quoted as saying that the rank and file officers 'desperately wanted to go in hard and sort out the criminals'. Some serious incidents occurred during this period on the Broadwater Farm Estate, such as an attack on police by youths which resulted in one officer sustaining a bad head wound, and a series of attacks on an Asian-owned supermarket. Senior police officers appeared to play these incidents down, but black youths complained that off the estate they were increasingly harassed by the police. During the week before the riots a stop and search operation was conducted at the entrance to the estate, and young blacks said that they were unfairly picked on and subjected to abuse and rough treatment.

The incident which triggered the riots began with police officers stopping a car driven by Floyd Jarrett, a 23-years-old black man. Jarrett is well-known in the area as a worker at the Broadwater Farm Youth Association, and in the BMW car with him was his pregnant girl friend. The police officers stopped him because his tax disc was out of date, and he explained that this was because he had only just returned from a youth exchange trip to Jamaica. The officers searched his car for stolen goods, but Jarrett says that he became concerned about his girl friend and requested to move off. A row developed which ended with Jarrett being arrested for assaulting an officer, although he and his girl friend denied that any such assault took place. What happened after Jarrett arrived at the police station is subject to dispute. The arrested man claims that he was assaulted, detained for five hours without being allowed to make a phone call, and then released with his possessions returned to him minus the front door key to his mother's house. The police state that he was treated correctly. The Jarrett family claim that five police officers used Floyd's key to enter his mother's home, whereas the police stated that they found the door open.

What is certain, however, is that during the search of the house, Mrs Jarrett collapsed and died. The family allege assault by police officers, and negligence in summoning an ambulance, the police firmly deny this. The incident occurred during the early evening of Saturday 5 October 1985, and the story spread round the estate during the evening. The next day, after sporadic anti-police incidents, violent disorder erupted.

## CHOOSING THE WRONG ROUTE: COERCION, RIOTS AND GHETTOS

Unfortunately, the reactions to the disorders were all too predictable. Simplistic explanations abounded, and as in 1981 the press and a number of police officers and politicians seemed particularly attracted by the conspiracy theory. The *Daily Express*, in its 'Tottenham Riot Special' edition of 8 October, managed to reach new depths of fantasy. Under its headline *Moscow-training hit squad gave orders as mob hacked PC Blakelock to death* KILL! KILL! KILL!, the *Express* explained:

> The thugs who murdered policeman Keith Blakelock in the Tottenham riots acted on orders of crazed Left-wing extremists.
> Street-fighting experts trained in Moscow and Libya were behind Britain's worst violence.
> The chilling plot emerged last night as detectives hunted a hand-picked death squad believed to have been sent into North London hell-bent on bloodshed.

Police officers, while not going as far as the press, suggested that agitators had fostered the disorder. Mr Norman Tebbit ascribed the riots to 'wickedness', but, as a correspondent to the *Guardian* remarked, since there were no post-war riots until 1980 the stock of human wickedness must have risen alarmingly after the election of Mr Tebbit's Conservative Party to government. Douglas Hurd, Home Secretary, said after the Handsworth disorder that it was 'not a social phenomenon but crimes'.

Surprisingly, some Labour Party politicians such as Roy Hattersley and Jeff Rooker seemed to agree with Mr Hurd in the aftermath of the Handsworth riot. More generally though, the response from Labour Party figures, and from those in community groups, local government, the churches and trade unions was to stress social deprivation, racial disadvantage and unemployment as causes of the disorders. Gerald Kaufman asked how, if the disorder was simply crime and not related to other social and economic factors, it occurred in areas such as Handsworth, Brixton and Tottenham but not in the delightful area of Witney in Oxfordshire, which is the Home Secretary's constituency. Mr Neil Kinnock attacked the Government's complacency, and the cuts in support for councils running the inner-city areas; it is, he said, government by 'lethargy and conflict'.

Kaufman's remarks seem well made, for as in 1981 the areas which experienced disorder in 1985 share common characteristics. Unemployment is high, particularly amongst the young and especially amongst young black people. Housing is poor and often overcrowded, environmental decay is evident, social problems are widespread and facilities are poor. A high proportion of the population in each area is Afro-Caribbean or Asian, and these are the people who tend to experience the social and economic disadvantages particularly acutely, and who are subjected to racial discrimination, racist abuse and sometimes physical attacks. These areas are also characterised by relatively high levels of crime, and by the common use by young people of cannabis. There is however little evidence of a hard drugs problem in the areas in which disorder occurred in 1985, despite media assertions to the contrary.

Handsworth, Brixton, Toxteth and Tottenham also seem to share two other characteristics. First, they are areas where *political* disadvantage is widespread in that there are few institutions, opportunities and resources for articulating grievances, and for bringing pressure to bear on those with political power. Many citizens in these areas lack the resources to voice politically their demands and complaints, and hence they are politically as well as materially dispossessed. The second common characteristic of these areas is that allegations of police misconduct have been frequently made in the recent past, tension between police and youths has been rising and there is evidence of police 'heavy handedness', if not downright harassment. Lord Scarman found all these factors evident in Brixton in 1981, and in paragraph 2.38 of *The Brixton Disorders* he stated:

> Taken together, they provide a set of social *conditions* which create a disposition towards violent protest. Where deprivation and frustration exist on the scale to be found among the young black people of Brixton, the probability of disorder must, therefore, be strong.

His remarks can be applied with equal force to the areas in which disorder occurred in 1985.

The depressingly familiar reactions to the disorders, by Government ministers, police officers and media commentators, suggest that little has been learned from the 1981 riots and Lord Scarman's report. The view that riots are 'alien to our streets' is a dramatic case of historical amnesia, and the responses that the disorders are 'senseless' crimes caused by agitators, subversives and 'wickedness' lead inexorably to tougher measures to combat 'the enemy within'. However, wiser counsellors down the ages have known that while repression may work in the short-term, although at great cost, it cannot be a lasting solution. As Edmund Burke wrote in 1775:

> the use of force alone is temporary. It may subdue for a moment, but it does not remove the necessity of subduing again.

The use of CS gas and plastic bullets, the adoption of foreign police tactics to crush disorder and the imposition of more stringent penalties and sanctions will not remove the underlying causes of the riots. Indeed, there is considerable evidence to show that repression leads to even greater disorder. Gurr has pointed to a strong relationship between an increase in force by a regime and the occurrence of disturbances (see for example *Why Men Rebel*) and Johnson in *Revolutionary Change* found that repressive measures often lead to a greater potential for collective violence.

The increased use of coercion is likely to erode many citizens' perceptions of the regime's legitimacy, to undermine the authority of the state and its agents such as the police, and to fuel feelings of injustice. As consent diminishes, non-compliance and 'hostile outbursts' increase and so greater coercion is required, leading in turn to less consent. Thus policing and disorder can enter a vicious circle, because the response to the initial rioting fails to tackle the root causes. Is this the route that the British Government has chosen to take? There seem to be a failure to appreciate that when people are dispossessed, politically excluded and deprived of hope they become frustrated, indignant and angry. If they experience police harassment and abuse, or if they believe that the police are behaving unjustly, they may erupt in fury, although such an outburst is likely to be shortlived and cathartic.

The Government steadfastly refused to hold a public inquiry into the 1985 disorders, preferring to requisition reports by the police forces involved. It seems quite incredible that rioting as serious as that which occurred should not be subject to an inquiry under the Police Act 1964. Indeed, in view of the disorders and the deterioration in relations between many black people and the police, which is the subject of this chapter, and the increasing politicisation and criticism of the police there is now an overwhelming case for a Royal Commission on the Police. Unfortunately, under the present administration this course of action looks most unlikely, and instead tougher measures, and unconditional support for whatever chief constables decide, is the order of the day.

And so the spiral of decline in police relations with local people, black and white, in many inner city areas looks set to continue. Heavy-handed methods, frequent use of stop and search powers, and hard policing in general will cause increased hostility and resentment and a consequent decrease in cooperation and information, making it more difficult to clear up crime. The police in such areas will feel even more beleaguered and hostile, and the gulf between them and local people, especially the black and the young, will grow even wider. Let us hope that this is an unduly pessimistic view and that wiser counsels on all sides prevail. However, the portents are not promising. The Government has introduced new legislative measures for controlling public order, which look likely to inflame rather than heal. It is surely no coincidence that the last Public Order Act was passed in 1936, at a time of high unemployment, social deprivation and antagonism between the police and certain sections of the public, and that its successor act is to be passed fifty years later in similar circumstances. It also seems that many police officers are determined to go on the offensive. This was illustrated graphically at 7 a.m. on 30 October 1985 when about 100 officers raided seven houses in Brailsford Road and Arlingford Road in Brixton. The police were looking for property stolen during the riots a month earlier, but none was found. The officers used sledgehammers to break down the doors of the houses, and then took photographs of the occupants. Mr Patrick Highland, aged 74, was photographed as he lay in bed. One resident was quoted as saying 'I asked an officer why they hadn't knocked on the door or rung the bell to be let in, rather than smash the door down. He said "It's a form of habit".' The chairman of the Community Police Consultative Group for Lambeth described the raids as brutal, irresponsible and provocative, and pointed out that they were carried out without knowledge of the police community liaison officer.

If determined action was taken the spiral of decline could be reversed. Instead it seems that palliatives are to be applied, which in fact are likely to exacerbate the underlying causes of unrest and disorder. Ghettos are being created, characterised by deprivation and neglect, tough policing and repressive measures, and, disintegrating political authority and a lack of social cohesion. Is this to be the real legacy which the Thatcher Government bequeathes to the nation?

## NOTES

1. The author gratefully acknowledges the award of a Research Fellowship by The Leverhulme Trust, and consequent financial support towards the production of this chapter.

2. Mr Ian Lloyd, Conservative MP for Havant and Waterloo: House of Commons Official Report, Parliamentary Debates (*Hansard*), Session 1980–81, Sixth Series, vol.8, col.575 (9 July 1981).

3. Mr Roy Hattersley, Labour MP for Birmingham Small Heath and Shadow Home Secretary: House of Commons Official Report, Parliamentary Debates (*Hansard*), Session 1980–81, Sixth Series, vol.8, col.22 (6 July 1981).

4. Quoted in J. Clare, 'Eyewitness in Brixton', in John Benyon (ed.), *Scarman and After: Essays reflecting on Lord Scarman's Report, the riots and their aftermath* (Pergamon Press, 1984) p.50.

5. G. Murdock, 'Reporting the riots: images and impact', in John Benyon (ed.), *Scarman and After*, op. cit., pp.83–5. Of course British history reveals many instances of riots, see for example G. Rude, *The Crowd in History*, New York: Wiley, 1967; E. J. Hobsbawm, *Primitive Rebels*, Manchester: University Press, 1959; John Stevenson, *Popular Disturbances in England, 1700–1870*, London: Longman, 1979.

6. *The Brixton Disorders 10–12 April 1981: Report of an Inquiry by the Rt. Hon. the Lord Scarman, OBE*, London: HMSO, 1981 (Cmnd. 8427), para.3.108.

7. This was Lord Scarman's view, see *ibid.*, ch.6; see also S. Field and P. Southgate, *Public Disorder*, Home Office Research Study No.72, London: HMSO, 1982.

8. *The Brixton Disorders*, op. cit., para.4.1.

9. Quoted in the *Guardian*, 1 Sept. 1976, cited by Paul Gordon, *White Law: Racism in the Police Courts and Prisons* (Pluto Press, 1983).

10. Select Committee on Race Relations and Immigration, Session 1976–77, *The West Indian Community*, vol. 1, *Report*, vols 2 and 3, *Evidence* HC 180, (HMSO, Feb. 1977). vol.2, 'Memorandum by the Community Relations Commission' (14 Oct. 1976) p.532, para. B13.

11. For an account of the area before the riot, which predicted that disorder would break out, see Ken Pryce, *Endless Pressure* (Penguin, 1979).

12. Quotation attributed to the Liverpool 8 Defence Committee in *The Times*, 13 Nov. 1981.

13. Michael Nally, 'Eyewitness in Moss Side', in John Benyon (ed.), *Scarman and After*, op. cit., pp.54–62.
14. Home Office, *Statistical Bulletin*, Issue 20/82, 13 Oct. 1982 (Home Office, 1982) pp.1–9.
15. See for example Derek Humphry, *Police Power and Black People* (Panther, 1972); Maureen Cain, *Society and the Policeman's Role* (Routledge & Kegan Paul, 1973); J. R. Lambert, *Crime, Police and Race Relations* (Oxford University Press, 1970); *Police Against Black People* (Institute of Race Relations, 1979); Stuart Hall *et al.*, *Policing the Crisis: Mugging, the State and Law and Order* (Macmillan, 1978); Paul Gordon, *White Law: Racism in the Police, Courts and Prisons* (Pluto Press, 1983).
16. G. Greaves, 'The Brixton Disorders', in John Benyon (ed.), *Scarman and After*, op. cit., p.67.
17. Clare Demuth, *'Sus': a Report on the Vagrancy Act* (Runnymede Trust, 1978).
18. Philip Stevens and Carole Willis, *Race, Crime and Arrests*, Home Office Research Study No. 58 (HMSO, 1979) pp.31–3.
19. House of Commons, *Race Relations and the 'Sus' Law: Second Report from the Home Affairs Committee, Session 1979–80*, HC 559 (HMSO, 1980).
20. Anne Brogden, ' "Sus" is dead but what about "Sas"?', *New Community*, vol.9, no.1 (Summer 1981); Merseyside Police Authority, *The Merseyside Disturbances: the Role and Responsibility of the Police Authority* (Merseyside County Council, 1981); Peter Southgate, 'The Disturbances of July 1981 in Handsworth, Birmingham' in Simon Field and Peter Southgate (eds), *Public Disorder*, op. cit., pp.50–1; Mary Tuck and Peter Southgate, *Ethnic Minorities, Crime and Policing*, Home Office Research Study No.70 (HMSO, 1981).
21. Carole Willis, *The Use, Effectiveness and Impact of Police Stop and Search Powers*, Research and Planning Unit Paper 15 (Home Office, 1983).
22. *Police and People in London*, vol.1: David J. Smith, *A Survey of Londoners*, PSI No.618 (Policy Studies Institute, 1983) ch.4, pp.89–154.
23. Ibid., pp.117–18.
24. *The Brixton Disorders*, op. cit., paras 4.37–4.40.
25. Stevens and Willis, *Race, Crime and Arrests*, op. cit., pp.15–18. For a critical discussion of the Stevens and Willis study see John Lea and Jock Young, *What Is To Be Done about Law and Order?* (Penguin, 1984) pp.147–62.
26. *Police and People in London*, Vol.1: Smith, *A Survey of Londoners*, op. cit., pp.118–26.
27. *Police and People in London*, vol.3: David J. Smith, *A Survey of Police Officers*, PSI No.620 (Policy Studies Institute, 1983) pp.88–91.
28. Select Committee on Race Relations and Immigration, Session 1976–77, *The West Indian Community*, op. cit.
29. Ibid., vol.3 'Memorandum by the Community Relations Commission' (14 Oct. 1976) pp.529–32 and 'Commentary by Professor Morris on the Memorandum by the Metropolitan Police', pp.548–54.
30. Select Committee on Race Relations and Immigration, Session 1971–72, *Police/Immigrant Relations*: vol. 1, *Report*, HC 471 (HMSO, Aug. 1972) p.71, para.242.
31. Lea and Young, *What Is To Be Done about Law and Order?*, op. cit., pp.135–8; see also J. Lea and J. Young, 'Urban Violence and Political Marginalisation: the Riots in Britain, Summer 1981', *Critical Social Policy*, no.3 (1982); J. Lea

and J. Young, 'Riots in Britain: Alienated Cultures', *Chartist*, no.87 (Oct./Nov. 1981); J. Lea and J. Young, 'A Missed Opportunity', *New Socialist* (Jan./Feb. 1982); J. Lea and J. Young, 'Race and Crime', *Marxism Today* (Aug. 1982).

32. Lee Bridges and Paul Gilroy, 'Striking Back', *Marxism Today* (1982); see also Lee Bridges, 'Policing the Urban Wasteland', *Race and Class*, vol.25 (Autumn 1983); Lee Bridges, 'Extended Views: the British Left and Law and Order', *Sage Race Relations Abstract* (Feb. 1983); Paul Gilroy, 'The Myth of Black Criminality', *Socialist Register 1982* (Merlin, 1982).

33. Stuart Hall, Chas Critcher, Tony Jefferson, John Clarke, Brian Roberts, *Policing the Crisis: Mugging, the State and Law and Order* (Macmillan, 1978) p.338.

34. 'The Police and the Black Wageless', *Race Today* (Feb. 1972).

35. House of Commons Official Report, Parliamentary Debates (*Hansard*), Session 1975–76, Fifth Series, vol.917 (19 Oct. 1976), *Written Answers*, cols 368–9.

36. *Report of the Commissioner of Police for the Metropolis* (HMSO, 1964), cited in Hall *et al.*, *Policing the Crisis*, op. cit., p.5.

37. *The Times*, 10 June 1863; *The Times*, 7 Nov. 1862; *The Times*, 1 Dec. 1862; see Geoffrey Pearson, *Hooligan: a History of Respectable Fears* (Macmillan, 1983) pp.128–42; see also K. Chesney, *The Victorian Underworld* (Penguin, 1972).

38. Stanley Cohen, *Folk Devils and Moral Panics* (Granada, 1973) p.9.

39. Derek Humphry, 'Danger Signals from the Streets of Lambeth', *Sunday Times*, 5 Jan. 1975.

40. See Select Committee on Race Relations and Immigration, Session 1976–77, *The West Indian Community*, op. cit., vol.2, 'Memorandum by the Community Relations Commission' (14 Oct. 1976) p.430, para B6; see also vol.3, appendix 21, 'Additional Memorandum by the Metropolitan Police', pp.689–96; an abridged version of the confidential Brixton study is printed as Annex 'A', pp.696–702.

41. *The Times*, 13 Jan. 1975; *Evening News*, 15 Jan. 1975; *Sunday Express* 19 Jan. 1975.

42. Judge Gwynn Morris quoted in the *Daily Mail*, 16 May 1975, cited by Hall *et al.*, *Policing the Crisis*, op. cit., p.333.

43. House of Commons Official Report, Parliamentary Debates (*Hansard*), Session 1975–76, Fifth Series, vol.917 (19 Oct. 1976) *Written Answers*, col.369.

44. Select Committee on Race Relations and Immigration, Session 1971–72, *Police/Immigrant Relations*, op. cit., vol.1, *Report*, p.22, para 66.

45. Maureen Cain, *Society and the Policeman's Role* (Routledge & Kegan Paul, 1973) p.117.

46. Joseph A. Hunte, *Nigger-Hunting in England?* (West Indian Standing Conference, 1966).

47. See Select Committee on Race Relations and Immigration, Session 1976–77, *The West Indian Community*, op. cit., vol.3, *Evidence and Appendices*, 'Additional Memorandum by the Metropolitan Police' (Dec. 1976), Annex A, p.701, paras 13–14.

48. See Jim Bulpitt, Chapter 1 in this book.

49. Select Committee on Race Relations and Immigration, Sessions 1971–72, *Police/Immigrant Relations*, op. cit., *Report*, p.92, para.342.

50. Bulpitt, op. cit., p.37.

51. *The Brixton Disorders*, op. cit., paras 4.11–4.20.

52. H. Mannheim, *Comparative Criminology*, vol.1 (Routledge & Kegan Paul, 1965) p.114.
53. Louis Blom-Cooper and Richard Drabble, 'Police Perception of Crime: Brixton and the Operational Response', *British Journal of Criminology*, vol.22 (Apr. 1982) pp.184–7.
54. *Police and People in London*, vol.4: David J. Smith and Jeremy Gray, *The Police in Action*, PSI no.621 (Policy Studies Institute, 1983) p.128.
55. *The Brixton Disorders*, op.cit., para 4.22.
56. *Daily Mail*, 21 Jan. 1982.
57. For each reported offence the Metropolitan Police record the extent of any injuries. It appears that injuries ranging from slight to fatal occur in about half of *all* robbery cases and in less than one out of ten 'other violent thefts', that is 90% of 'other violent thefts' involve no injury at all: Stevens and Willis, *Race, Crime and Arrests*, op. cit., pp.36–7. This study also examined the degree of injury caused, by the ethnic group of the assailant, and found that contrary to popular perceptions *attacks by black people are much less likely to result in any injuries*; the analysis is for all crimes of violence, that is assaults, robberies and 'other violent thefts':

*Attackers in reported crimes of violence by injury caused*
*(Metropolitan Police District 1975 in percentages)*

|  | Attacker's identification | | | | |
| Degree of Injury | White (n = 7164) | 'Coloured' (n = 4553) | Mixed (n = 870) | Not known (n = 6527) | Total (n = 19114) |
| --- | --- | --- | --- | --- | --- |
| Fatal | 2.8 | 0.8 | 0.2 | 0.4 | 1.4 |
| Serious | 8.8 | 5.5 | 8.6 | 5.8 | 7.0 |
| Slight | 66.7 | 49.4 | 53.2 | 63.8 | 61.0 |
| None | 21.8 | 44.2 | 37.9 | 30.0 | 30.7 |
| Total | 100.1 | 99.9 | 99.9 | 100.0 | 100.1 |

SOURCE Stevens and Willis, *Race, Crime and Arrests*, op. cit., p.37.

58. J. Shirley, 'Mugging: Statistics of an "Unacceptable Crime" ', *Guardian*, 14 Mar. 1982.
59. 'Black, White and Full Statistics', *Guardian*, 24 Mar.1983.
60. Working Party into Community/Police Relations in Lambeth, *Final Report* (Borough of Lambeth, Jan. 1981).
61. Francis Wheen, 'Living in a State of Siege', *New Statesman*, vol.101, no.2602 (30 Jan. 1981) p.10.
62. *The Brixton Disorders*, op. cit., para.4.33.
63. Greaves, 'The Brixton Disorders', op.cit., p.64.
64. *Standard*, 23 Apr. 1982; *The Times*, 24 Apr. 1982, 'Law Report'; *Daily Telegraph*, 24 Apr. 1982; *Guardian*, 24 Apr. 1982.
65. *Police Against Black People* (Institute of Race Relations, 1979); Derek

Humphry, *Police Power and Black People* (Panther, 1972); Paul Gordon, *White Law: Racism in the Police, Courts and Prisons* (Pluto Press, 1983).

66. Select Committee on Race Relations and Immigration, Session 1971–72, *Police/Immigrant Relations*, op. cit., vol.2, *Evidence*, p.72, para. 221.

67. Select Committee on Race Relations and Immigration, Session 1976–77, *The West Indian Community*, op. cit., vol.3, *Evidence and Appendices*, pp.432–3, para. 1103.

68. *Rights*, vol.7, no.1 (Spring 1983) p.6.

69. Select Committee on Race Relations and Immigration, Session 1971–72, *Police/Immigrant Relations*, op.cit., vol.2, *Evidence*, 'Memorandum by "B" Division of the Metropolitan Police', pp.213–14; 'Memorandum by London Council of Social Services Committee for Inter-Racial Co-operation', pp.231–2 and 265–7; vol.3, *Evidence, Documents and Index*, 'Memorandum by the National Council for Civil Liberties', p.623, 'Memorandum from the Institute of Race Relations', p.770; See also Gordon, *White Law*, op. cit., pp.39–40.

70. House of Commons Official Report, Parliamentary Debates (*Hansard*), Session 1980–81, Sixth Series, vol.8, col. 1425 (16 July 1981).

71. House of Commons Official Report, Parliamentary Debates (*Hansard*), Session 1980–81, Sixth Series, vol.10, cols 991–998 (29 Oct.1981); House of Commons Official Report, Parliamentary Debates (*Hansard*), Session 1982–83, Sixth Series, vol.41, col.372 (28 Apr. 1983); *Policing London*, no.8 (June/July 1983) pp.6–7; *New Law Journal*, vol.133, no.6100 (22 Apr. 1983) p.363; *Report of the Police Complaints Board 1982*, HC 278 (HMSO, 12 Apr. 1983) p.1.

72. Peter Southgate and Paul Ekblom, *Contacts between Police and Public: Findings from the British Crime Survey*, Home Office Research Study No.77 (HMSO, 1984) pp.23–4.

73. *Report of the Police Complaints Board 1983*, HC 391 (HMSO, 25 Apr. 1984) pp.5–8 and 16–22.

74. Philip Stevens and Carole Willis, *Ethnic Minorities and Complaints Against the Police*, Research and Planning Unit Paper 5 (Home Office, 1981).

75. *Police and People in London*, vol.1: Smith, *A Survey of Londoners*, op. cit., p.325 and ch.9, 'Views about standards of police conduct', pp.236–73.

76. Peter Fryer, *Staying Power: the History of Black People in Britain* (Pluto Press, 1984) pp.395–6; Bethnal Green and Stepney Trades Council, *Blood on the Streets: A Report on Racial Attacks in East London* (the Trades Council, 1978); see also Commission for Racial Equality, *Brick Lane and Beyond: an Inquiry into Racial Strife and Violence in Tower Hamlets* (CRE, 1979).

77. Tony Jefferson and Roger Grimshaw, *Controlling the Constable: Police Accountability in England and Wales* (London: Muller, 1984) p.105. See also: Gordon, *White Law*, op. cit., pp.29–30; Unofficial Committee of Inquiry, *Report: Southall 23 April 1979* (NCCL, 1980); Unofficial Committee of Inquiry, *The Death of Blair Peach* (NCCL, 1981); State Research, *State Research Bulletin* (June–July 1979).

78. *Daily Telegraph* (24 Apr. 1979) quoted in Unofficial Committee of Inquiry, *Report: Southall 23 April 1979*, op. cit., pp.159–60.

79. Southall Rights, *23 April 1979: a Report* (Southall Rights, 1980).

80. Home Office, *Racial Attacks: Report of a Home Office Study* (HMSO, Nov. 1981); Francesca Klug, *Racist Attacks* (Runnymede Trust, 1982); Greater London Council Police Committee, *Racial Harassment in London* (Greater

London Council, 1984); see also, Joint Committee Against Racialism, *Racial Violence in Britain* (JCAR, 1981); *Searchlight* June 1982 and Aug. 1982; Ealing Community Relations Council, *Racialist Activity in Ealing 1979–81* (CRC, 1981); Commission for Racial Equality, *Racial Harassment on Local Authority Housing Estates: a Report prepared by the London Race and Housing Forum* (CRE, 1981).

81. *Guardian*, 8 Dec. 1983 and 9 Dec. 1983; *Policing London*, no.11 (Feb./Mar. 1974) pp.54–5.
82. Reported in *Policing London*, vol.3, no.16 (Jan./Mar. 1985) pp.22–3.
83. See for example the *TV Eye* programme (Thames Television) entitled 'Racial Outlaws' broadcast on 17 Jan. 1985; 'East End Asians Bear the Brunt of Growth in Racist Attacks', *Guardian*, 17 Jan. 1985; 'Reporting Racial Harassment', *Guardian*, 28 Jan. 1985; 'Policing the Race Hate Gangs', *The Times*, 8 Feb. 1985 and 9 Feb. 1985.
84. Paul Gordon, *Passport Raids and Checks* (Runnymede Trust, 1981); Gordon, *White Law*, op. cit., pp.35–42.
85. Colin Brown, *Black and White Britain: The Third PSI Survey* (Heinemann, 1984) table 138, p.276; see also tables 57 and 119, pp.122 and 221.
86. Humphry, *Police Power and Black People*, op. cit., p.11.
87. Royal Commission on Criminal Procedure (Chairman: Sir Cyril Philips), *Report*, Cmnd 8092 (HMSO, Jan. 1981).
88. For a discusson of the Police and Criminal Evidence Act in particular, and policing problems in general, see John Benyon and Colin Bourn (eds), *The Police: Powers, Procedures and Proprieties* (Pergamon Press, 1986).
89. Robert Reiner, *The Blue-Coated Worker* (Cambridge University Press, 1978) pp.225–6.
90. Peter Southgate, *Police Probationer Training in Race Relations*, Research and Planning Unit Paper No.8 (Home Office, 1982) pp.9–12.
91. See 'The enormous price of "a slip of the tongue" ', *Police*, vol.16 (June 1984) p.3.
92. *Police and People in London*, vol.4. Smith and Gray, *The Police in Action*, op. cit., pp.109 and 127.
93. *Coventry Evening Telegraph*, 26 Nov. 1981; *The Brixton Disorders*, op. cit., para.5.15.
94. Police Training Council, *Community and Race Relations Training for the Police* (Home Office, 1983); C. Bainbridge, 'Pilot Study of Racism Awareness Training', *Police Journal*, vol.57, no.2 (1984) pp.165–9; Peter Southgate, *Racism Awareness Training for the Police*, Research and Planning Unit Paper No.29 (Home Office, 1984); Michael Banton, 'Back to the Drawing Board', *Police*, vol.17 (Feb. 1985) pp.34 and 44; Maureen Baker, 'Come Down to Earth, Professor', *Police*, vol.17 (Apr. 1985) p.48.
95. A. Colman and L. Gorman, 'Conservatism, Dogmatism and Authoritarianism in British Police Officers', *Sociology* (Feb. 1982); A. J. P. Butler letter in *The Times*, 5 Oct. 1981; P. A. J. Waddington, 'Conservatism, Dogmatism and Authoritarianism in the Police: a Comment', *Sociology*, Nov. 1982; A. Colman, 'Rejoinder', *Sociology*, Aug. 1983; 'Police Racism in the Making', *Policing London*, no.4 (Nov. 1982) pp.1–2; P. Taylor, 'How Hendon Police Cadets are Wooed Away from Racialism', *Police*, vol.15 (Aug. 1983).
96. *Police and People in London*, vol.4: Smith and Gray, *The Police in Action*, op.

cit., pp.150–4; David Wilson, Simon Holdaway and Christopher Spencer, 'Black Police in the United Kingdom', *Policing*, vol.1, no.1 (Autumn 1984) pp.20–30.

97. M. Hough and P. Mayhew, *The British Crime Survey: First Report*, Home Office Research Study no.76 (HMSO, 1983); Southgate and Ekblom, *Contacts between Police and Public*, op. cit.; David Moxon and Peter Jones, 'Public Reactions to Police Behaviour: Some Findings from the British Crime Survey', *Policing*, vol.1, no.1 (Autumn 1984) pp.49–56.

98. *Police and People in London*, vol.1: Smith, *A survey of Londoners*, op.cit., pp.181–5 and 219–24.

99. Hough and Mayhew, *The British Crime Survey*, op. cit., p.29.

100. Southgate, *Police Probationer Training in Race Relations*, op. cit., pp.4–15.

101. Robert Reiner, *The Politics of the Police* (Wheatsheaf, 1985) pp.126–7 and 134.

102. See G. Greaves, 'The Brixton disorders', op. cit., pp.69–71; for a discussion of the concept see David Mason, 'After Scarman: a Note on the Concept of "Institutional Racism" ', *New Community*, vol.10 (Summer 1982) pp.38–45.

103. Gordon, *White Law*, op. cit., p.137.

104. Salman Rushdie, 'The New Empire within Britain', *New Society*, 9 Dec. 1982.

105. John Rex, 'Law and Order in Multi-Racial Inner City Areas – the Issues after Scarman' in Philip Norton (ed.), *Law and Order and British Politics* (Gower Press, 1984) p.107.

106. Simha Landau, 'Juveniles and the Police', *British Journal of Criminology*, vol.21 (Jan. 1981).

107. See for example Robert Mark, *Policing a Perplexed Society* (Allen & Unwin, 1977) and R. Mark, *In the Office of Constable* (London: Collins, 1978).

108. *Guardian*, 17 Mar. 1982.

109. 'Anderton Attacks Political Policing', *Guardian*, 8 June 1985.

110. *The Brixton Disorders*, op. cit., paras 5.3 and 5.58.

111. P. A. J. Waddington, ' "Community policing": a Sceptical Appraisal', in Philip Norton (ed.), *Law and Order and British Politics* (Gower Press, 1984) p.95.

# Index

Action Group on Immigration and
Nationality, 101–2
Afro-Asian Caribbean Convention,
80
Alliance, SDP–Liberal, 114, 116–22
and black votes, 173
and immigration issue, 11
1983 Manifesto, 120–1
see also Liberal Party and Social
Democratic Party
Alton, David, 115, 117–18
Alderson, James, 261
Anti-Nazi League, 37, 101, 250
Apartheid, 50–1
Atkinson, Norman, 110
Attlee, Clement, 27
Avebury, Lord, 115, 119

Barker, Martin, 45–6, 58, 60
Bell, Ronald, 56, 82
Berkshire Education Authority, 194
and Education for Equality, 194
Biffen, John, 57
Birmingham Immigration Control
Association (BICA), 47
Black People's Manifesto (1979),
102
Blakelock, P.C. Keith, 265
Brittan, Leon, 95
Bristol riots, 59, 80, 87, 100, 212,
228–8, 263
Brixton, 105, 107, 210
crime in, 91, 237, 241
police raids in, 247–8, 270
riots in, 1, 37, 60, 65, 87–8, 100,
163, 229, 231, 244, 259,
264–5, 268
Budgen, Nicholas, 62
Burke, Edmund, 269

Butler, R.A.B., 47, 49

Callaghan, James, 38, 54
Campaign Against Racial
Discrimination (CARD), 55
Casey, John, 59–61
Centre for Disadvantage, 190
Chamberlain, Joseph, 32
Churchill, Winston, 27
Churchillian rhetoric, 49
Collett, Charles, 47
Colonial Office, 28
Commission for Racial Equality
(CRE), 2, 5, 9, 36–9, 62–4, 74,
82–3, 97, 114, 119, 153, 204,
209–13, 215–17, 219
Code of Practice on Employment,
10, 214
ethnic question in census, 109
investigation of by HASC, 142–3
investigation of immigration
controls, 92–3, 101
Lord Scarman Report, 219–20
Unemployment and Homelessness
(1974), 212
Youth in Multi-Racial Society
(1980), 212
Commonwealth, British, 20, 25, 50,
52
loss of faith in, 48, 86
migration in, 27–8
Commonwealth Immigrants
Advisory Committee, 189
Commonwealth Immigrants Act
(1962), 3, 26, 28–30, 32
Commonwealth Immigrants Act
(1968), 105, 111
Communalism, 56
Asian, 66

Community Relations Commission (CRC), 33, 36, 102, 211
 and *Unemployment and Homelessness* (1974), 207
Conservative Party, Central Council of, 76
 Conference of (1961), 47–8
 Home Affairs Committee, 148
 ideology of, 8, 10, 45–6, 58–9, 67
 and immigration, 8, 11, 75, 82, 91, 95–6
 manifesto of (1979), 39, 76–7, 79, 82, 86, 91
 and 'new right', 45–6, 55
 One Nation Conservatism, 53, 65, 67
 political vocabulary of, 60
 *The Right Approach*, 57, 75
 and 'wets', 46
Cowling, Maurice, 59, 64
Crawshaw, Richard, 115–17, 121
Crewe, Ivor, 102
Criminal Evidence Act (1984), 12
Crossman, Richard, 11
Curtis, Leslie, 255

Deedes, William, 55, 245
Department of Education and Science (DES), 134–7, 191
 Circular 7/65, 189
 Green paper on *Education* (1977), 192, and LEAs, 193
 Report on *Educational Disadvantage and the Needs of Immigrants*, 190
 English for Immigrants (1965), 189
Department of the Environment (DoE), 113, 135–6
 and Merseyside Task Force, 37, 89, 125
 and urban aid programme, 36
Department of Health and Social Security (DHSS), 135–6
Dubs, Alf, 108

Eden, Anthony (Lord Avon), 27
Education, 13
 anti-racist education, 12
 multi-cultural education, 12
 and Swann Committee, 12
Elton, Lord, 49–50
Empire, British, 20, 52
 Imperial Conference (1921), 28
Employment policy, 13
 *see also* Youth Training Scheme
Ennals, Martin, 48
Ethnic Groups/Local Grants Bill, 162

Fisher, Nigel, 48
Foot, Paul, 3, 53
Foreign Office, 28
Frazer, John, 247

Gaitskell, Hugh, 31
Gordon-Walker, Patrick, 5, 30
Greater London Council (GLC), 36, 97, 113, 122, 219, 251
 and Greater London Training Board, 219
Greaves, George, 229–30
Griffiths, Peter, 51–3
Gummer, John Selwyn, 66

Hailsham, Lord, 8, 74
Hall, Stuart, 45, 235
Halsey, A. H., 207
Hancock, Keith, 56
Handsworth riots, 1, 5, 13, 263–5, 267–8
Hart, Judith, 110
Hattersley, Roy, 85, 105–7, 109, 112–13, 267
Heath, Edward, 5, 31–2, 54, 73–4, 76
 Heath government, 57–8
Heseltine, Michael, 37, 40, 89, 163
 *see also* Merseyside Task Force
Home Affairs Committee (HAC), 126–7, 129–31, 144, 148, 152
Home Affairs Sub-Committee on Race and Immigration (HASC), 13–14, 86, 108, 116, 125–54
 report on British Nationality Fees, 96, 138–9
 and British Overseas Citizens, 140

and ethnic and racial questions in the census, 138
investigation of CRE, 142
proposed new immigration rules, 140, 142
Report on Race Relations and the 'sus' Law, 80–1, 132, 145–7, 230
Report on Racial Disadvantage, 88–9, 100, 133–5, 138, 147, 153
Second Report on 'sus' Law, 81–2, 132
Home Office, 96, 104, 127–8, 134–7, 152–3, 190, 251
and CRE, 92, 142–3
and educational funding, 189
Equal opportunities and Community Programme Section, 137
and Franks Report, 77
and mugging, 238
and report of Police Complaints Board, 248
Report on Racial Attacks, 91, 251–2
Study of Ethnic Minority Attitudes, 91, 251–2
and urban programme, 33, 36
and virginity tests, 108
Honeyford, Ray, 196
Hume, David, 46, 58–9
Hunt, John, 131, 146
Hunte, Joseph, 239
Report on *Nigger Hunting in England?* (1966), 239
Hurd, Douglas, 263, 267
Huxley, Elspeth, 48, 50

Idrish, Mohammed, 94
Illegal Immigration Intelligence Unit, 253
Immigration, consensus on, 31
control of, 26–7, 32, 37, 74, 92, 94–5, 119, 182–3
illegal influx of, 93–4
Indian, 32–3, 86, 92
new rules on (1979), 78–9, 86, 91–2, 100, 117, 140

as political issue, 168–9, 171–2, 175, 177
and repatriation, 82
and virginity tests, 92
Immigration Act (1971), 11, 38, 50, 57, 60, 72, 76, 112, 178, 253
Immigration White Paper (1965), 13, 45
Inner London Education Authority, 194, 197
Institute of Economic Affairs (IEA), 57
Institute of Race Relations, *Police Against Black People*, 245
Institutional racism, 12, 14, 22, 258–9

Jenkins, Roy, 75, 115–17
Jewish voters, 180
John, Gus, 208
Johnson, Peter, 255
Joint Campaign Against Racialism, 115
Joseph, Sir Keith, 59, 67

Kassam, Mrs Shamira, 253
Katznelson, Ira, 160, 164–5
Kaufman, Gerald, 268
Kelland, Gilbert, 242
Keynesian economic policies, 29
Kinnock, Neil, 268
Knight, Jill, 81

Labour Party, 56, 59, 104, 106–9, 115, 121
and black voters, 21, 104, 171, 173–6, 178
campaign for black sections, 7
Home Affairs Committee, 111, 148
Human Rights Committee, 104, 110
and immigration, 11, 31, 102, 110
and inner city disorders, 267–8
Labour's Programme (1982), 110, 113
NEC Working Group on Race Relations, 111–13
*The New Hope for Britain*, 114

policy on Nationality, 111
Race Action Group, 103, 105, 108
and Scarman Report, 109
Lambeth, 229
  Community Policy Consultative
    Group in, 270
  Community relations in, 244
  Council for Community Relations
    in, 244
  Crime in, 231, 237, 241
  Working Party with
    Community/Police Relations
    in, 243–4
Lane, David, 64
Lawrence, Errol, 46
Levin, Bernard, 75
Lewis, Gordon, 63
Leyton, by-election in (1965), 30, 45
Liberal Party, 114, 116, 121
  Community Relations Policy
    Panel, 119–20
  and immigration control, 114
Liverpool, black population in, 88–9
  riots in, 89, 100, 229
Lloyd-George, David, 28, 32
Local Government Act (1972), 34
Local Government Assistance Act
  (1966), 29, 89, 113, 162, 189,
  195
Local Government Grants (Ethnic
  Groups) Bill (1979), 36, 38
London Government Act (1963), 34
Lubbock, Eric, *see* Lord Avebury
Lyon, Alex, 38, 108, 128–30, 133,
  135, 141, 143, 148
Lyons, Edward, 121

Macmillan, Harold, 5, 27, 47
Mangat, Kulwant Singh, 252
McNee, Sir David, 81, 227, 245
Manpower Services Commission,
  89–90, 96, 204, 211–17, 218
  London Regional Office Report
    (1982), 210
Mark, Sir Robert, 228, 238, 261
Merseyside Task Force, 89, 163
Migrants Action Group, 93
Miles, Robert, 46, 63
Mill John Stuart, 62

Monday Club, 9, 30, 55–6, 62, 66,
  82, 95, 102
Morris, Professor Terrence, 233–4
Moss Side, disorders in, 229
'Mugging' incidences of, 241
  panic on, 236–8
Mullard, C., 193
Multi-cultural education, 188, 198–9
  and LEAs, 188
Muslim Education Council, 192
Muslim Parents Association
  (Bradford), 192

National Anti-Racist Movement in
  Education, 193
National Association for
  Multi-Racial Education, 193
National Council for Civil Liberties
  (NCCL), 48
National Front, 3, 8, 11, 30, 32, 37,
  57, 60, 66, 75, 101, 103, 250
  demand for ban on NF marches,
    109
Nationalism, British ideology of, 10,
  18, 52–3, 64
  electoral appeal of, 54
  Tory philosophy of, 60–1, 64
Nationality Act (1981), 11, 37, 66,
  76, 79, 86–7, 96, 111, 119, 121,
  161, 178
  Bill (1980), 83–5, 104–6
Newman, Sir Kenneth, 252, 265
Newham, attacks in, 252
'New racism', 45–7
Newsam, Peter, 142
Notting Hill, Carnival in, 228
  crime in, 238
  Mangrove Restaurant raid in, 247
  riots in (1958), 162

Osborne, Cyril, 47
Owen, David, 120

Page, Sir Graham, 128, 152
Pannell, Norman, 47–8
Partnership Scheme, 89
Peckham, crime in, 238
  disturbances in, 265
Phizacklea, Annie, 46, 63

Pitt, Bill, 115–16, 121
Plowden Report, 190
Police
  and Asians, 249
  Association of Chief Police
    Officers, 90, 246, 261
  and blacks, 161, 163, 240, 246,
    264
  black views on, 172, 175, 262
  complaints on, 248
  Dear Inquiry, 247
  in Merseyside, 80
  Metropolitan Police, 80, 88, 247,
    259
  and black crime, 233–4, 237–9,
    241, 243
  and National Reporting Centre,
    260
  Police Act (1964), 83, 260, 270
  Police Complaints Board, 248
  Police Federation, 81, 90, 261
    (conference of (1984), 255)
  Police Superintendents
    Association, 90
  Police Training Centre, 256
  PSI Study of (1983), 230–2,
    241–2, 249, 253–7
  public confidence in, 257
Police and Criminal Evidence Act
  (1984), 230, 254–5
  as Bill, 87
Powell, Enoch, 3, 10–11, 30, 52–6,
  62, 74, 82, 102
  political influence of, 32
Powellism, 11, 46–7, 54–5, 60, 62
  'Rivers of Blood' Speech, 31, 55,
    177
Pressure for Economic and Social
  Toryism (PEST), 55
Procter, Harvey, 10, 62, 243
Pym, Francis, 96

Race Relations Act (1965), 13, 55,
  161
  (1968), 56, 161
  (1976), 36, 216, 38, 63, 74, 82,
    161, 179, 216 (and local
    authorities, 36, 38)
Race Relations Board, 33, 36, 55

Racial integration, 56, 63
Radice, Giles, 15
Raison, Timothy, 81, 93, 106
Rampton Report, 101
Rees, Merlyn, 79, 81, 104, 117, 147
Richardson, Jo, 108
Rooker, Jeff, 267
Rose, Richard, 4, 180
Rushdie, Salman, 259

Salisbury, Lord, 24
*Salisbury Review*, 9, 61, 196
Scarman, Lord, 89, 107, 135, 221
  *Report*, 7, 9, 37, 63, 88–9, 107,
    109, 116, 145, 163, 192, 205,
    218, 244, 247, 268–9
  and policing, 12, 90, 228, 241–3,
    254, 256, 258–9, 261–2
  and *Swamp' 81*, 230–1, 242
Scruton, Roger, 61
Select Committee on Procedure,
  First Reform, 150
Select Committee on Race
  Relations
  and West Indian crime, 234
  and police–black relations, 240
Selsdon Group, 57
Sherman, Sir Alfred, 60
Smethick, election in (1964), 30, 45
Smith, Dudley, 245
Social Democratic Party (SDP),
  115–17, 119–20
  Green Paper on Citizens Rights,
    119–20
  Green Paper on Urban Policy,
    120
South Africa, 29, 56
Southall, 65, 100, 199, 250
  'Battle of Southall', 250
Special Patrol Group (SPG), 104,
  241, 244, 250
Speed, Keith, 75–6
Stanbrook, Ivor, 10, 63, 85–6
Standing Advisory Council, 179
Steel, David, 116
Stevas, Norman St. John, 130
Stokes, John, 62, 65
Suez Crisis, 28, 49, 52
Summerskill, Shirley, 104

'sus' Law, 80–1, 239
    House of Commons debate on,
        132
    Report of, 133, 230
    'Scrap the sus' Campaign, 102
*Swamp' 81*, 231, 241, 261
    *see also* Scarman, Lord
Swann Committee, 136, 187, 195,
    199

Tebbitt, Norman, 267
Thatcher, Margaret, 57, 64–6, 72,
    74–5, 96, 103, 115
    and Conservative governments,
        35
    and law and order, 87–8
    'swamping' speech, 8, 39, 46, 63,
        75, 166
    Thatcherism, 39, 57–8, 65–6
    and Victorian values, 10
Tilley, John, 105–6
Tory Reform Group, 66
Tottenham
    riots in, 1, 5, 13, 165–8
Toxteth, 88, 116, 210
    riots in, 1, 37, 60, 87, 100, 106,
        229, 265, 268

Unemployment, among blacks, 38,
    204, 213–15
    joint working party of MSC and
        CRE on (1981), 213
    and policing, 205
    as political issue, 166–8, 170–2

White paper on (1985), 222
Urban aid programme, 30–1, 33, 36,
    38, 89–90, 113, 136, 161–3
Utley, T. E., 64


Waddington, David, 95
Walker, Peter, 76, 96
Webb, David, 263
West Indian Standing Conference
    (WISC)
    Memorandum to Select
        Committee (1972), 245
Wheeler, John, 86, 129–30, 141,
    148, 153
Whitelaw, William, 8, 74–5, 81,
    84–5, 88, 117, 220
Willey, Fred, 38
Williams, Shirley, 115
Wilson, Harold, 5, 31, 45, 54
Wolverhampton Council for Racial
    Harmony, 53
Worsthorne, Peregrine, 259


Yorkshire Campaign to Stop
    Immigration, 56
Young, George, 55–6
Young, Sir George, 136
Young Conservatives, 66
Youth Training Board, 214
Youth Training Scheme (YTS), 12,
    90, 211, 218–19
    equal opportunities policy in,
        213–14